# COMPENSATION FOR POLLUTION DAMAGE

ORGANISATION FOR ECONOMIC CO-OPERATION AND DEVELOPMENT

The Organisation for Economic Co-operation and Development (OECD) was set up under a Convention signed in Paris on 14th December 1960, which provides that the OECD shall promote policies designed:
- to achieve the highest sustainable economic growth and employment and a rising standard of living in Member countries, while maintaining financial stability, and thus to contribute to the development of the world economy;
- to contribute to sound economic expansion in Member as well as non-member countries in the process of economic development;
- to contribute to the expansion of world trade on a multilateral, non-discriminatory basis in accordance with international obligations.

The Members of OECD are Australia, Austria, Belgium, Canada, Denmark, Finland, France, the Federal Republic of Germany, Greece, Iceland, Ireland, Italy, Japan, Luxembourg, the Netherlands, New Zealand, Norway, Portugal, Spain, Sweden, Switzerland, Turkey, the United Kingdom and the United States.

THE OPINION EXPRESSED AND ARGUMENTS EMPLOYED
IN THIS PUBLICATION ARE THE RESPONSIBILITY OF THE AUTHORS AND
DO NOT NECESSARILY REPRESENT THOSE OF THE OECD

Publié en français sous le titre:

INDEMNISATION DES DOMMAGES
DÛS À LA POLLUTION

\*\*

# TABLE OF CONTENTS

Environmental pollution can result, and often has resulted in serious damage to the health of people, to their property and to natural eco-systems. Such damage may result from the accumulation of toxic chemicals in the food chain, as in the case of Minimata disease. It may result from the sudden release of a toxic substance into the air or water as in the case of Seveso. Catastrophic accidents such as large oil spills can cause massive damage to coastal property, tourism and to the commercial interests dependent on them. Decisions to alter patterns of land use for example, the location of an autoroute or an airport in a previously undisturbed area, can significantly affect property values.

In the past, health and property damage from environmental pollution was viewed, for the most part, as a kind of "normal" or "unavoidable" disamenity associated with modern industrial life. More recently, however, some Member countries of OECD have gradually developed systems of compensation for victims of certain types of pollution. Under these schemes compensation is sometimes paid by the person responsible for the damage, sometimes by the industrial sector concerned and sometimes by the State. The victims of major sources of noise like airports now qualify for damage compensation in some countries. In other countries certain industries have to pay compensation year by year for damage to the health of victims or even to damage to flora and fauna in their neighbourhoods. In Japan, for example, oil burning industries cover health costs of persons suffering from ailments caused by sulphur contained in the fuel.

Various methods of compensation are being tried. Generally the victim tries to establish the liability of the polluter and then obtains compensation if the polluter is identified, liable and solvent. During the last two decades, special efforts have been made on both the national and international level to develop schemes that would guarantee payment of compensation for damage caused by accidental pollution from nuclear facilities or from oil tankers at sea. Attempts are currently being made to extend compensation schemes to cover damage from other sources of accidental pollution. Attention has been given lately to the establishment of State or industry supported funds out of which compensation for damage may be paid up to certain ceilings.

All compensation schemes face numerous problems. It is often difficult to establish the true nature and extent of the damage or to give it a monetary value. It is sometimes difficult to establish the precise cause of the damage. Even where this is possible, establishing the exact source and the person or industry liable for it can be fraught with controversy. These difficulties are perhaps less pronounced where there is a system of strict no-fault liability which is the case for water pollution damage in a number of Member countries such as France and Germany. Similarly, the establishment of a fund for certain types of damage can avoid some problems. Even here, however, the increasing size of the risks involved, the growing importance attached to indirect damage and continuing inflation make it more likely that the ceilings established for compensation will be exceeded. As a result, efforts are being made to set up funds with very high ceilings. At the same time, new types of insurance policies are being developed to provide better coverage for potential polluters and to protect them against the considerable financial risks that can be connected with pollution accidents and ecological catastrophies.

Compensation for victims of transfrontier pollution raises a number of issues. In 1974, the OECD Council stressed the need to establish "practical procedures promoting the prompt and equitable compensation of persons affected by transfrontier pollution" and later recognised that the international liability of States for transfrontier pollution may be a source of difficulty as regards the redress of foreign victims of transfrontier pollution.

Recourse to the courts of the polluting State would offer an acceptable solution provided there was genuine equality of treatment and access for all claimants. Studies made by OECD on this subject were published in "Legal Aspects of Transfrontier Pollution".

Other solutions could be envisaged and are discussed in the present work. Their purpose is both to facilitate compensation and to avoid the occurrence of damage by preventive measures.

This book considers the experience of Member countries to date with compensation and examines some of the legal and economic problems associated with the establishment and administration of compensation systems. It looks at possible alternatives to existing practice. It examines the questions from both a national and international perspective. It is based on a series of studies undertaken for the Transfrontier Pollution Group and the Group of Economic Experts of the OECD Environment Committee.

Jim McNeill
Director, Environment Directorate
OECD

# COMPENSATION FOR "INDIRECT OR REMOTE" POLLUTION DAMAGE IN INDIVIDUAL COUNTRIES AND AT INTERNATIONAL LEVEL

by

Emmanuel du Pontavice
Professor at the University of Law,
Economics and Social Sciences of Paris

and

Patricia Cordier
diplômée d'études supérieures de droit européen

In any system of third-party liability, although certainly there can be no compensation without damage, it is equally certain that not all damage will introduce a right to compensation. National and international law is unanimous in considering that only damage which is a direct consequence of the act complained of ("dommage direct") may be the subject of compensation. Compensation may only be paid where there is a causal relationship between the damage and the event which gave rise to it. The need to establish a causal relationship is nevertheless a source of many difficulties in cases of pollution damage, a field to which it seems particularly unsuited.

As had been said by Despax, "lawyers, since Pothier, have a decided aversion to damage which results indirectly from the wrongful act and will sever the chain of causality with a clear conscience for reasons of convenience. Yet, ecology teaches us that animate beings and inanimate objects together form a complex whole which is not easily divisible and that the phenomenon of interdependence is a fundamental feature of the universe".(1) The release of polluting substances into the environment is the cause of numerous cases of damage to property and of physical injury or "moral damage" to persons, as may be seen from a daily perusal of the newspapers. In one case, injuries of various kinds result from exposure to ionising radiation, in another the discharge of chemicals causes the death of hundreds of fish and makes breeding impossible, in yet another the wreck of an oil tanker or the blow-out of an oil well release tons of oil which spread over many kilometres of beach.

---

1) La défense juridique de l'environnement. Réflexions à propos de quelques décisions de jurisprudence concernant la pollution de l'eau et de l'atmosphère, J.C.P. 1970. I. 2359.

Some of these forms of damage may have "indirect" economic repercussions. Thus, pollution of beaches may result in a considerable
financial loss for persons who make their living from the sea or from
the tourist trade. Although the fouling of beaches does not directly
affect individual interests but rather concerns state-owned public
property, it may nevertheless discourage tourists and lead to a loss
of profits for seaside hotel keepers and restaurant owners. Similarly,
an oil spill may "indirectly" result in financial loss for fishermen
when they are unable to sell their fish as a result of the public's
fears. Profits will also fall if a large number of fish are destroyed.

Are the victims of such so-called "indirect or remote" damage,
but the economic dimension of which may nevertheless be considerable,
to be refused compensation at both national and international levels?
This is the question that this report sets out to examine, by discussing
in Part I "The concept of remoteness in relation to pollution damage"
and in Part II "Consequences as regards compensation".

Part I

## THE CONCEPT OF REMOTENESS IN RELATION TO POLLUTION DAMAGE

The concept of remoteness of damage (i.e. damage caused indirectly) has to be defined, hence that of causal relationship, in order to determine whether the financial losses referred to above are from the legal standpoint too remote and therefore not subject to compensation.

Salvioli, in his course on liability and the award of damages by international courts (1) at the Academy of International Law in The Hague states the problem in a nutshell: "Damage is considered to be caused indirectly, taking this term in its broadest sense, in the event where an unlawful act has caused damage x and there subsequently occurs another damage y. Should compensation be paid for the second damage? The answer to this question should be sought in the chain of causation between the unlawful act, the first damage and the second. Where damage y occurs due to the occurance of damage x, the second damage y appears in its turn as a consequence - although an indirect one - of the unlawful act which caused the first damage, and as such calls for redress. "Y" is remote damage giving rise to a duty of redress."

### A. THE ORDINARY LAW OF LIABILITY

#### a) Domestic law

Directly caused damage (préjudice direct) is generally understood as damage which is linked by a direct causal relationship to the event which gives rise to it.

In French Law, Article 1151 of the Civil Code, which relates specifically to contract but also covers tort, states that "Damages awarded in respect of loss suffered or deprivation of profit shall only cover such items as are the immediate and direct consequence of the failure to perform the agreement". Taken literally, this Article would prevent compensation from being paid for pollution damage.

--------

1) RCADI, 1929, III, p. 246.

In the extreme case all pollution damage may be regarded as
being indirectly caused. In pollution matters it should thus be
pointed out that the relationship between the cause and the damage
itself is rarely a direct one, but take place through the agency of
the environment, i.e. the air or water which receives and transmits
the pollution.(1) A physical description of the process which takes
place may thus serve to show that there is no direct cause or relationship between the damage and the polluting substance. "When a polluting
substance is discharged, it has a direct effect on the environment
which receives it; regardless of the facts of the case, it is the air
or the water which first suffers 'damage' and only insofar as these are
themselves 'used' in the exercise of a specific right is such right in
its turn indirectly affected".

"Thus, where an industry discharges its waste water into a river,
the immediate damage is caused to the water in the river and to the
animal and plant life which it contains; the liability mechanism will
not come into play until a third party (fisherman, farmer or manufacturer) who needs to 'use' the water of the river for his own purposes, finds that he is unable to do so owing to the pollution of the
water".(2)

The French courts do not give a literal interpretation of
Article 1151 of the Civil Code. The courts describe as "directly
caused" that damage which is necessary, i.e. damage which is the
necessary consequence of the incident. To the extent that the incident is held to have played a necessary role in the occurrence of the
damage, compensation will be awarded.(3)

Thus, in a case where a motor vehicle crashed into a hair-
dressing saloon, resulting in the establishment's closure and the
staff's unemployment, the court held that the damage suffered by the
employees "is a direct and necessary consequence of the fault committed by the person responsible for the accident". The fact that it
was indirectly caused from the standpoint of the injured parties was
unimportant, since there existed a direct chain of cause and effect.

---

1) Martine Remond-Gouilloud, Note re: Tribunal Grande Instance of
   Bastia, 8th December 1976, D 1977 J.429 et seq., especially p. 430.
2) Gilles J. Martin, De la responsabilité civile pour faits de pollution au droit à l'environnement, thesis, Nice, October 1976,
   typed, pp. 106-107.
3) Mazeaud, Leçons de droit civil, T.2 4th edition, by M. de Juglart,
   1969 No. 570. Mazeaud and Tunc, Traité théorique et pratique de
   la responsabilité civile délictuelle et contractuelle, T.II 6th
   edition 1970 No. 1666 et seq. Le Tourneau, La responsabilité
   civile, 2nd edition 1976 No. 546 et seq. On trends in French case
   law which, "without accepting the principle of compensation for
   indirectly caused damage is increasingly inclined to extend the
   notion of directly caused damage", see Patrick Simon, Essai d'inter-
   prétation des clauses obscures ou ambiguës des chartes-parties,
   Droit maritime français, 1978 page 46 and note 10, at ordinary law
   and maritime law.

"Every person who suffers damage as a direct result of the same wrongful act derives his right to compensation from the existence and proof
of direct personal damage, irrespective of whether he is the immediate
or secondary victim, since several persons may be incidentally affected.(1) Although it is true that unemployment of the staff was not an
"immediate" consequence of the accident, it is nevertheless clear that
a direct cause of destruction of the premises was unemployment of the
people who worked there.

The same reasoning may be applied to pollution cases. While in
fact the loss of earnings by hotel keepers, restaurant owners or
fishermen is not the "immediate" consequence of the discharge of polluting substances, it is however clear that the pollution of beaches
and the destruction of fish lead directly to a loss of earnings by
people who make their living from them.

The French administrative courts have admitted such claims on
several occasions.(2) Damages have been awarded to a restaurant owner
for loss of prospective earnings resulting from pollution of the
river Seine due to discharge from the Paris sewer system.(3) Similarly,
the operator of a washing and bathing establishment obtained compensation for loss of prospective earnings due to pollution of the
Seine.(4) Compensation was also awarded to a fisherman for loss of
prospective earnings due to pollution of the Seine by the Paris sewer
system.(5)

More recently, on 3rd November 1965 (6) the Court of Appeal at
Rennes did not dispute the principle of redress for damage to the
tourist trade, but asked for proof that the damage had actually
occurred. Following the discharge of oil by an oil tanker, several
resorts claimed to have suffered "moral damage" by being brought into
disrepute as a result of oil pollution. The court held as follows:

> "It is difficult to conceive how a town can be held to suffer
> 'moral' damage, meaning that the feelings of all inhabitants

---

1) T.G.I. Nanterre, 22nd October 1975 G.P. 1976 I, p. 392. Dupichot,
   Des préjudices réfléchis nés de l'atteinte à la vie ou à l'inté-
   gralité corporelle. See also the "chronique" by Georges Durry
   which shows that the damage suffered incidentally by the relatives
   of a seriously injured victim no longer requires, in order for
   compensation to be awarded, to be of exceptional gravity (Deuxième
   Chambre Civ. Cass. 23rd May 1977, Revue trimestrielle de droit
   civil 1977, 768, No. 2).
2) Despax, La pollution des eaux et ses problèmes juridiques, 1968,
   No. 40.
3) C.E. Ville de Paris v. Giquel, 4th March 1914, Rec. Lebon 1914,
   p. 298.
4) C.E. Ville de Paris v. Héritiers Pottier, 4th March 1914, Rec.
   Lebon 1914, p. 299.
5) C.E. Ville de Paris v. Deshayes, 4th March 1914, Rec. Lebon 1914,
   p. 298.
6) Captain of the World Mead v. Towns of La Baule, Pornichet, Le
   Pouliguen, Le Croisic, DMF 1966, p. 466.

in their capacity as town citizens should be affected; the
loss of reputation which they allege, namely that as a result
of oil spillage the high public regard for their beaches may
have been jeopardised, constitutes a form of financial loss
which is unsupported by any evidence."

If, as has been claimed,[1] the damage to the tourist trade was too
remote, and consequently not subject to compensation, the court would
not have made any reference to it. But in this case the claim by the
towns was refused on the grounds that they had not produced evidence
in support of the alleged damage. The court did not deny the principle
of redress for damage to the tourist trade.[2]

Even more clearly, on 8th December 1976 a decision (referred to
above) of the High Court of Bastia pronounced in favour of the Bastia
Fishermen's Association and the two Corsican departments in their
claim owing to smaller catches due to pollutants discharged in the
fishing grounds, damage to tourist traffic and to amenity, and other
"disastrous consequences such as the fall in value of coastal property,
the absence of tourists in hotels, restaurants and bathing establishments, and finally for the losses incurred by local authorities in the
form or reduced revenue due to the pollution".[3]

Similarly, the Toulouse Court of Appeal has recently awarded compensation for loss of prospective earnings by a fisherman whose customers were reluctant to buy his fish as a result of pollution of the
river Garonne.

"Whereas the chief occupation of Delmas is that of fisherman,
and as such he has had to pay his general expenses, fishing
rights, taxes, insurance and motor-vehicle expenses for the
period in which he was unable to fish and did not receive any
profit from the sale of his fish to his many customers: it
seems natural that such customers should during the period of
pollution have been somewhat reluctant to buy and consume fish
from the Garonne; the loss suffered by Delmas therefore cannot
be denied and was considerable".[4]

---

1) Rousseau, Chron. des faits internationaux, RGDIP, 1967, p. 1092
   et. seq.
2) E. du Pontavice, La pollution des mers par les hydrocarbures "A
   propos de l'affaire du Torrey Canyon", 1968, pp. 44-45. And by the
   same author, La pollution des eaux de mer par les hydrocarbures:
   problèmes juridiques de la réparation, G.P. 1969, II, p. 168.
3) D.1977.J.427, note by M. Remond-Gouilloud, DMF 1977.669. This
   decision was appealed by the defendant, the Montedison Company, on
   the grounds of lack of jurisdiction and concurrent proceedings in
   another court. This application was dismissed by the Bastia Court
   of Appeal (Haute-Corse) on 28th February 1977 (unpublished decision,
   Société Montedison v. Prud'homie des Pêcheurs de Bastia and others).
4) Court of Appeal of Toulouse, 3rd February 1977. Guerbadot, BOS,
   Szilagyi v. Ministère Public et Parties Civiles, unpublished.

The Court has also held that directly caused and certain damage for which compensation can be claimed is suffered by the Federations of Fishing and Fish-breeding Associations which lose the subscriptions of members who have not renewed their annual fishing cards due to the fact that there were no or very few fish or that fishing had had to be discontinued following pollution.(1)

Most national legislation and decided cases known to the author take a similar view of directly caused damage and the causal relationship. To our knowledge, directly caused damage is not interpreted in the sense of "immediate damage" which would suggest that only the damage initially suffered may be subject to compensation. The issue is not one of temporal or geographical proximity. Once a relationship of cause to effect exists between the incident and the damage, then the loss suffered should be made good, however remoet it may be in the causal chain.

It appears from the majority of decided cases that directly caused damage is the "necessary damage", that which is the "normal" consequence of the incident. Thus, in Soviet law "if the damage is a necessary and direct result of the unlawful act, such damage is deemed to be direct. On the other hand, the damage is 'indirect' if its essential cause is to be found in the circumstances which accompanied the unlawful act".(2) Similarly, in English law, directly caused damage was defined by Judge Scrutton in the Polemis case: "The damage is in fact directly traceable to the negligent act and not due to the operation of independent causes having no connection with the negligent act".(3)

Although damage which is a direct result of the unlawful act is sometimes compared with foreseeable damage,(4) this test should not prevent redress for economic losses resulting from pollution. The English and United States courts have sometimes maintained that only those events whose harmful consequences can reasonably be foreseen are a cause of damage.(5) Likewise, under Dutch law, the defendant is only held liable for the foreseeable consequences of the wrongful

1) Court of Appeal of Toulouse, Criminal Appeals Division, 3rd February 1977, Guerbadot, Bos, Szilagyi v. Ministère Public et Parties Civiles, unpublished.
2) Fridieff, La responsabilité civile en droit soviétique, Revue internationale de droit comparé, 1958, p. 581.
3) /1921/, 3KB, p. 527.
4) Mazeaud and Tunc, op.cit., No. 1441, p. 531.
5) Marty, La relation de cause à effet (Etude comparative des conceptions allemande, anglaise et française). Revue trimestrielle de droit civil, 1939, p. 695, et.seq. Tunc, Les récents développements des droits anglais et américain sur la relation de causalité entre la faute et le dommage dont on doit réparation, Revue internationale de droit comparé, 1953, p. 5 et seq. John Wilson, Un arrêt important en matière de causalité: le "Wagon Mound", Revue internationale de droit comparé, 1962, p. 575 et seq.

act. The courts however sometimes deliberately ignore this rule, notably in environmental cases.(1)

The concept of damage which is reasonably foreseeable does not prevent redress for financial loss due to a polluting act. A fact that can reasonably be foreseen is that the discharge of harmful substances will result in the death of fish and pollution of beaches causing loss of earnings for persons obtaining their living from the sea.

b) International law

A similar approach may be detected at international level. A study on damage under international law shows that the question of whether damage is caused directly by the unlawful act may be determined by reference to two types of causal relationship. The relationship may be either "pure" or "transitive".(2) If the damage follows clearly and without any intermediate stage from a given event, the causal relationship is "pure". This hypothesis may be represented by the formula $E_1 \rightarrow D$. The damage is directly caused in the strict sense of the term.

If the event causes initial damage $D_1$ which gives rise to damage $D_2$ and so on until $D_n$, should it be held that $D_2$, $D_3$, .. $D_n$ are indirect consequences of the event? Insofar as it can be shown that $E_1$ is the sole cause of $D_1$, that $D_1$ is the sole cause of $D_2$ and so on until $D_n$, in other words that there exists a pure causal relationship between $E_1$ and $D_1$, $D_1$ and $D_2$, $D_2$ and ... $D_n$, the causal relationship between the event and the damage will be described as "transitive".(3) Although the damage may then be seen as being indirectly caused as regards the physical sequence, from the legal standpoint it will nevertheless be seen as "directly caused although remote".(4) Confusion arises perhaps from the fact that transitive damage has frequently been described as "indirect" although there is no doubt that compensation is payable for it. This view is supported by international case law.

Under the terms of administrative decision No. 2 of the Joint German-American Commission of 1st November 1923 "All indirect losses are covered provided only that in legal contemplation Germany's act was the efficient and proximate cause and source from which they flowed".(5) Most of the cases also concede the right to compensation

---

1) Lambers, Compensation for environmental damage under Dutch Law, OECD, Environment Directorate, Working Paper No.3, 9th August 1977, pp. 9-10.
2) B. Bollecker-Stern, Le préjudice dans la théorie de la responsabilité internationale, Pédone, 1973, pp. 186-187.
3) Bollecker-Stern, op.cit., p. 187.
4) Case of British property in Spanish Morocco, RSA II, p. 615, 659.
5) RSA VII, pp. 29-30.

for transitive or "indirect" damage. Eagleton considers that it is the existence of an uninterrupted pure or transitive chain of causality which enables us to say what damage should be subject to compensation. "All damages which can be traced back to an injurious act as the exclusive generating cause, by a connected though not necessarily direct, chain of causation should be integrally compensated."[1] According to Personnaz "should be treated as consequences of an injurious act, hence considered for the purposes of assessing compensation, all those facts connected to the original act by a link of cause to effect; in other words all those facts which may be traced back to the original act through an uninterrupted sequence".[2]

Truly "indirect" damage, not subject to compensation, is therefore damage which can only be traced to the original event through an unforeseen sequence of exceptional circumstances due only to the presence of extraneous factors. As noted by Mme. Bollecker-Stern "the very existence of exceptional circumstances which allowed the damage to occur should be regarded as an external event and the resulting damage extraneous rather than transitive".[3] The concept of "indirect" transitive damage appears quite appropriate when applied to damage from pollution. Transitive damage involves the formula $E_1 \rightarrow D_1 \rightarrow D_2$. What happens in pollution cases, in particular those involving damage to the tourist trade?

A discharge of oil ($E_1$) causes pollution of beaches ($D_1$) which results in fewer tourists ($D_2$). Damage to the tourist trade takes the form of a loss of profits or prospective earnings. The beach and the sea are "commodities" and are the source of economic and commercial activities, hence provide a means of livelihood for some groups of the population, just as fish to fishermen. If it is true that pollution of beaches has driven away tourists due to the unsightly aspect of water covered in oil, foam resulting from the use of detergents or the foul smell, then hotel-keepers, restaurant owners and bathing establishments should be awarded compensation for the consequent loss of earnings.

This approach runs into the difficulty that the "economic" loss [4] is incurred indirectly by third parties (hotel-keepers, fishermen) and not by the original victim, in this case the State. It is true that for Salvioli the principles applicable remain exactly the same where subsequent damage is suffered by a person other than the first victim, whether the same person or instead a third party is

---

1) The responsibility of states in international law, New York, 1932, p. 202.
2) La réparation du préjudice en droit international public, Thesis Paris, 1938, p. 136.
3) Op.cit., p. 212.
4) On the concept of "economic" loss, see Doyen Claude-Albert Colliard, Loi et usage concernant le contrôle de la pollution en France, 1974, p. 84, No. 3.1.8.b.

affected.  Once a sufficient causal relationship exists between the
initial act and damage to the third party, then redress is required.(1)

However, it appears from international decisions that a third
party who indirectly suffers damage cannot claim compensation for his
loss from the person responsible for the initial damage.

In the Chorzow factory case the P.C.I.J. stated "it should first
be observed that, in estimating the damage caused by an unlawful act,
only the value of property, rights and interests which have been affected and the owner of which is the person on whose behalf compensation
is claimed, or the damage done to whom is to serve as a means of
gauging the reparation claimed, must be taken into account.  This
principle, which is accepted in the jurisprudcnce of arbitral tribunals,
has the effect, on the one hand, of excluding from the damage to be
estimated, injury resulting for third parties from the unlawful act
and, on the other hand, of not excluding from the damage the amount
of debts and other obligations for which the injured party is responsible".(2)

According to Salvioli, the principle laid down by the P.C.I.J.
with the effect "of excluding from the damage to be estimated, injury
resulting for third parties from the unlawful act" cannot be justified
if viewed separately.  "The court", he considers, "is undoubtedly re-
ferring to a case where a State claiming on behalf of person A would
not have authority to claim for another person B, even where B had
been solely and directly injured".(3)

B. Bollecker-Stern refutes this interpretation, which is contrary
to the facts of the case since it concerned compensation for damage
suffered indirectly by the German tax authorities, on whose behalf
Germany was certainly entitled to claim.(4)  She considers that the
principle stated in the Chorzow factory case, far from being an exception, is confirmed by several other decisions.

It will be noted, however, that the cases she quotes in support
of her view involve contractual or family relationships between the
first person who suffers the initial damage and the third party.  It
is precisely this relationship which constitutes, according to B.
Bollecker-Stern, the external factor, the unrelated cause which im-

---

1) La responsabilité des Etats et la fixation des dommages et intérêts
   par les tribunaux internationaux, R.C.A.D.I., 1929, III, p.251,
   note 1. Likewise under French law, the courts will award compensation for damage suffered as an after-effect by persons other than
   the first victim, if it is established that such damage unquestion-
   ably stems from the original fault.  Mazeaud et Tunc, op.cit.,
   No. 1676, p. 794; see above a) TGI Nanterre, 22nd October 1975,
   GP 1976 I p. 392, Weill and Terre, Les obligations, 2nd Edition
   No. 606, Durry, Chronique RTD Civ. 1977.  768 No. 1. Vedel, Droit
   administratif, 1968, p. 344.
2) P.C.I.J., Collection of judgements, series A, No. 13, p. 31.
3) Op.cit., p. 251, note 1.
4) Op. cit., p. 232.

plies that damage is indirectly caused. Put in another way the relationship acts as a "driving belt" in producing the damage. The two victims are not wholly independent. The damage rebounds onto a third party whose interests are linked to those of the person who suffers damage in the first place.

In line with the definition usually given of indirectly caused damage, such damage is accessory to the main damage; it usually takes the form of damage incidentally affecting a person other than the one who suffered the main damage; it is due in part to extraneous causes.(1)

B. Bollecker-Stern considers that in the case of damage to a third party, the extraneous factor is "precisely the special relationship which exists between such party and the first victim, which results in the damage rebounding on the third party. Since such a factor is always present where damage is caused incidentally to a third party, such damage will never be subject to compensation"(2).

Where loss to the tourist trade following pollution damage is concerned, the extraneous factor however does not exist since there is no relationship between the initial victim (the State) and third parties (hotel-keepers, restaurant owners). The loss to the tourist trade cannot therefore be described as being indirectly caused. It is not the fact that the State has suffered loss which results in hotel-keepers being affected as a consequence. The damage suffered by the hotel-keeper is independent of any relationship with the initial victim. The damage is not related to the initial victim but to the damaged property itself. In such case, the external cause or extraneous factor therefore appears to be missing. If this is so, redress for the economic loss suffered would be admissible.

Moreover, in most of the cases where the principle laid down in the Chorzow factory case has allegedly been applied, it may be asked whether it was not the absence of a causal relationship rather than the impact on a third party which underlay the decisions.

Thus, in connection with the damage caused by the torpedoing of the Lusitania, the Joint German-American Commission refused to indemnify the insurance companies for compensation which they had been obliged to pay, on the grounds that "the accelerated maturity of the insurance contracts was not a natural and normal consequence of Germany's act in taking the lives, and hence not attributable to that act as a proximate course"; hence that such act could not be considered the direct cause.(3) On the other hand, the Commission order

---

1) Rousseau,Droit international public, Sirey, 1953, p. 634. Cavare, Le droit international public positif, T.2, 1969, 3rd edition, updated by J.P. Queneudec, p. 505.
2) Op. cit., p. 230.
3) Joint German-American Commission, Witemberg I, p. 103 et seq. See also under French Law Le Tourneau op. cit., No. 107, p. 49, Mazeaud and Tunc, op. cit., No. 1676, note 1 in fine.

Germany to pay compensation for damage suffered by relatives of victims who had previously been supported by them and who could normally
expect to continue receiving financial support. "Its view was that
the members of the families of those who lost their lives on the
Lusitania and who were accustomed to receive and could reasonably expect to continue to receive pecuniary contributions from the decedents,
suffered losses which, because of the natural relations between the
decedents and the members of their families, flowed from Germany's act
normal consequence thereof, and hence /were7 attributable to Germany's
act as a proximate cause."

Assuming that compensation for financial loss is refused, could
not the State "take over" the losses to the tourist trade suffered by
its nationals and in addition to the damage done to beaches refer to
that affecting related interests (damage to the tourist trade), as
would appear to be possible under certain agreements concerning pollution?

B. POLLUTION LAW

a) Oil

Several provisions in recent agreements concerning pollution cover
both damage to tourism and damage suffered by fishermen. Under the
Brussels Convention of 29th November 1969 relating to Intervention on
the High Seas in cases of Oil Pollution Casualties which came into
force on 6th May 1975, "Parties to the present Convention may take
such measures on the high seas as may be necessary to prevent, mitigate
or eliminate grave and imminent danger to their coastline or related
interests from pollution or threat of pollution ... (Article 1)."

"Related interests means the interests of a coastal State
directly affected or threatened by the maritime casualty, such as:

a) maritime coastal, port or estuarine activities, including
   fisheries activities, constituting an essential means of
   livelihood of the persons concerned;
b) tourist attractions of the area concerned;
c) the health of the coastal population and the well-being
   of the area concerned, including conservation of living
   marine resources and of wildlife;" /Article II(4)7.

It is apparent from this definition that the tourist attractions
of a region and its fisheries activities are interests "directly"
threatened by an incident at sea in the same way as are the living
resources of the sea itself.

The French Act of 7th July 1976 concerning the prevention and
control of marine pollution due to dumping from ships and aircraft

and the control of accidental marine pollution (1) which authorises
the State to take action in accordance with the 1969 Brussels Convention refers back to the Convention itself for the definition of "related interests" (Section 16).

Identical provisions to those in the 1969 Brussels Convention
are contained in the Protocol concerning Co-operation in Combatting
Pollution of the Mediterranean Sea by Oil and other Harmful Substances
in Cases of Emergency, signed in Barcelona on 16th February 1976.
Under Article 1 the Contracting Parties are to co-operate in taking
the necessary measures in cases where the presence of massive quantities of oil or other harmful substances which are polluting or threaten
to pollute the waters of the Mediterranean, constitutes a grave and
imminent danger to the marine environment, the coasts or related
interests of one or more parties.

"The term 'related interests' means the interests of a coastal
State directly affected or threatened and concerning, among others:

a) activities in coastal waters, in ports or estuaries,
   including fishing activities;
b) the historical and tourist appeal of the area in question,
   including water sports and recreation;
c) the health of the coastal population;
d) the preservation of living resources" (Article 2).(2)

Provisions in agreements under private law are undoubtedly to be
interpreted in the same way.  Indeed, it would be strange if Conventions under public law were to cover damage to the tourist trade and
damage to fishing interests if this was not also the case in private
law agreements.

Under Article 1.6 of the Brussels Convention of 29th November
1969 on Civil Liability for Oil Pollution Damage "pollution damage
means loss or damage caused outside the ship carrying oil by contamination resulting from the escape or discharge of oil ..."  An identical definition appears in the London Convention of 17th December 1976
on Civil Liability for Oil Pollution Damage due to Exploration and
Exploitation of Mineral Resources of the Seabed /Article 1 (6)7.

It is understood that the term "contamination" appears in both
definitions in opposition to fire and explosion which does not cause
pollution damage as defined by the two Conventions.

---

1) Journal Officiel of 8th July 1976.
2) On extension of the definition in the 1969 Convention to that of
   1976, see Michel Buhl, La Convention de Barcelone du 16 février
   1976 pour la protection de la Mer Méditerranée contre la pollution,
   in Travaux of the UER de Droit de Saint-Etienne, Vol. 1-1977,
   p. 83 et seq. and in particular p. 119.

As concerns the scope of the expression "any loss or damage caused outside the ship" and in particular what precisely is covered by the term "loss", it should be noted that this is a question of interpretation which will depend on the law of the court which hears the case. It may well be, however, that many courts will interpret this expression so as to cover not only damage to property - or injury to persons, although this is less usual in oil pollution cases - but also loss consequent upon such damage, i.e. loss of prospective earnings. The conventions would therefore apply to compensation for property contaminated as a result of oil spills (polluted beaches, dead fish) and consequent loss of income (damage to tourism, fishing interests).(1)

Thus, under the law of the State of Maine in the United States the polluter is liable for "damage to real and personal property and loss of income attributed to pollution".(2) Similarly, the protection fund of the State of Maine provides compensation for financial loss. Under Section 551 of the Oil Discharge Prevention and Pollution Control Act of 1970 "Anyone claiming to have suffered damages to real estate or personal property of loss of income directly or indirectly as a result of a (prohibited) discharge of oil, petroleum products or their by-products ... may apply within six months after the occurrence of such a discharge to the commission stating the amount of damage he claims to have suffered as a result of such discharge".(3)

Similar provisions are to be found in Canadian legislation. A national level the Marine Pollution Compensation Fund set up by the 1970 Canadian Shipping Act pays compensation to victims of damage due directly or indirectly to pollution by ships, where the polluter cannot be identified or where the victim is unable to recover sums due to him under a judgment against the person responsible for the pollution. The Fund will compensate any fisherman who suffers a loss of

---

1) E. du Pontavice, La convention internationale pour la responsabilité civile pour les dommages dus à la pollution par les hydrocarbures du 29 novembre 1969, Colloque sur les problèmes juridiques posés par les dommages de pollution survenant à l'occasion d'opération d'assistance à des pétroliers, Institut Méditerranéen des Transports Maritimes, Marseille, 24-25 octobre 1975, p. 34.
2) Edgar Gold, "Oil Pollution, a Survey of Worldwide Legislation", published by Gard Protection and Indemnity Insurance Club of Norway, p. 17, paragraph 3, quoted by Thomas A. Mensah, "Pollution Risks and Shipowners Liabilities", p. 13 (unpublished text of a statement by Mr. Mensah, Legal Adviser to IMCO (Inter-governmental Maritime Consultative Organisation), at a seminar of Arab countries on marine insurance held in Mohammedia, Morocco, from 1st to 4th September 1975. Reproduced by the author under the title "International Environmental Law: International Conventions concerning Oil Pollution at Sea, in Case "Western Reserve", Journal of International Law, Vol. 8, 1976, p. 110-130.
3) Thiem, Environmental Damage Funds, OECD, 25th October 1977, Working Paper No. 6, p. 25-28.

income as a result of pollution due to a discharge by a ship and who is unable to recover the amount of his losses (Section 746).(1)   Likewise a 1970 Act of Manitoba Province, the Fishermen's Assistance and Polluters Liability Act, provides compensation for fishermen who have suffered or will suffer financial loss as a result of their activities being interrupted due to pollution.(2)

Likewise under German case law a restaurant owner has been awarded compensation for loss of goodwill where his turnover declined as a result of offensive smells due to flooding by the river next to the restaurant.(3)

The US case law also provides compensation for losses in production of oyster-breeders from the dumping of mud on oyster-beds as a consequence of dredging.(4)   Similarly, the Courts recognise:  "the right of fishermen to "maintain private actions for damages based upon alleged tortious invasion of public rights.";  "the right of commercial fishermen to recover for injuries ... caused by pollution .. is a pecuniary loss of a particular and special nature".(5)

In the Union Oil case, the Court stated that the "alleged diminution of the aquatic life of the Santa Barbara Channel claimed to have resulted from this occurrence (an oil spill) constitute(s) a legally compensable injury to the commercial fisherman claimants".(6)

W. Rodgers (7) has stated that the interests of the commercial fishermen in Oppen "appear indistinguishable from charter boat operators, motel owners and beach concessionaires with an economic stake in the integrity of public waters."

Under these reasoning, such business interests would also be able to recover lost profits resulting from pollution of the ocean.(8)

---

1) Thiem, op.cit., p. 29; Lefebvre and Leonetti, Etude comparative des législations nord-américaines et européennes relatives à la pollution par les hydrocarbures, Institut du Droit, de la Paix et du Développement de l'Université de Nice, p. 20, Reprint in "Le Pétrole et la Mer" (PUF, Paris, 1976, pp. 166-167; Council of Europe, La contribution du droit pénal à la protection de l'environnement, Report submitted by M. Beale, Document DPC/CEPC/XXXIV(74)1, Strasbourg, 23rd April 1974, p. 77.
2) Tancelin, Rapport sur la protection juridique du voisinage et de l'environnement au Canada, Journées de l'Association Henri Capitant, 1976, pp. 14-15, Reprint in "La protection du voisinage et de l'environnement, Travaux de l'Association Henri Capitant, 28th May-2nd June (1979), p. 73; Thiem, op.cit., pp. 29-30.
3) Steiger with the collaboration of Demel, Prévention et récupération des pollutions venant du large, Rapport sur le droit allemand, Deuxième Congrès de la Société Française pour le Droit de l'Environnement, La Protection du Littoral, Bordeaux, 6th-7th-8th October, 1977, p. 13.
4) Petrovich v. US, 421 F. 2d 1364 (Cc. Cl., 1970).
5) Accord, National Sea Clammers Assoc. v. City of New York, 12 ERC 1118, 1128 (NJ, 1978).
6) Union Oil Co. v. Oppen, 501 F. 2nd 558,570 (9 Circ., 1974).
7) W. Rodgers, Handbook on Environmental Law, 147-148 (1977).
8) Stephen McCaffrey, Legal Remedies for existing or threatened pollution damage to Canada and the United States. A study prepared for the Environment Directorate, OECD, June 1979, p. 49 et seq. and footnote page 50.

Professor McCaffrey (1) gives many examples of such damages in the United States case-law which are rejected by the Canadian case-law (which is often lagging behind the Canadian written law):

> "Special damages may also be recovered in the nuisance cases
> for various forms of direct injury to personal as well as
> real property ... in contrast to the Canadian position.
> Thus plaintiff may be compensated for loss of egg production,
> loss of chickens and hogs, decrease in milk production,(2)
> loss injury to domestic animals, plants and clothes on a
> line,(3) and even for destruction of fish in a stream running
> through plaintiff's land."(4)

Compensation is also recoverable for damages to ornamental trees.(5)

Even where there is neither lost profit nor loss of rental income from damage to plaintiff's property, recovery has been allowed for the loss of the special value of the property to the plaintiff himself.(6)

Various forms of economic injury are compensable. For example, damages have been awarded in pollution cases for injuries to fishing privileges,(7) loss of patronage (8) and even loss of anticipated profits.(9)

---

1) See McCaffrey supra, p. 49 et seq.
2) Seaboard Oil Co. v. Britt, 208 Ky. 723,271 S.W. 1038 (1925);
   Fairview Farms, Inc. v. Reynolds Metals Co., 176 F. Supp. 178
   (D.C. Or. 1959) (decrease in milk production).
3) Griffin v. Northbridge, 67 Cal. App. 2d 69, 153 P. 2d 800 (1944)
   (flowers); Wheat v. Freeman Coal Mining Corp., 23 Ill. App. 3d 14,
   319 N.E. 2d 290 (1974) damage to clothes and housepaint by coal
   dust).
4) Hodges v. Pine Products Co., 135 Ga. 134 68 S.E. 1107 (1910).
5) Pettinghill v. Turo, 159 Me. 350, 193 A.2d 367 (1963).
6) Nitram Chemicals v. Parker, 200 So. 2d 220 (Fla. App. 1967); Adams
   Const. Co. v. Bentley, 335 S.W. 2d 912 (Ky. 1960). See generally
   D. Dobbs, Handbook on the Law of Remedies 345 56 (1973).
7) Hodges v. Pine Products Co., 135 Ga. 134, 67 S.E. 1107 ((1910);
   Masonite Corp. v. Steede, 198 Miss. 530,547, 23 So. 2d 756 (1945);
   Hampton v. No. Carolina Pulp Co., 223 N.C. 535, 27 N.E. 2d 538
   (1943) damages also awarded for loss of anticipated profits);
   Carson v. Hercules Powder Co. 250 Ark. 887, 402 S.W. 2d 640; and
   Union Oil Co. v. Oppen, 501 F. 2d 558 (9th Circ. 1974).
8) Ft. Worth and R.G.R. Co. v. Hancock, 386 S.W. 335 (Tex. Civ. App.
   1926); Love v. Nashville Agricultural and Normal Institute, 146
   Tenn. 550,243 S.W. 304 (injury to the reputation of a spring as
   furnishing pure medicinal water).
9) Fort Worth & Rio Grande Ry. Co. v. Hancock, 286 S.W. 335 (Tex.
   Civ. App. 1926) (pollution of river injured plaintiff's swimming
   business); Union Oil Co. v. Oppen, 501 F.2d 558 (9th Cir. 1974)
   (damage to commercial fishery by oil spill); Hampton v. No.
   Carolina Pulp Co., 223 N.C. 535, 27 S.E. 2d 538 (1943) (interference with riparian's fishing business); Storley v. Armour Co.,
   107 F.2d 499, 507 (8th Cir. 1939) (interference with farming by
   river pollution); Conley v. Amalgamated Sugar Co., 74 Ideho
   416,263 P. 2d 705 (1953); Gano v. Hall, 188 Kan. 491, 363 P. 2d
   551 (1961). See generally D. Dobbs, supra, at 345.

Even where there is neither lost profit nor loss of rental income from damage to plaintiff's property, recovery has been allowed for the loss of the special value of the property to the plaintiff himself.(1)

Various forms of economic injury are compensable. For example, damages have been awarded in pollution cases for injuries to fishing privileges,(2) loss of patronage,(3) and even loss of anticipated profits.(4)

In cases involving damage to land, recovery has been allowed for expenses incurred in protecting against future injury as well as for sums expended in minimising damages.(5)

Examples of such defensive action by plaintiff for which damages could be allowed are installation of soundproofing, insulation and air conditioning.(6)

The two Conventions on third party liability referred to above do not confine compensation to damage physically caused by the polluting substance but also cover expenses incurred in preventing or limiting the damage.

The Conventions thus state that pollution damage includes the cost of preventive measures and any loss or damage caused by such measures. "'Preventive measures' means any reasonable measures taken by any person after an incident has occurred to prevent or minimise

---

1) Nitram Chemicals v. Parker, 200 So.2d 220 (Fla. App. 1967); Adams Const. Co. v. Bentley, 335 S.W. 2d 912 (Ky. 1960). See generally D. Dobbs, Handbook on the Law of Remedies 345 56 (1973).
2) Hodges v. Pine Products Co., 135 Ga. 134, 67 S.E. 1107 (1910); Masonite Corp. v. Steede, 198 Miss. 530, 547, 23 So.2d 756 (1945); Hampton v. No. Carolina Pulp Co., 223 N.C. 535, 27 N.E.2d 538 (1943) (damages also awarded for loss of anticipated profits); Carson v. Hercules Powder Co., 240 Ark. 887, 402 S.W. 2d 640; and Union Oil Co. v. Oppen, 501 F.2d 558 (9th Cir. 1974).
3) Ft. Worth & R.G.R. Co. v. Hancock, 286 S.W. 335 (Tex. Civ. App. 1926); Love v. Nashville Agricultural and Normal Institute, 146 Tenn. 550, 243 S.W. 304 (injury to the reputation of a spring as furnishing pure medicinal water).
4) Fort Worth & Rio Grande Ry. Co. v. Hancock, 286 S.W. 335 (Tex. Civ. App. 1926) (pollution of river injured plaintiff's swimming business); Union Oil Co. v. Oppen, 501 F.2d 558 (9th Cir. 1974) (damage to commercial fishery by oil spill); Hampton v. No. Carolina Pulp Co., 223 N.C. 535, 27 S.E. 2d 538 (1943) (interference with riparian's fishing business); Storley v. Armour Co., 107 F. 2d 499, 507 (8th Cir. 1939) (interference with farming by river pollution); Conley v. Amalgamated Sugar Co., 74 Idaho 416, 263 P. 2d 705 (1953); Gano v. Hall, 188 Kan. 491, 363 P.2d 551 (1961). See generally D. Dobbs, supra at 345.
5) See D. Dobbs, supra, at 346.
6) See, e.g. Schatz v. Abbott Laboratories Inc., 51 Ill. 2d 143, 281 N.E. 2d 323 (1972) (air conditioning and insulation). See also Stratford Theater, Inc. v. Town of Stratford, 140 Conn. 422, 101 A.2d 279 (1953) (installation of lateral sewer lines to alleviate overflow caused by defendant); Piedmont Cotton Mills, inc. v. General Warehouse No. Two, Inc., 222 Ga. 164, 149 S.E. 2d 72 (1966); and Annot., 41 A.L.R.2d 1064 (1955). See generally, W. Rodgers, supra, at 148.

pollution damage." (Article 1(7) Convention of 1969, Article 1(7) Convention of 1976). Any private individual or public body which takes measures to prevent pollution damage will therefore be entitled to compensation. The London Convention of 1976 nevertheless lays down that measures to contain oil-wells and to protect, repair or replace an installation are not deemed to be preventive measures. As a result of this narrow definition, where the fracture of a pipe leads to the escape of oil, measures taken to plug the leak will be deemed "repairs" to the installation and hence not preventive measures. To be treated as such, measures must be taken outside the installation, i.e. the use of chemical products and mechanical processes such as pumping or laying barriers.

On the other hand, it is clear from the 1969 Convention that where repairs are carried out on board ship to plug an oil leak, such steps are seen as preventive measures, as are operations to pump oil out of an oil tanker where this is done to prevent or limit pollution. Thus, pumping operations on the Bohlen, estimated to have cost around F.100 million, are to be treated as a preventive measure.(1)

It may be asked whether the cost of air surveillance of oil slicks is a preventive measure. The answer is yes where pollution is hence prevented or limited as where information is provided on the trend of the oil slick, its course and appropriate steps can accordingly be taken.

Costs of cleaning beaches are also covered by the definition of preventive measures. Long before the adoption of the 1969 Convention such costs were however already regarded as directly caused damage and the courts had never hesitated to order their reimbursement. Thus on 3rd November 1965 in the case referred to above, Captain of the oil tanker World Mead v. the towns of La Baule, Pornichet, Le Pouliguen and Le Croisic, the Court of Appeal of Rennes, after noting the causal relationship between the escape of fuel oil and beach pollution compensated the resorts for the costs of cleaning their beaches. "Whereas it has been proved that the towns of La Baule and Pornichet were obliged to undertake more extensive cleaning operations for their beaches than in previous years, and that it was necessary to extract and remove sand saturated with fuel oil; that the Court of First Instance was correct in allowing the expenditure incurred by the towns, as verified by the expert, amounting to F.20,753.30 for the commune of La Baule and F.16,906.87 for the commune of Pornichet ... Upholds the decision of the lower court in ordering the Master of the World Mead to "pay such sums to the two communes as compensation for their material loss".(2)

---

1) La Revue Maritime, November 1977, p. 1225; Journal de la Marine Marchande, 25th August 1977.
2) DMF 1966, p. 466.

Similarly, the Court of Appeal of Toulouse accepted that expenses incurred by the Prefects of the departments of Haute-Garonne and Tarn et Garonne in cleaning the river Garonne and assisting fishing companies affected by the pollution, were a result of the pollution and "were the direct consequence of the offences with which the accused were charged".(1)

Insofar as compensation is designed to restore the victim to the position in which he would have been if the event giving rise to the damage had not occurred, the courts will accept that the victim is entitled to reimbursement of the cost of restoring the damaged property to its original state. In the case of oil pollution of beaches, the measure of the damage is therefore the sum required to restore the beaches to their original condition, i.e. the cost of removing the oil or of cleaning.

Likewise, expenses incurred in restoring animal life in the polluted area are to be treated as preventive measures. This was stated by the Court of Appeal of Toulouse in the decision mentioned above: "Whereas the Federations of Fishing and Fish-Breeding Associations of the two departments affected by the pollution, required by Sections 2 and 3 of the Decree of 11th April 1958 to ensure the reproduction and protection of fresh water fish, are legally entitled to claim compensation for the direct and certain loss which they have suffered by reason of the additional expenses incurred in restocking the river with fish and maintaining the biological potential of water courses affected by the pollution.(2)

The law of several countries in regard to pollution makes provisions for the reimbursement of cleaning expenses. Thus in the United States the owner of a ship is required to reimburse the State for expenses incurred in removing oil.(3)

Likewise in Canada an Act for the Prevention of Pollution of those parts of the Arctic sea close to the continent and to the islands of the Canadian Arctic (4) states that where the Governor in Council directs any action to be taken to repair or remedy any condition that results or may reasonably be expected to result from the deposit of waste, the costs and expenses of and incidental to the taking of such action, to the extent may, that such costs and expenses

---

1) Court of Appeal of Toulouse, Criminal Appeals Division, 3rd February 1977, Guerbadot, Bos, Szilagyl v. Ministère Public et Parties Civiles, unpublished.
2) Court of Appeal of Toulouse, 3rd February 1977, Guerbadot, Bos, Szilagyi v. Ministère Public et Parties Civiles, unpublished.
3) Water Quality Improvement Act 1970, Section II f (1).
4) Arctic Waters Pollution Prevention Act, S.R.C. 1970, C.2 (1st suppl.). On this Act see in particular Donat Pharand "The Law of the Sea of the Arctic with Special Reference to Canada", Ottawa, 1973, p. 224 et seq.

can be established to have been reasonably incurred in the circumstances, are recoverable by Her Majesty in right of Canada from the person or persons liable /Section 6(2)7.

It will be recalled, as regards private arrangements, that under the TOVALOP agreement (Tanker Owners Voluntary Agreement concerning Liability for Oil Pollution, 7th January 1969) in the event of an oil spill all reasonable expenses by the ship-owner to prevent or limit the damage are to be reimbursed, in addition to cleaning costs incurred by governments. A further private agreement knowns as CRISTAL (1) covers the cost of protective measures designed to prevent and limit pollution damage as well as damage caused by such measures themselves.

Likewise, in cases of off-shore pollution, Opol (2) will reimburse the cost of protective measures taken by the operator and by any government or other public authority to prevent, reduce or eliminate pollution, with the exception of measures for well control or measures to protect, repair or replace the installation.

## b) Other harmful substances

Although the first treaty provisions only dealt with damage to the tourist trade or to fishing when this was due to oil pollution, more recent provisions also cover pollution by "other harmful substances", e.g. the Barcelona Protocol mentioned above.(3)

Moreover, in several cases pollution has been defined in general terms which ought to enable compensation to be paid irrespective of which polluting substances are involved.

Thus under Article 4 of the Soviet-Finnish Agreement on frontier waters signed in Helsinki on 25th April 1964 states the Contracting Parties agree to take measures to prevent the frontier waterways system being polluted by harmful industrial wastes, by domestic waste water, by waste caused by the floating of timber, by discharges from ships or by any other substances liable to cause immediate or subsequent water pollution, degradation of water consistency, interference with fishing, any instable blighting of the landscape, danger to human health or entail other harmful consequences for the population or the economy".(4)

At its meeting in Ottawa in November 1971, the Intergovernmental Working Party on the Pollution of the Seas adopted the following definition: "Marine pollution is defined as the introduction by man, directly or indirectly, of substances or energy into the marine environment (including estuaries), resulting in such deleterious effects as harm to living resources, hazards to human health, hindrance to

---

1) Contract regarding an interim supplement to tanker liability for oil pollution, 1st April 1971.
2) Offshore Pollution Liability Association Limited, 4th September 1974.
3) See above.
4) Text in RTNU, Vol. 537, p. 231.

marine activities including fishing, impairment of quality for use of
sea water, and reduction of amenities."(1)  This definition, restated
in the Stockholm Declaration (Principle 7), also appears in the Conventions of Oslo, London (immersion) and Paris (land-based pollution).
The Contracting Parties thus undertake to take all possible measures
to control marine pollution by substances liable to create hazards to
human health, to harm living resources and marine life, to damage
amenities or interfere with other legitimate uses of the sea.  Similarly, the definition in the Barcelona Convention covers interference
with maritime activities including <u>fishing</u>, impairment of the quality
for use of sea water and reduction of amenities (Article 2).

Lastly, the single revised negotiating text, submitted on 6th
May 1976 by the Chairman of the Third Commission at the end of the
Fourth Session of the United Nations Conference on the Law of the Sea
in New York contains an identical definition (Article 1).(2)

This general agreement as to the definition of pollution should
make possible the compensation of damage deemed to be "indirectly
caused" regardless of which polluting substances are involved.

c) <u>Lessons to be drawn from the Torrey Canyon case</u>

The Torrey-Canyon case did not really shed any light on the
question of so-called indirect damage.  Under an agreement concluded
in London on 11th November 1969 by the British and French Governments
with the owners and charterers of the Torrey Canyon on the other, the
two governments, who had borne the costs of controlling the pollution
and cleaning their coasts, accepted an overall sum of £3 million
sterling (a little over F.40 million), to be shared equally between
them, in full and final settlement of the dispute.  In addition, the
shipowners and shippers undertook to pay private individuals compensation in an amount not exceeding £25,000 sterling (about F.335,000)
in all, to be shared in the same proportion as for the two governments.(3)

As there is no information on the exact nature of the damage
alleged by private individuals, we do not know whether so-called "indirect" damage was in fact the subject of compensation.(4)

It is clear from the above that financial losses incurred by
fishermen as a result of declining sales could be compensated either
by direct payment to the fishermen as in the Red Sludge Case, or
through payments by the State to its nationals out of sums obtained

---

1) UN Document A/CONF 48/1 WGMP II/5 of 22nd November 1971.
2) UN Document A/CONF.62/WP.8/Rev.1/Part III.
3) Journal de la Marine Marchande 1969, p. 2601 and 2679;  Rousseau,
   Chronique des faits internationaux, RGDIP 1970, p. 1087.
4) Ballenegger, La Pollution en Droit International, 1975, p. 216.

from the person liable. Under Article 14 of the French Civil Code "a foreigner, even if not resident in France, may be the subject of proceedings before the French courts for the discharge of obligations contracted in France ... (or) contracted abroad vis-à-vis French citizens". It follows from this Article, which has been extended by the courts to all debts, even where not resulting from contract, that French citizens may bring proceedings against foreigners in a French court, which will in practice be the one of the place where the damage occurred or of the place of residence of the plaintiff. Such courts will apply French law as being the law of the place where the damage occurred.(1) If the damage occurs on the high seas, French law is still applicable as being the lex fori.

What has been said above would suggest that such a court would award compensation for loss of prospective earnings by fishermen. Although financial loss following on pollution is seen as indirectly caused from the standpoint of the physical chain of events, it should from the legal standpoint nevertheless be described as directly caused and compensation should therefore be awarded.

---

1) E. du Pontavice, La pollution des mers par les hydrocarbures. A propos de l'affaire du Torrey Canyon, LGDJ, 1968, No. 46.

Part II

## CONSEQUENCES AS REGARDS COMPENSATION

This paper does not propose to study compensation mechanisms and procedures, which have been discussed on many occasions.(1)  As regards pollution it has been seen that a number of conventions have introduced systems of limited, guaranteed redress, often supplemented by a compensation fund.  These apply to the compensation of financial loss which has been discussed above.  They will not be referred to here, since they apply to pollution damage in general and not specifically to so-called "indirect" damage.

On the other hand, consideration will be given to problems of evidence which victims have come up against, i.e. proof that the damage actually occurred and proof of the causal relationship.

## A. REFUSAL TO AWARD COMPENSATION

A person who suffers damage should, in principle, be restored to the situation which would have prevailed had the event which gave rise to the damage not occurred.  The compensation should be equal to the amount of loss suffered but should not afford additional financial advantage to the victim.  This would be the case if compensation were awarded for purely hyoothetical or unproved damage.

A loss of earnings should only be the subject of compensation insofar as its existence and amount can be established as probabilities. This principle of domestic law is also to be found in international law.(2)  The loss of earnings must therefore be "objective" (3) and its occurrence must not merely as foreseen by the claimant's own

---

1) See in particular within the OECD, E. du Pontavice, Compensation for Transfrontier Pollution Damage (1974) published in "Legal Aspects of Transfrontier Pollution", OECD, 1977, p. 409; M. Remond-Gouilloud, Compensation for Marine Pollution, ENV/TFP/77.1(Rev. 1). Compensation for Pollution Damage, ENV/ECO/77.18, 21st September 1977;  Thiem, Environmental Damage Fund, Working Paper No. 6, 25th October 1977.
2) Mazeaud and de Juglart, op.cit. No. 410 et seq.;  Judgement No. 1 of the PCIJ, speech by the French agent, publications of the PCIJ, C.3.1, p. 229 et seq.
3) Personnaz, La réparation du préjudice en droit international, Thesis 1938, p. 117.

calculations, but must also be such as to warrant consideration by the court. The latter must, as stated by the umpire in the William case,(1) consider "if the owner of the ship could rely with certainty on the passengers or if this were only a possibility". Compensation will therefore not be awarded for loss of earnings which is purely hypothetical. The claimant must establish that it is probable - and not merely possible - that he would have earned the sum in question if the unlawful event had not occurred.(2)

The cases show that the occurrence of the prospective loss does not have to be an absolute certainty in order for compensation to be awarded. Thus, in the Cape Horn Pigeon case, the umpire stated "the general principle of civil law, according to which damages must include a compensation, not only for the damage incurred but also for the profit lost, does equally apply on international lawsuits. In order to apply this principle it is not necessary that the amount of profit lost can be established with certainty, but it is sufficient to prove that in the natural order of things, one could have made a profit, that is lost due to the fact that gave rise to the claim."(3)

Loss incurred by fishermen and by the tourist trade should therefore be compensated as loss of prospective earnings, provided that the probability of the occurrence of such loss and of its expected amount can be proved. Compensation will not be awarded to a victim who is unable to provide evidence of his loss.

Thus, a claim was not successful when submitted by a restaurant owner who was unable to establish that he had suffered damage due to the alleged loss of his regular customers following pollution by the River Seine.(4) Likewise, compensation was refused to resort towns which alleged that they had been brought into disrepute by reason of the oil pollution of their beaches but were unable to establish that proceeds from the tax on tourists and summer residents had diminished as a result of the pollution.(5)

The High Court of Bastia in its judgement of 8th December 1976, previously referred to, also stated "that local authorities which levy taxes of various kinds on tourists, summer residents and in some cases on certain real-estate dealings, are entitled to claim compensation for loss incurred in the form of a decrease in revenue due to pollution". But the Court held that it did not have sufficient evidence at its

---

1) La Pradelle et Politis, Recueil des arbitrages internationaux R.A.I., I, 470.
2) Case of Fabiani, La Fontaine, Pasicrisie, p. 365, cited by B. Bollecker-Stern, op.cit., p. 201, No. 534.
3) R.S.A., IX, p. 65.
4) C.E., 7th March 1962, Société des Auberges du Fruit Défendu, JCP, 1963, II. 13094.
5) Court of Rennes, 3rd November 1965, D.M.F. 1966, p. 466.

disposal to evaluate the loss suffered by the two Corsican departments, and appointed an expert to determine the amount of damage caused by the discharge of industrial waste and evaluate the resulting losses; the principle of compensation was therefore accepted but the departments concerned had to provide evidence of the decrease in revenue and of the causal relationship between the discharge of waste and such lower revenue.

Lastly, the Bastia Court agreed, in the same judgement, to award compensation for future damage which was deemed to be probable, on the same basis as damage which had actually occurred "the pollution ... is going to have disastrous consequences ...".(1)

The US case law also requires proof of the certainty of the damage. In the Union Oil case already mentioned the Court stated that: "in order to recover the plaintiff must prove that 'the oil spill did in fact diminish aquatic life and that this diminution reduced the profits the plaintiffs would have realised from their commercial fishing in the absence of the spill. This reduction of profits must be established with certainty and must not be remote, speculative or conjectural.'"


## B. PROOF OF THE CAUSAL RELATIONSHIP

### a) Problems of evidence in pollution cases

A person who has suffered loss can only obtain redress if he establishes that his loss was directly caused by the fault or at least by the activity of another person. As has already been noted, the problem of the causal relationship is a problem of evidence.(2)

Even where the principle of absolute liability is accepted proof of the causal relationship is a precondition for any compensation. The courts are very strict on this point.

Thus, as regards damage due to aircraft, even where liability "is ipso jure absolute and material, it is still necessary for a causal relationship to be established between the damage and the act of the aircraft".(3) The relation of cause to effect must be established with certainty "and otherwise than by hypothesis, however likely this may appear to be".(4)

---

1) M. Remond-Gouilloud, op. cit., p. 431.
2) Pelzer, Problèmes posés par l'établissement du lien de causalité entre l'accident et le dommage nucléaire, in Droit Nucléaire Européen, 1968, p. 49.
3) Tribunal d'instance of Arcachon, 5th February 1965, RGAE, 1965, p. 144.
4) Tribunal de Grande Instance of Montpellier, 19th March 1964, RGAE, 1965, p. 155, Note by Goy.

Proof of the causal relationship will often be difficult, since pollution may be widespread and its causes difficult to trace. In order to assist victims, the courts have sometimes resorted to presumptions of causality. Some presumptions have also been laid down in legislation.

## b) The presumptions of causality

1. In sonic boom cases, the court may infer the existence of a causal relationship between the passing overhead of a supersonic aircraft and the collapse of a building, from a series of "weighty, clear and concordant presumptions".(1)

For several years French courts have thus been inclined to establish the link in a negative fashion. Sufficient presumption may be derived from the fact "that no earth tremor, storm or hurricane had occurred, that the weather was normal, and that no quarry, mining, major work project, clearing of land or underground work site existed in the vicinity".(2)

Similarly, in relation to the pollution of a watercourse, the court found "that between the Sayo factory and the place where the witnesses were situated, there is no farm, no other factory and no vine-growing area. This is sufficient to establish that this particularly serious pollution originated in the Sayo factory even though it is not possible to explain the blueish colour of the water."(3)

2. In addition to presumptions established by the cases, presumptions set out in legislation also assist action by victims.

Thus in the nuclear field, Section 10 of the French Act of 30th October 1968 on civil liability in the matter of nuclear energy provides that in the event of a nuclear incident, a decree will be issued containing "a list, not intended to be exhaustive, of diseases which shall be presumed, unless the contrary be proved, to derive from the incident".(4) The Austrian Act of 29th April 1964 on civil liability in nuclear matters also contains a presumption regarding the causal relationship: "Where several nuclear events originating from different installations or different nuclear substances may, in a given case and according to the circumstances, be suspected of being 'the cause of the damage', it shall be presumed that the damage was caused jointly by such events. It shall be possible to rebute such presumption by proving that the damage is unlikely to have been caused by one or more such nuclear events".(5)

---

1) Cassation Civile, 2nd Chamber, 4th and 31st May 1972, D.1972, summary p. 166.
2) Cassation Civile, 2nd Chamber, 13th October 1971, JCP 1971. II. 17044, note by de Juglart and du Pontavice.
3) Tribunal de Grande Instance of Bordeaux, 28th February 1969, JCP, 1970.oo.16529, quoted by Girod, in La réparation du dommage écologique, LGDJ, 1974, p. 129, note 25.
4) Official Journal of 31st October 1968, p. 10195.
5) Pelzer, Problèmes posés par l'établissement du lien du causalité entre l'accident et le dommage nucléaire, in Droit nucléaire européen, 1968, p. 47.

In regard to water pollution, an Austrian Bill states that "concerning damage caused by polluted water, it shall be presumed until the contrary be proven, to have been caused by the riparian owner who is geographically nearest to the place of the damage, having regard to the kind of activity in which he engages".(1)

In Japan, Act No. 142 of 25th December 1970 on offences involving public nuisance causing damage to human health contains a presumption of causality vis-à-vis the person discharging toxic substances where, within a given area, damage affecting public health is caused by toxic substances similar to those which have been discharged within the same area.(2)  Thus, where physical injury is found to have been caused by a discharge of toxic substances, all similar health damage occurring in the same area will automatically be the subject of compensation.(3)

Lastly, in Canada, the Act of 1970 of the Province of Manitoba referred to above, states that any polluting discharge into the watercourses of Manitoba involves the liability of the polluter for all damage, without it being necessary for the chain of causation to be established.(4)  Under this Act, fishermen compelled to cease work due to water pollution are compensated directly by the provincial authorities, which in their turn have a right of action against those responsible for the pollution.  The fishermen who are victims of the damage are thus spared the necessity of proving the existence of a causal link.  This instead is done by the authorities.(5)  This trend towards greater flexibility in the need to show a relation of cause to effect ought to be continued in relation to pollution.

According to P. Dupuy, "the determination of a 'substantial relationship' should vary depending on whether a system of liability based on fault or one based on the theory of the risk created is being applied:  whereas in the first case the court must determine exactly to what extent the fault of the person doing the damage is the cause of the loss sustained, in the second case, that of the 'risk created', one consideration alone is important, namely protection of the victim.

In the first case, should intermediate causes intervene so that the damage suffered is only partially attributable to the wrongful act, assessment of compensation may be directly affected since the fault is thereby lessened.  Total or partial exoneration is in fact

---

1) Quoted by Pierard, Responsabilité civile, énergie atomique et droit comparé, 1963, p. 119.
2) Rodière, Traité général de droit maritime, l'armement, 1976, addenda, No. 514.
3) M. Remond, Compensation for marine pollution, ENV/TFP/77.1(1st rev.), p. 11.
4) E. du Pontavice, La protection juridique du voisinage et de l'environnement en droit civil et commercial, Journées de l'Association Henri Capitant 1976.
5) Tancelin, op. cit., p. 14 et seq.

involved. But any such consideration appears of little relevance where the interest of the victim urges that the entire damage be attributed to the activity covered by the system of liability which offers the greatest protection. Although there are qualifications, systems of 'no fault' liability tend to produce 'absolute' liability by providing for automatic compensation.

Hence to insert an implied exoneration clause by requiring a direct link between 'an unusually dangerous activity' and the loss suffered would be contrary to the logic of the system."(1)

CONCLUSION

Contrary to what has often been said, <u>financial loss following an act of pollution</u>, generally described as indirect and hence not subject to compensation, is at law if not in fact, connected by a causal link to the event which gave rise to it.

Such damage does indeed appear to be indirectly caused from the standpoint of the sequence of events. From the legal standpoint it must however be deemed to be directly caused and hence <u>subject to compensation</u>. Thus, although it is true that the loss of earnings by hotel keepers, restaurant owners or fishermen is not an "immediate" consequence of the discharge of polluting substances, it is nevertheless clear that the pollution of beaches and the destruction of fish lead as a direct consequence to a loss of earnings on the part of people who make their living from them. Where pollution of the beaches drives away tourists and where fish are killed by water pollution, hotel keepers, restaurant owners and fishermen should be compensated, in the author's opinion, for their loss of prospective earnings.

As has been seen, the reasoning adopted in international case law as well as recent provisions contained in conventions dealing with pollution, enable compensation to be paid for such damage. Likewise, at national level, most of the cases seem to treat as directly caused not only that damage which is immediate (which would restrict compensation to the first harmful consequence) but also that damage which is "necessary". Should any legislation or court decisions happen to be found which confine directly caused damage to immediate damage, then it would be well if the States in question were to bring their interpretation into line with the broad one prevailing in other States.

Although it is a matter for some satisfaction that the courts are adopting a favourable attitude towards compensation for financial loss resulting from pollution (the decision referred to of the Bastia

1) P. Dupuy, La responsabilité internationale des Etats pour les dommages causés par les activités technologiques et industrielles, Thesis, Paris II, 1974, p. 182 (p. 57 of the 1976 edition by Editions A. Pedone, Paris).

Court in the "Red Sludge" case is a recent example), yet much remains to be done, in French law among others, to provide <u>redress for any damage to the ecology and to tourism which does not have financial repercussions</u>.

When the discharge of polluting substances damages the marine environment and marine life, the courts will, in principle, not enter tain an action brought by a <u>private individual</u> or by an association, for the purpose of protecting the environment. A decision to the effect that the courts have jurisdiction to hear an action brought by a mere stroller or an individual fisherman, has never been taken, on the grounds that such persons have no personal interest in the matter. As has been stated by Despax "the specific nature of pollution damage is such that private individuals are in many cases unable to obtain justice. The fact that the harm done to them as individuals when, for example, they breathe air full of evil-smelling fumes, is the common fate of the whole community, far from giving more weight to their claim, will be regarded as evidence of the absence of any direct and personal damage such as to warrant effective legal proceedings".[1] Holiday-makers who are denied access to beaches polluted by oil or who are unable to indulge in their favourite water sport will be unable to obtain compensation for ecological damage or loss of amenity, due to the absence of any personal interest in the matter.

On the other hand, right or proprietary interest in real estate may be sufficient justification for legal proceedings.[2] The courts will entertain proceedings by the owner of a residence or a person who rents a stretch of water and who claims compensation for loss of amenity due to pollution. Compensation has thus been awarded to an owner for loss of amenity when ditches and canals were invaded by silt and reeds following water diversion.[3] As the action by the owner or the tenant is designed to protect their rights in real estate, the courts will accept that they have a personal interest.[4] Dutch case-law appears to follow the same reasoning.[5]

This is the case for the US courts which allow compensation to the owners of houses situated along a beach who are denied full enjoyment of their property after an oil spill. The Court states that these damages could include "compensation for annoyance, inconvenience and discomfort suffered by particular claimants." (Petition of N.J. Barging Corp. 168 F. Supp. 925 (S.D.N.Y. 1958).

---

1) Obs. JCP 1970.I.2359.
2) Martin, <u>op. cit.</u>, p. 132.
3) CE 26th April 1907, Sieur de Reiset v. Ville de Paris, Recueil Lebon 1907, p. 394.
4) Despax, La pollution des eaux et ses problèmes juridiques, <u>op.cit.</u>, No. 40, p. 127 and note 11, No. 35 p. 115; Pau, 25th February, 1970, JCP 1970.II.16532 comment by Despax.
5) Lambers, Compensation for environmental damage under Dutch law, OECD, Working Paper No. 3, 9th August, 1977, p. 14-15.

The attitude towards ecological proceedings brought by associations is no better than that accorded to private individuals.
Action by associations is held to be inadmissible since they are unable to establish the existence of personal damage distinct from that
to the community as a whole, the protection of which is the responsibility of the Public Prosecutor.(1)

A nature protection association cannot obtain compensation for
damage to the marine environment unless it has incurred expenditure
which owing to pollution has been totally wasted, as in stocking water
with young fish.(2)  The French Cour de Cassation has thus denied any
right to compensation on the part of a Federation of Fishing and Fish
Breeding Associations of a department since, "apart from the expenditure which it has been forced to incur in restocking the river in
young fish, it has not established any personal loss due to the fact
that the river has become and will for a time remain less rich in
fish".(3)

This strict approach adopted by the courts seems even more un-
fortunate in cases where associations are responsible for seeing that
animal species are preserved through protection of their natural environment.  Fishing and fish breeding federations are thus instructed
"to provide for the control of poaching, for the protection and reproduction of freshwater fish and, in general, for increasing the
value of fresh waters".(4)

This attitude is not specific to the French courts.  In Canada,
proceedings brought by a private individual will be dismissed unless
he provides evidence of a personal loss which is special and distinct
from that sustained by the inhabitants as a whole.(5)  The fact that
the latter form themselves into an association does not increase their
chances of success.(5)

Similarly in the US, in the case Burgess v. M/V Tamano (370 F.
Supp. 247. 251 (D. Me. S.D., 1973)), the Court stated that shopkeepers
with premises in the vicinity of polluted beaches could not obtain
compensation.  "They complain only of loss of customers indirectly
resulting from alleged pollution of the coastal waters and beaches in
which they do not have a property interest.  Although in some instances

---

1) Likewise under Dutch law.  See Lambers, op. cit., p. 4-36.
2) M. Remond-Gouilloud, La mise en application en France des règles
   internationales relatives à la lutte contre la pollution des mers
   venant du large, in La Protection du Littoral, Second Congress of
   the Société Française pour le Droit de l'Environnement, Bordeaux,
   6th, 7th and 8th October 1977; by the same author, see note to
   Tribunal de Grande Instance of Bastia, 8th December 1976, D.1977,
   p. 432.
3) Cassation Criminelle, 28th February 1957, Bulletin Criminel, 1957,
   No. 209, p. 356.
4) Decree of 11th April 1958, Section 3.
5) Lucas, The Legal Control of Pollution in Canada, in Proceedings
   of the Eighth International Symposium of Comparative Law, Ottawa,
   1971, p. 17.

their damage may be greater in degree, the injury of which they complain, which is derivative from that of the public at large, is common to all businesses and residents of the Old Orchard Beach area."

This position is more restrictive than that which was adopted in the Court of Rennes in the aforementioned World Mead case. In this case the judges in no way refused redress for the damage to tourism but required the evidence of damage be established.

Only recognition of a general right to the environment which could be relied on by both private individuals and associations in court proceedings would ensure protection of those interests described as collective.

The United States has taken the initial steps in this direction. Under Section 101 (c) of the National Environmental Policy Act of 1969, "the Congress recognises that each person should enjoy a healthful environment". Moreover, the comprehensive Clean Air Amendments of 1970 recognises the right of citizens to take legal proceedings against government or against private individuals who do not comply with the specified standards. These provisions have led to many cases, the novel feature of which is that "the plaintiffs are private citizens, not public agencies ... they are not as property owners nor as protectors of any conventional private interest, but as members of the general public asserting rights they claim simply as members of the public".(1) Likewise, proceedings by associations for the protection of the environment appear to be given favourable consideration.(2)

In France the emergence of a "trend in favour of legal action intended to protect individuals against damage to community interests" may be noted.(3) Several recent measures have recognised the right of environmental protection associations to take legal action in environmental matters subject to certain conditions. Section 26 of the Act of 15th July 1975 on the disposal of waste and the recovery of materials (4) grants such a right to associations recognised to be of public benefit. Under Section 40 of the Nature Conservation Act of 10th July 1976 (5) such proceedings may only be instituted by those associations which are approved in accordance with a procedure laid down by decree.

To ensure participation by environmental protection associations "is in the interest of citizens who, since admittedly they are most

1) Joseph L. Sax, Pollution et nuisances devant les tribuneaux américains, The UNESCO Courier, July 1971, p. 20.
2) Girod, op. cit., pp. 235-236.
3) G. Viney, note under 1st Civ., 27th May 1975, D.1976, p. 318.
4) Journal Officiel of 16th July 1975, p. 7281.
5) Journal Officiel of 13th July 1976, p. 4206.

directly threat ed by environmental degradation, are also in the best position to protest against it. But it is also in the interest of the courts themselves, for easier access to them can but increase their credit".(1)

1) Girod, op. cit., p. 238; Lucas, op. cit., p. 33. Unfortunately, the Criminal Division of the French Cour de Cassation, in line with its narrow approach to the cases, manages to avoid giving effect to the new measures which, as has been seen, to some extent admits action by associations, on the grounds that in the circumstances the "claim for damages by an association in criminal proceedings is inadmissible where the facts upon which such association relies are not covered by the measures in question (referred to above) and where moreover the association does not allege any personal loss distinct from that of its members (Cassation Criminelle, 30th November 1977, JCP 1978, éd., G. IV, 33 and 34).

COMPENSATION FOR ECOLOGICAL DAMAGE

by

Gilles J. Martin

Assistant Lecturer, Teaching and Research Unit
for Law and Economics, Nice University

( 10 D )

Whereas in the long term the desirable goal is to prevent damage
from occurring, in the short and medium term an effective system of
redress is certainly important.  Two arguments may be advanced in support of this affirmation:  first the existence of an effective system
of redress may be regarded as a prerequisite for undertaking activities
which prove socially useful although productive of damage (a fact
which should not be scorned in periods of crisis);  moreover, it must
be recognised that in spite of any precautions taken, accidental or
residual pollution is - and will continue to be - the cause of considerable damage which will require compensation.

Omitting the study of mechanisms designed for guaranteeing compensation for such damage in kind (by restoring matters to their former state), the present article will analyse the methods by which victims are compensated for the disamenities they suffer, meaning that
only methods of monetary compensation for ecological damage will be
discussed.

In this context an attempt will first be made to bring out the
leading aspects and main shortcomings of the system of compensation
for ecological damage as it operates under positive law.  On this
score the contradiction noted between the method and basis of compensation will be emphasised.

During a second stage it will be useful to study possible measures
for ultimately improving the system.


I. THE CONFLICT BETWEEN METHOD AND BASIS
IN COMPENSATING FOR ECOLOGICAL DAMAGE


A mark of the present situation is that compensation for ecological damage is not formally governed by any specific body of law.  With
few exceptions it still comes under the law relating to tortious or
quasi-tortious liability.  Evidence of this is provided by the provisions of international agreements, and the reference made by the
French courts to Articles 1382 et seq. of the French Civil Code.

Logically this situation should lead to a number of conditions having to be met before polluters can be held liable;  similarly it should also have specific consequences at the stage of damage compensation.

The conditions usually required for triggering tortious or quasi-tortious liability are three in number:  first the person liable must be shown to have committed "a fault", save in cases where a special legislation enables such liability to be incurred in view of the risk created by the activity in question;  secondly, damage must exist, it being understood that all damage gives a right to redress;  and lastly a causal connection should be established between the fault (or injurious act) and the damage.

As for the results of legal action alleging liability, these should be of two kinds:  on the one hand, such action should provide full redress for the injury suffered, and on the other, result in cessation of the unlawful situation.

Such is the formal and theoretical legal framework of compensation for ecological damage.

When positive law is considered, however, it is noted that in connection with ecological processes such legal techniques and traditional concepts are in many ways modified and substantially distorted (A), with the ultimate result that the law relating to compensation for ecological damage is based on a fundamental contradiction (B), while no effective protection for the victims is provided (C).

(A) Modifications and distortions in the traditional law governing civil liability

a) First, in regard to the conditions under which liability will arise, such modifications and distortions may be noted at every stage.

1. Thus fault, a traditional prerequisite for liability, no longer appears as such in the law governing compensation for ecological damage.

While continuing to refer to Articles 1382 et seq. of the Civil Code, the courts in fact apply the principle that the polluter is liable even in a case where no fault has been found against him.(1) Going further, they recognise the liability of a polluter who has scrupulously complied with all administrative orders or who has even

---

1) Among many examples may be mentioned a recent decision of the Cour de Cassation of 3rd November 1977 (D. 1978.434, note F. Caballero): "The decision dismissing an owner's claim for redress ... on the grounds that no right or easement nor any legal or regulatory provision was disregarded ... without ascertaining whether the alleged prejudice ... exceeded normal inconveniences common among neighbours, shall be rescinded."

tried to improve upon them by adopting sophisticated techniques for controlling pollution.(1)

Strict liability is also applied in the few national texts establishing specific liability regimes. Legislation in regard to aircraft is a case in point, where Article L. 141-2 of the French Civil Aviation Code makes the aircraft operator "liable" without demonstration or presumption of fault"(2) for any disturbance caused to third parties on the ground. An identical principle prevails under the Act of 30th October 1968 regarding the liability of nuclear energy operators. The "heretical" nature of this provision from the standpoint of traditional law is all the greater as, for technical reasons owing to the needed establishment of a system of financial security, liability is "channelled" towards the operator alone, even in cases where the latter materially has had nothing to do with producing the damage.

The principle of no-fault liability has similarly been adopted from an international standpoint. The most significant example in this regard is no doubt that of "maritime" conventions.(3) Although liability due to fault is traditional in maritime matters and although many voices were raised for maintaining it in agreements dealing with liability for damage due to pollution,(4) it is a converse principle which has been adopted in various agreements already in force or still awaiting ratification.

In the light of these comments, one might of course be inclined to think that ecological litigation involves fault giving way to a substitute concept. Such however is not the case. All authors agree in stating that nothing has replaced fault other than the hazy idea that it seems equitable to compensate the victims of damage caused by socially useful activities.(5)

2. Moreover, further analysis shows that the shift away from the principles of ordinary law is quite as substantial where the condition regarding damage is concerned.

---

1) Here again may be mentioned as examples decisions of the Cour de Cassation of 22nd October 1964 (D. 1965.44, note Raymond) and 8th May 1968 (J.C.P. 1968.II.15595, note M. de Juglart and E. du Pontavice).
2) T.G.I. Nice, 9th December 1964 (D. 1965. 221, note F. Derrida).
3) See for example the Brussels Convention of 29th November 1969 or the London Convention of 1976.
4) See for example Cl. Legendre, Projet de convention internationale sur la responsabilité civile en matière de pollution par les hydrocarbures, Droit Maritime Français, 1969. 131.
5) One author sums up the situation by mentioning the "equitable nature" of what he merely defines as a "no-fault duty of redress" ("devoir de réparation sans faute"). A. Tunc, in "Traité théorique et pratique de la responsabilité délictuelle et contractuelle", with H. and L. Mazeaud, T. 1, No. 621-2); see also the opinion of F. Caballero, above-mentioned note, No. 4, p. 436.

41

Whereas the principle is redress for any damage, compensation for ecological damage is only provided when the damage is of some seriousness.

Thus in decisions regarding private nuisance, the damage must without exception "exceed the measure of ordinary obligations of neighbourship",(1) or, according to other terminologies, must be "excessive" or "abnormal".

It is no less interesting to note that in the matter of noise affecting third parties on the ground, a requirement is the abnormal character of the prejudice suffered, even though special legislation (2) lays liability on the aircraft operator.

Similarly it has been noted that in nuclear matters the set of definitions and exceptions in Articles 1, 2 and 3 of the Paris Convention of 29th July 1960, and adopted by the Act of 30th October 1968 (Section 2) had the effect of limiting the system of liability to "disaster risks" alone.(3)

With respect to water pollution, one author notes that "the use of water must result in some amount of degradation, and to prohibit any pollution would be tantamount to disregarding the user rights of riparians".(4) This comment is given concrete form in international instruments when these provide that only "reasonable" expenditure - that is warranted by a certain level of damage - shall be taken into account.(5)

Here again, the justification advanced in support of such shifts away from the ordinary law is pragmatic. As the polluter is liable without having to be found at fault, it is considered in the natural order of things that he should be made liable only for damage of some importance. According to this view, the public usefulness of polluting activities would imply that the victims should bear a part regarded as "normal" of the harmful consequences of such activities.

3. It is again with reference to equity that the novel way of establishing the causal connection - the third indispensable requisite for invoking liability - in ecological matters can be explained.

---

1) See for example the decisions rendered by the Cour de Cassation on 18th July 1972 (J.C.P. 1972. II. 17203, Fabre report) and on 28th April 1975 (D. 1976. 221, note E. Agostini and J. Lamarque).
2) T.G.I. Nice, 9th December 1964, mentioned above; Cour de Cassation, 8th May 1968, mentioned above; T.G.I. Paris, 13th July 1977, D. 1979. 427, note Rodière.
3) G. Viney, "Le déclin de la responsabilité individuelle", L.G.D.J. 1965, No. 354, p. 294.
4) M. Despax, "La pollution des eaux et ses problèmes juridiques", Librairie Technique, 1968, No. 48.
5) See for example Article V, para. 8, of the Brussels Convention of 29th November 1969.

As the often scattered character of ecological damage makes it difficult to determine its connection with the injurious act,(1) in order to protect the victims the courts are thus induced to adopt an approach different from the conventional one. It is in fields where the causal connection is naturally slackest that the most daring solutions have emerged.

Thus in regard to damage following sonic boom, the courts, approved by the Cour de Cassation, have adopted a negative approach - by elimination - in determining the connection between the shock wave and damage caused on the ground. Noting, at the time of a building's destruction, that no earth tremor had been recorded, that no mine gallery weakened the ground underneath and that no vehicle had struck the building, the court deduced that only the detonation heard several hours before when an aircraft was passing over at supersonic speed could have caused the damage.(2) An identical approach is that adopted by a court which, after dismissing the arguments of a polluter aiming to show that several, largely unknown causes might have been responsible for the death of a plaintiff's bees, concluded that "in the absence of any other cause, the death of the bees could therefore only be due to fluorine poisoning".(3) As pointed out by the annotator, such an approach "rhetorically constitutes motivation of a hypothetical character".

Moreover, significant is the fact that legislators should also have felt the need to amend the rules of ordinary law. In this regard may be mentioned the provisions of the Act of 30th October 1968, which in Section 10, institutes a presumption regarding the origin of bodily injury noted following a nuclear accident.(4) In arranging for the preparation of a "non-limitative list of diseases which, in the absence of proof to the contrary, shall be presumed to originate with the accident", The French Act does not however go so far as the Austrian Act of 29th April 1964, which introduced a whole system of presumptions, entirely based on probability considerations. A reversal of the burden of proof in favour of the victim also emerges from the Japanese Act on pollution-related illness. In force from 1974 this Act provides for the establishment of different exposure zones (categories I and II0 within which the causal link between the damage and the pollution will be presumed to exist.(5)

---

1) V.G.J. Martin, Chronique de jurisprudence judiciaire, Revue Juridique de l'Environnement, 1979, No. 2.
2) See for example Rennes, 13th November 1967, Revue Française du Droit Aérien, 1968, p. 465; Cour de Cassation, 12th October 1971, J.C.P. 1972. II. 17044, Note Juglar and du Pontavice.
3) T.G.I. of Albertville, 26th August 1975 (J.C.P. 1976. II. 18384, note Rabinovitch).
4) For nuclear accidents during maritime transport, Article 2 of the Act of 29th November 1968 institutes an identical presumption.
5) Environmental policy in Japan, Background report prepared by Japan (Env./Jap./76.1) and report by the Secretariat (Env./Jap./76.2).

The above brief analysis shows the extent to which the law relating to compensation for ecological damage has moved away from the principles and techniques of the ordinary law of liability so far as the conditions under which liability will arise are concerned. The prevailing impression nevertheless remains that these "deviations" have not led to the emergence of a new coherent system, but seem rather to be the outward sign that the law is having difficulty in coping with problems of a new type. This feeling of "hesitancy" in the law is also encountered upon investigating the results of legal proceedings for liability.

b) It is traditionally maintained that liability proceedings should lead, first, to full redress for the damage caused and secondly to "cessation of the unlawful situation". The originality of the results of such proceedings in relation to ecological matters is highlighted on closer analysis.

1. First, as regards "cessation of the unlawful situation", it is easy to demonstrate that in this particular field it is hardly ever effective. This is the consequence of legal or "para-legal" constraints (1) to which the courts are subject. Three of these may be listed.

* In the first place it must be noted that a large number of activities which cause pollution are carried on pursuant to an administrative authorisation, and judges in the ordinary courts do not feel entitled to encroach on the powers of the administration or to reverse administrative decisions. This attitude on the part of the courts is apt to be sharply criticised and judges reproached for their lack of spirit.(2) Two observations may however serve to explain, if not justify, such an approach: first, the court is faced with two adversaries, one of whom, the polluter, relies on a "positive" right - an authorisation - while the other, the victim, can only invoke a general and negative right, namely that he should not suffer damage without redress; last but not least, to expect the ordinary courts to reconsider the authorisation given to the polluter would mean their having to redefine the public interest in the administration's stead without there being any justification for such a transfer of powers. The reservations on the part of the ordinary courts are likely to be even greater in the future insofar as under the Act of 19th July 1976 the administration will be deemed to have taken into consideration the protection of nature and the environment before issuing its authorisation.

* Secondly, it must not be overlooked that, apart from any question of authorisation, these activities play an essential role

---

1) P. Girod, La réparation du dommage écologique, L.G.D.J. 1974, p. 165 et seq.
2) Ibid., p. 156 et seq.

in the life of the community from the economic and social standpoints.
The courts are rarely deaf to this argument. An example of this is
the reasoning of the Toulouse Court of Appeal when refusing to impose
any drastic solution on a polluter: "It is clear that the operation
of a factory, such as that at Sabort, inevitably results in disamenities for the neighbourhood, and the sole concern of the administration is that such disamenities be reduced to the minimum compatible
with operation of the factory. Consequently, the claim by Mr. and
Mrs. F. that the Pechiney Company be ordered to take all necessary
measures to prevent the escape of fluorides, is dismissed ..".(1)

    * Thirdly and lastly, these polluting activities are usually
carried on without it being possible to establish that any fault has
been committed. Although it has long been admitted that compensation
could be awarded in the absence of any fault, it has never been accepted that the court could order the cessation of the injurious acts
when the activity giving rise to them was not unlawful.(2) The court
could only do this in cases where the polluter misused the natural
environment by engaging, as in a recent example,(3) in "improper
practices unconnected or, at any rate, without any necessary connection with normal commercial activity".

    In short, as can be seen, these solutions are advocated on the
grounds of equity and expediency. From this standpoint, to penalise
the polluter too heavily by preventing him from carrying on his activity would be to disregard the positive aspects of that activity for
the community. But this attempt to achieve equity and proper balance
should likewise cause full account to be taken of the position of
the victim by at least guaranteeing him full compensation.

    2. This is however not the case: full compensation is only
rarely awarded for ecological damage.

    In the first place it should be pointed out that some kinds of
damage are not compensated at all, insofar as they do not affect any
legally protected "victim".(4) Thus the compensation awarded is
never based on damage to the environment itself, but only on the
use which another person may have made of it. In this respect the
example concerning compensation for damage to fish stocks is of particular significance: "... fish, being res nullius, are in no way
the property of the owner of the fishing rights, which means that
compensation cannot be based on the value of fish destroyed".(5)

1) Toulouse, 17th March 1970, J.C.P. 1970. II. 16534, note M. Despax.
2) See G.J. Martin, Le droit à l'environnement - De la responsabilité
   civile pour faits de pollution au droit à l'environnement - P.P.S.
   1978, No. 89, p. 99, and references cited.
3) Cour de cassation, 26th April 1977, D. 77, informations rapides,
   p. 359.
4) Cf. G.J. Martin, Le droit à l'environnement, op.cit., No. 31 and
   68 et seq.
5) M. Despax, La pollution des eaux et ses problèmes juridiques,
   op.cit., No. 37, p. 118 and 119.

It may moreover be noted that where any such victim does exist the courts are inclined to weigh the respective activities of the polluter and the pollution victim one against the other and to favour the industrial undertaking to the detriment of mere "idle ownership". One writer has summarised the situation by stating: "In general, the court will spontaneously qualify the extent of the damage subject to compensation by weighing it against the economic or social benefits which the activity concerned provides".(1) This is borne out by decisions which refer to the "prosperity" that a region derives from its industries,(2) to "the collective utility" of the activity challenged (3) or to "the wealth" which polluters "bring into the valley in the form of wages and jobs of various kinds".(4) Of course it is difficult to evaluate the precise amount of these unstated "reductions" of compensation by the court, but there can be no doubt whatsoever of their existence.

An examination of national and international instruments dealing with liability in the nuclear energy field leads to an identical conclusion: all of them provide for limited compensation,(5) in some cases laying down "equitable criteria for apportionment" among victims in the event of the maximum sums available being insufficient (6) or a flat-rate system of compensation modelled on compensation for injury due to industrial accidents.(7)

The same observation may be made concerning the international conventions on third-party liability for pollution arising in connection with oil exploration (8) or transport.(9) The protocols to private agreements (Tovalop, Cristal, Opol) also follow this general trend. In all cases where a limit is set on the liability of polluters or the cover provided for them, no full compensation will thus ensue whenever the damage exceeds the prescribed ceiling.

It is therefore possible to conclude by noting that damage caused by pollution is never compensated in full: where not specified a priori in special legislation, the court will be a process of reasoning share the burden of the damage between the polluter and the victim. Two arguments are advanced in support of solutions of this type: one is of a technical and financial nature while the second is more general.

----

1) P. Girod, op.cit., p. 170 et seq. and the examples referred to below.
2) Civil Court of Saint-Etienne, 5th February 1844, D.P. 1848. 1. 122.
3) Paris, 16th May 1970, J.C.P. 1970. II. 16399, note D.S.
4) Criminal Court of Tarbes, 14th January 1976, cited by M. Despax, op. cit., p. 17, note 37.
5) See the comparative analytical study by the European Nuclear Energy Agency, Nuclear Legislation - Nuclear Third Party Liability, Publication of the OECD, 1967.
6) Article 8 of the Brussels Supplementary Convention of 31st January 1963.
7) Section 13 of the French Act of 30th October 1968.
8) See the Convention on Civil Liability for Oil Pollution Damage from Offshore Operations (London, 1976), Article 6.
9) See the Brussels Conventions of 1969 and 1971.

In the first place it is asserted that in cases where a financial security mechanism is set up - as is the case in the nuclear field and for oil pollution - limitation of the amount of compensation payable is indispensable since the "ceiling" to damage subject to compensation must be known beforehand.

More generally, it is noted that it is equitable that victims should bear a part of the damage without compensation so that activities deemed essential can continue to be developed. This is one of the explanations which can be given for the requirement that ecological damage must be abnormal in nature, a requirement found even in cases where the liability of polluters is dealt with in special legislation (e.g. liability of aircraft operators). The general interest of the activity in question - e.g. air traffic - would explain why pollution victims are expected to bear the resulting damage up to a certain limit. This should be seen merely as the transposition to private relationships of the concept which accounts for - although in our view does not justify - the absence of compensation for damage resulting from the creation of public utility rights.(1)

However this may be, the above solutions, although formally a part of the law of third-party liability, are in complete contradiction with the principles upon which that law is based.

From this brief outline of the specific features of legal proceedings for compensation for ecological damage, it is possible to draw a number of conclusions illustrating the fundamental contradiction upon which compensation for ecological damage in positive law is based.

(B) The contradiction in the positive law concerning compensation for ecological damage

a) First, the affirmation that compensation for ecological damage is a consequence of the obligation not to cause harm to others does not seem to be confirmed by the facts, which in most cases show that compensation goes hand in hand with recognition of a "right to cause harm" - a right to pollute - more or less positively stated. This is seen particularly whenever the courts refuse to order the cessation of the injurious act and confine themselves to awarding compensation to the victim, not only for past damage, but also for the future damage that continuation of the polluting activity will inevitably cause. The case may be one of an award of damages against a livestock breeder whose animals are reducing the market value of a neighbouring building,(2) or against a firm authorised to operate a castor-oil

---

1) See A. de Laubadère, Traité élementaire de droit administratif, 5th edition 1970, T.2,L.G.D.J. No. 817.
2) Cour de Cassation, 22nd January 1970, D. 1970, Summary 131.

47

factory (causing considerable damage) and where fully effective preventive measures are impossible.(1) Some decisions are of particular significance in this connection. There is no denying, for example, that the court accepts the existence of a right to pollute in return for an indemnity when, in awarding compensation, it includes, upon calculating the amount of damages, the removal and re-installation expenses incurred by the victim following his forced departure due to continuation of the polluting activity.(2) The situation is identical where in addition to damages awarded for loss suffered up to the date of judgement the court directs future annual payments by the polluter for so long as the pollution continues.(3) The desire not to interfere with the activity of the polluter and confirmation of his right to cause damage in return for payment of compensation is also apparent where the court does no more than award damages to the owner of a house who had brought proceedings for increased disamenity following the adoption of new technology by a nearby factory.(4) In such cases, the award itself implies acceptance of the polluter's right to continue his injurious activity.

It is noteworthy that polluters themselves, in cases where serious incidents have occurred, have not hesitated to pay compensation to victims before any proceedings have been commenced, hoping that such an attitude would avoid any challenging of their activities. This was the case in Seveso where the directors of the companies responsible for the disaster agreed in advance to pay compensation for the damage and injury caused.(5) More recently, it appeared that following serious pollution of the river Rhone, the chemical firm Ugine-Kuhlmann had met claims by fishing federations in five French departments by local authorities and by private individuals. In return for this the company wished to avoid any criminal liability being incurred by its directors, i.e. that the ecological offence should not be recognised as such.(6) As the public knows, the criminal courts did not however accept this contention of the polluter.(7)

1) Cour de Cassation, 27th October 1964, J.C.P. 1965. II. 14288.
2) Cour de Cassation, 15th December 1971 (D. 1972, Summary, p. 96): "After awarding compensation for damage resulting, first, from the depreciation in value of a villa ... and, secondly, from the inconvenience caused over a period of eight years by a noise nuisance, it is a matter for the sole discretion of the court to assess the extent and amount of loss incurred by the owners of the villa and award further compensation to cover removal and re-installation expenses, such noise nuisance being likely to continue indefinitely".
3) Toulouse, 17th March 1970, J.C.P. 1970, II 16534, note M.D.
4) This decision was rendered by the Cour de Cassation on 28th April 1975, Bull. civ. 1975, II. No. 123, p. 100.
5) Le Monde, 13th August 1976.
6) Le Monde, 5th and 20th October 1977.
7) Le Monde, 9th November 1977. This decision proves, if such proof were required, that compensation in no way excludes other more "direct" pollution control measures.

Paradoxically, the attitude of pollution victims or of the government authorities often strengthens the polluter in his belief that he has a right to cause damage in return for payment of compensation. This is so where victims accept the compensation offered by the polluter in the form of an agreed settlement. In cases of damage to fish stocks, one writer considered that this was the outcome in eight out of ten cases.(1)

Such a right has moreover in some cases been embodied in legislation. Thus for example, in view of the total incompatibility of fishing and the oil industry in the Etang de Berre, legislation was introduced in 1957 accepting the rights of the polluters and prohibiting fishing in return for payment of F.450 million compensation to the "expropriated" owners of the fishing rights.(2)

Solutions adopted by the public authorities to deal with the position of residents in the vicinity of Paris airports reveal the same approach. In return for payment of a parafiscal tax intended in particular to cover the "costs incurred in the acquisition of dwelling accommodation and where necessary the rehousing of their occupants ..",(3) aircraft operators were given the right - not expressly stated but nevertheless real - to continue their polluting activity.

In the light of the above examples it can be affirmed that the present state of our positive law and legal practice implies recognition of the existence of "lawful" pollution - since it is allowed to continue, at least in the short term - but which nevertheless gives a right to compensation.

b) The second conclusion which can be drawn from our analysis of the existing situation lies in the fact that ecological damage gives rise to compensation with some highly original features.

First, it emerges that such compensation may be awarded in cases where it would be excluded under the ordinary law of liability. The polluter is thus frequently required to compensate the victim, even though no fault has been proved against him and no special legislation makes him otherwise liable. This desire to compensate the victim even where he is not protected by the ordinary law is surely the equitable counterpart of acceptance of the polluter's right to pollute. The desire for equity also leads the courts and the legislator to ease the ordinary rules concerning proof of the causal link.

Second, however, the same concern with equity leads the courts and legislation to take account, in the opposite direction, of the situation of the polluter. Contrary to the provisions of the ordinary law, the polluter will only pay compensation for abnormal loss, and the amount of damages payable by him will only cover part of the

1) P. Girod, op. cit., p. 231.
2) Act No. 57 - 397 of 7th August 1957, J.O. 8th August 1957, p.7813.
3) Section 3(2)(b) of Decree No. 73 - 193 of 13th February 1973.

prejudice suffered.  It would be inappropriate to make the burden of compensation excessively onerous since in some cases the activity of the polluter will be considered socially useful and his wish not to pollute may run up against technical limits.  Final compensation awards can thus be seen as the end product of a delicate balancing process between the different interests involved, the final result having no other real justification than that of equity.

c) If an attempt is made to summarise the above observations, it has to be admitted that the words used and the formal framework within which compensation of ecological damage takes place do not reflect the real situation.

Far from being the consequence of liability for violating an obligation, compensation is seen as a pre-condition for the exercise of a right.  Moreover, far from providing any real _redress_ for damage, it merely _compensates_ - usually in part - for it.  This means, in other words, that compensation for ecological damage, as now existing under positive law, is in reality simply the equitable counterpart of a right to cause damage accorded to polluters on technological, economic and social grounds.  This in turn clearly shows the gap existing between the legal technique of awarding compensation and its underlying legal basis.  Based on the wish to pay pollution victims the "just price" for disamenity caused by activities of value to the community, and for this reason deemed lawful, compensation is awarded by means of techniques originally intended to penalise undesirable behaviour.  It may perhaps be thought that the need to meet new requirements is sufficient justification for such an adjustment of traditional legal techniques.  This point of view could little be argued against were it not for the consequences of the contradiction between the underlying basis of compensation and the techniques used, which prevent achievement of the desired objective.

(C) The negative consequences of the positive law concerning compensation for ecological damage

These negative consequences may be set out for convenience under three main headings.

a) The present system of compensation for ecological damage results, first, in uncertainty of compensation.  The need to resort to the courts and bring proceedings for liability are the two main causes of this uncertainty.

The bringing of proceedings in itself has a deterrent effect on pollution victims.  In addition to factors commonly referred to (cost of proceedings, delays, etc.) there is here another specific factor relating to the nature of the adversary.  Polluters - as had been demonstrated (1) - do not hesitate to use the threat of layoffs, particularly effective in times of economic crisis, to avoid conviction.

1) P. Girod, _op. cit._, p. 167 et seq.

Also and more particularly, his economic "weight" and ability to fight a long and complex legal "battle" often make the polluter a formidable opponent.

This fear is all the greater as the victim will have to prove to the court - in spite of the modifications to the law of liability - the existence of a number of factual elements difficult to establish and which are often likely, for technical and financial reasons, to be in the control of the defendant. In many cases this marked inequality means that pollution victims will only take action where the damage is obvious and can be attributed beyond any shadow of doubt to a given polluter. Compensation may thus not be obtained in cases where the damage is clearly a reality but difficult to prove. At the most, the injured parties may attempt to reach a compromise settlement offering inadequate compensation but less risky from the legal standpoint. A recent example illustrates perfectly this type of situation and highlights the unsatisfactory nature of the results obtained. Although the new Paris express metro line (RER) to Cergy passes within five metres of the windows of a villa - making normal life impossible - the authorities have refused to expropriate the property, on the grounds that the French railways did not require any private land for their installations. However, in view of the resulting situation and after "discreet negotiations" the victim was awarded as compensation the ownership of a strip of 300 square metres of land alongside the railway line.(1) There is no doubt that in the absence of clear and easily implemented legal solutions, such "arrangements" will continue to be reached to the detriment of the victims concerned. Although there are no statistics to show the extent to which such compromises are practised, it is likely that they concern a fair number of cases.(2)

b) The positive law relating to compensation for ecological damage also produces unequal compensation. This inequality takes two forms.

Our analysis of the solutions adopted has demonstrated, first, that the inappropriateness of traditional legal techniques in dealing with problems of pollution damage had led the courts to qualify in a pragmatic and empirical way the rules of the ordinary law. On this basis, it is inevitable that the view taken of the facts and the solutions adopted should vary from case to case and from court to court. How indeed could all courts be expected to define the abnormality of damage in the same way?(3) How could they be expected

---

1) Le Monde, 27th September 1975.
2) See the examples given above, page    and notes.
3) F. Caballero (note cited above) protests against the fact that the Cour de Cassation will not review the condition of "abnormal damage" as applied by the lower courts.

to reduce to the same extent compensation due the victim in order to take account of the social and economic utility of the polluting acti- vity? Differences and contradictions between decisions are likely to be all the greater as in most cases questions of fact of unacknowledged solutions (e.g. reductions in compensation) are involved and the Cour de Cassation has no power of review. In this respect equity, used to justify such solutions, emerges far more as a source of arbitrariness rather as the guarantee of a more just law, while it is paradoxical - and disturbing - to see such a sensitive problem as pollution re- solved with reference so hazy and unreliable a concept.

But inequality in compensation also derives from the fact that alongside the ordinary methods of compensating victims - or more precisely offsetting their damage - are to be found a number of speci- fic compensation procedures based on special machinery and available to certain categories of victim. The most significant example is undoubtedly found in relation to aircraft. Whereas victims of air- craft noise in the vicinity of provincial airports can only obtain "redress" through ordinary proceedings under Article L 141 - 2 of the Civil Aviation Code and by action for private nuisance, in the Paris region victims of the same disamenity are protected by specific pro- visions brought into effect by the Decree of 13th February 1973 (with- out their being prevented from bringing "ordinary proceedings").

Distinctions are thus made between victims which may be seen as shocking from the standpoint of the Law ... and equity, and which are solely due to the lack of general and precise rules governing the right to compensation for ecological damage.

c) While uncertain and unequal, compensation for ecological damage is also costly. Costly in the first place for the victim who has to go to court to obtain his compensation, and just as costly for the polluter who, in addition to having to pay damages, will in most cases have to bear the costs of the proceedings. The cost in practice will be all the greater insofar as the uncertainty of both the subject matter concerned and the law surrounding it will encourage the pol- luter to contest the case. Lastly, such compensation is costly for the community as a whole, since with rare exceptions it presupposes the conduct of litigation.

As can be seen, the fact of continuing to compensate victims of ecological damage by using the techniques - albeit distorted - of tortious and quasi-tortious liability, whereas such compensation clearly is in fact awarded on entirely different grounds, is a source of numerous difficulties and produces unsatisfactory results. Such a finding justifies the making of a number of proposals.

## II. PROMOTING A NEW BODY OF LAW GOVERNING COMPENSATION
## FOR ECOLOGICAL DAMAGE

In view of the complex problems involved and the magnitude of the task, there can be no question in this paper of describing in detail what might be a system of compensation for ecological damage other than that prevailing under positive law. At most a few avenues of research and reflection can be suggested.

An initial affirmation is in order. For technical, economic and social reasons, it is idle - because mistaken - to go on saying that the body of law governing compensation for ecological damage is based on an obligation imposed on polluters not to pollute. The previous examples thus show that the facts are far different and that the right of a polluter to pollute is often recognised and sometimes even systematised. While such a right should not of course be stated as a general principle, no doubt the reasons explained above require that in the short and medium term it be recognised in specific cases and within limits to be defined.(1) It will be noted that such an assertion of a legal right to pollute adds nothing to positive reality (the right to pollute exists and is denied merely from a formal legal standpoint); the fact is simply duly reported so that the consequences regarding protection of the victims can be drawn. In this context compensation for ecological damage should be so organised that the evil effects of exercising such a right can be counterbalanced as fairly and effectively as possible. Thus regarded as the _price_ paid for "expropriating" the victims' environmental rights,(2) compensation for ecological damage might have four main features.

1. First, it is suggested that such compensation should in some measure be _automatic_. Freed from the contentious issue of liability, compensation could be made purely "objective" by resorting to previously devised machinery and quasi-administrative procedures. Such a largely automatic approach should in particular consist, when establishing proof of damage and determining the causal connection, in defining thresholds of pollution deemed injurious or in delimiting especially exposed areas. In this regard partial foreign or French experience concerning, for example, compensation for damage due to aircraft noise (Germany, United States, United Kingdom, France), engineering projects such as roads or motorways (Germany, the Netherlands, United Kingdom), or compensation for "health accidents" due to pollution (Japan) could serve as useful illustrations.

---

1) On the understanding that beyond these limits doing away with the disamenity can suffer no exception and that the object of all relevant policy must be to abolish such limits.
2) See G.J. Martin, "Le droit à l'environnement", _op. cit_.

Various advantages can be expected from such automatic action. In the first place it should enable litigation to be done away with or at least appreciably reduced. As the rights of the polluter and victim would be specified before any conflictual situation arose, it may thus be assumed that recourse to the courts would be unnecessary except in a few marginal cases or to enable the polluter to rebut a presumption wrongly causing him to bear the burden of compensation. The first effect might be to reduce the total cost of such compensation.

Moreover, and insofar as today the need for successfully carrying through the process causes certain victims to refrain from court action, the setting up of automatic compensation procedures would help to strengthen equality among those polluted. Since they would no longer have to face a court duel with an often feared, better informed adversary with greater resources, they would be less reluctant to assert their rights.

Yet the introduction of such procedures cannot be suggested without regard for the measures which should normally accompany them. It would first seem that the harmful effects of each type of pollution should be better ascertained and reliable measurement methods adopted. This is an indispensable requisite for determining the thresholds of pollution providing the right to "automatic" compensation, or for delimiting the areas deemed to be "exposed".(1)

From an entirely different aspect it would seem difficult to make polluters directly responsible for automatic compensation. Since this would no longer be the penalty for violating an obligation but be the "price" paid by the polluter for continuing his activity, "damping" mechanisms would have to be introduced. Essentially these would result from the constitution of a system of mutual cover, not the least advantage of which would also be to make the victims sure of receiving compensation.(2) Moreover significant is the fact that all current compensation experiments provide for such a system to be set up.

2. While compensation for ecological damage should be automatic, it should also be of a somewhat general character so that all the victims can avail themselves of the system's advantages. What this would actually mean calls for explanation.

No doubt it would neither be possible nor desirable to have a single system of compensation for all types of ecological damage. The diversity of pollutants and of the damage they cause necessarily calls for diversity of the forms of compensation. Yet the latter should

---

1) It will be noted in passing that the training of jurists with technical and scientific knowledge daily proves increasingly necessary.
2) Regarding the merits and limitations of the French pollution insurance scheme (GARPOL), see the record of a round table on industrial pollution published in the "Argus des Assurances", No.5535, p. 938.

not be matched by diversity of the underlying principles. In fact
the situation opposing the victim to the polluter is invariably identical, whether the latter be an aircraft operator or an industrialist
disposing of his waste water: in each case damage results from the
fact that the polluter "uses" the "environmental goods"(1) in such a
way that they lose all or some of their qualities and cannot be re-
used by others under the same conditions. It is therefore essential
that the victims of air pollution be afforded the same "right to compensation" as the victims of water or noise pollution. In other
words, this means that conceivably different techniques should serve
a single purpose: equality of compensation for ecological damage.
It is from this standpoint that one may speak of the""general" character of compensation.

Needless to say, the general character of an effective system of
compensation should also prevail in terms of geography. It would be
unacceptable for victims to be treated differently according to their
location on national territory.

The difficulties of such an undertaking cannot however be ignored. Acceptance of such a concept as general compensation for ecological damage implies that a definition of such damage also exists,
whereas in spite of the considerable amount of progress made by research, it must be admitted that the concept is still somewhat hazy.(2)
To remedy this inadequacy recourse must yet be had to "lists" showing
damage caused or presumably caused by some given type of pollution,
although the principle is unsatisfactory.(3)

Lastly, it is important to point out that the need for general
compensation strengthens that for a system of mutual cover. while
smoothness of operation will be ensured by pooling risks to a greater
extent.

3. Another feature of the system adopted should be to guarantee
the victims full compensation for the damage they incur.

In analysing the present situation we found that, in order to
take account of the economic and social value of some polluting activity, courts were inclined to make the victim pay for part of the
damage. Under an organised system of compensation such a solution
would be unacceptable. There are two main arguments against it:
first, it is hardly conceivable that a compensation system which aims
at being "objective" should include qualifications or restrictions
which cannot be justified by any clear-cut concept or effectively defined by any criterion; secondly and above all, it is obvious that
by letting the victim bear part of the damage, it is he alone who is

---

1) See G.J. Martin, Le droit à l'environnement, op.cit., Part II.
2) P. Girod, op.cit.
3) See the French Act of 30th October 1968 on the civil liability of
   nuclear energy operators.

asked to make a sacrifice for the common welfare. On this account it would be better to provide full compensation for the damage caused and allow the polluter to include, during a first stage, the burden he must bear in his cost price. In this way the users of the product whose manufacturer caused the damage would far more logically bear the expense indirectly.

The limitation of compensation is also advanced as a prerequisite for introducing a system of mutual cover. Here again two comments will show the weakness of such an argument. The existence of co-insurance and re-insurance techniques and the introduction of a general system of cover rather than one restricted to a few special risks would first provide a sound enough financial basis to compensate fully for any "ordinary" ecological damage. Where "disaster" risks are concerned, the setting up of governmental (or even intergovernmental) supportive agencies along the lines of those for nuclear energy would enable the same result to be achieved, or at least provide enough cover reasonably promising full compensation for any damage which occurred.

As may be noted, the goal of full compensation once again leads to the conclusion that the introduction of a system of mutual cover is an essential step.

4. The aim in advancing the preceding proposals is to guarantee full compensation for the victims with due regard for the position of the polluters. But in addition to this aspect, it must also be borne in mind that a system of compensation for ecological damage must also, perhaps primarily, play an _incentive_ role.

It is probably from this standpoint that development of a mutual system of cover is most obviously needed, and that its main features come into focus.

For this is the stage where the distinction already met with as between legal and illegal polluting acts again emerges. As the aim so far has been to ensure full compensation for the victims, there could be no question of introducing such a distinction, owing to the fact that, whether legal or illegal, an injurious polluting act calls for automatic, general and full compensation.

On the other hand the licit or illicit nature of the pollution is an essential subject for study when it is proposed that the system of compensation be of an _incentive_ kind.

Where illegal polluting acts are concerned, two principles might serve to guide legislative proceedings: first, the absolute necessity of halting the illegal action by reducing pollution to a level below the permitted threshold, and even in extreme cases - which would be marginal - by halting the injurious activity; secondly, the polluter would be made to bear all or part of the compensation. As the first of these principles is not within the scope of this paper, it will

not be further discussed.  As for the second, presumably only a mutual
cover scheme would enable it to be applied without jeopardising the
rights of the victim.  It should then be possible for the latter to
obtain full compensation for damage by applying to the insuring body,
which could later bring proceedings against the illicit polluter.  By
means of such a double-action mechanism the polluter could moreover be
made to bear a cost which did not depend on the damage caused but only
on the fault committed.  Conceivably a "minor" fault (as when an
authorised threshold is only slightly exceeded) might result in extensive damage, and whereas in this event the polluter should be penalised
it would be poor policy to make him pay for all the damage.  This snag
could be avoided by pro-rating his contribution to the seriousness ·of
his fault.  In the opposite case (a major fault resulting in minor
damage), it would however not seem possible to allow the insuring body,
when bringing action, to demand more than it itself has paid to the
victim:  this would in fact amount to letting the body amass money for
no valid purpose.  In this event penal action would be the only effective way of punishing the polluter.

The flexible quality of these devices should enable them to play
no little incentive role.(1)

In the matter of legal injurious pollution, it must not be for-
gotten that it is an evil (though perhaps a necessary one in the short
and medium term) which should be countered.  It is also within a system
of mutual cover that the most flexible and suitable solutions can be
found, provided the system can be smoothly adapted to the various
situations involved.  Here insurance techniques would undoubtedly
guarantee the best results.  By means of a careful rates policy allowing for the "danger content" of the different risks and for special
efforts made by each insured party to control pollution, and by introducing a no-claim-bonus scheme for rewarding prudent insured parties,
insurance techniques could thus be used for achieving the objectives
without affecting the rights of victims.

Along similar lines, it may be pointed out that the introduction
of a real system of compensation can lead to solutions which, beyond
indemnification strictly so-called, can help to improve or at least
conserve the environment.  Thus if the concept is accepted that compensation is a "price" paid by the polluter for continuing his activity, there is nothing to prevent this "price" from being fixed whenever feasible to compensate as closely as possible (from a qualitative
standpoint) for any damage caused.

The city of Marseilles has thus developed a scale for determining
the "real ecological value" of its trees, which takes account of their
age, appearance, beauty, and especially their location.  Whenever some

1) See G.J. Martin, Le droit à l'environnement, op.cit., No. 176
  · et seq., p. 186 et seq.

development project leads to cutting down a tree, the developer may be required to replace it by a number of shrubs corresponding to the tree's ecological value.  The city may thus require as many as 250 shrubs per adult tree cut down to be planted.(1)

In an altogether different regard, it is common knowledge that under an agreement concluded between the Ministry for Equipment and Regional Planning and the Electricity Authority, the latter promises to allocate part of the amount corresponding to the cost of building nuclear plants to the purchase of land which is to remain in its natural state and be open to the public.  Such amounts would either be paid to the coastal conservation agency or to local authorities near the installation.(2)

To conclude, it may be pointed out that the weakness of the present system governing compensation for ecological damage seems mainly due to the fact that the legal "tools" used utterly conflict with the objectives imposed by practice and logic.

Designed to penalise the violation of an obligation and to re-dress any injurious effect, the techniques concerning liability for tortious and quasi-tortious offences were paradoxically to be used to compensate for damage caused by activities regarded as legal. Qualified and even distorted by court decisions and legislation, such methods have lost their coherence without achieving their purpose. To amend these techniques is therefore not the solution.  Instead a specific body of law governing compensation for ecological damage, where techniques would be consistent with substance, should be built up.  Uncertain, incomplete, unequal and costly forms of redress could then give way to "objective", general mechanisms providing for full compensation and playing an incentive role.  Establishment of a system of mutual cover making use of insurance techniques could help to reach this goal.

---

1) Le Monde, 26th-27th June 1977.
2) Le Monde, 9th July 1977.

# COMPENSATING VICTIMS OF POLLUTION
## CAUSED BY ACTIVITIES AT SEA

by

Martine Rémond-Gouilloud
Chargée de conférences
University of Paris I

## INTRODUCTION

1. Looking back over the last twelve years, one could claim that
the occurrence of the Torrey Canyon incident in 1967 was a good thing.
Thanks to the Torrey Canyon, present-day society was made suddenly
aware of the seriousness of the problem of marine pollution.(1)  The
rules of traditional law were shown to be ill-adapted to meet the case
and compensation for victims of pollution damage largely hypothetical.

Meanwhile, the spectacular growth in off-shore oil prospecting
had made this gap still more conspicuous:  among pollution incidents
associated with such drilling, three took place in heavily-populated
coasts or in extensively fished waters - one in Santa Barbara,
California, in 1969;  another in Ekofiskfield, off Norway in April
1977, and the third, particularly serious, in the Gulf of Campeche
off Mexico in August 1969.(2)

Only public feeling could trigger off the unprecedented spate of
legislation which then developed;  through international conventions,
regional agreements and national legislation of all kinds, new mechanisms were introduced.

No doubt these mechanisms are still far from satisfactory:  as
early as 1967 the wrecks of the Boehlen and Olympic Bravery had re-
vealed various defects in them.  That of the Amoco-Cadiz in 1978
showed that the system was very inadequate where exceptionally large-
scale accidents were concerned.(2a)  Nevertheless, such mechanisms
are available and beginning to work.  Among them, the systems of compensation for victims of pollution damage stand out for their especial
novelty.

2. A difficult problem.  Such innovations were necessary on account of the novelty of the problem itself.  Compensation of victims
of pollution damage encounters two kinds of obstacle, one related to
the physical characteristics of the effluents involved and the other

to the complex nature of the legal system applicable to the sea.
Moreover, these two difficulties interact on each other.

a) The problem of proof results from the ease with which an effluent becomes diluted in the receptor medium. Thus oil slicks can,
in a matter of hours, spread over large areas of water. The effluent
is also carried hither and thither by wind, currents and tides. In
addition, it is frequently not seen: the most visible effluents discharged into the sea are not necessarily the most toxic ones.(3)
Mercury, cadmium, other heavy metals, and nuclear wastes pose a much
more serious threat. Yet, in order to obtain compensation, a victim
must prove not only his loss but also the origin of the loss, in other
words, the source of the pollution and more particularly the chain of
causation between the source of pollution and the damage. If he is
unable to establish that the loss was caused by a specific agent he will
obtain no compensation. Besides this, the traditional legal system requires him to prove that the discharge complained of is a result of a
wrongful act or omission ("fault"), in the absence of which the party
causing the damage cannot be required to make reparation.(4)

b) Catastrophic occurrences. Once the fact of damage has been
established and it has been proved that the polluter was at fault, it
is necessary that the latter be solvent if compensation is to be obtained from him. However, given the gigantic proportions of the
damage to users of the sea that may result from a pollution incident,
no one can be regarded as solvent.(4a) In the case of a drilling accident, the risk cannot even be measured in advance with any certainty,
since no one can predict how long it may take for a well or, worse, a
crack in the seabed to be plugged.(5)

As for damage calling for compensation, it is now beginning to be
realised that in addition to that affecting persons and property
through the agency of the sea, another kind which should be taken into
account is damage to the sea itself, its fauna and flora.(6) The
sometimes tragic depletion of fish stocks, and the recent development
of fish farming are contributing factors.(7) As a result, traditional
systems of individual liability no longer seem adequate in relation
to the scale of potential damage.

This is all the more true since most marine pollution is not due
to the spectacular accidents which arouse public opinion, but to the
daily operational leakages inherent in maritime transport. It is
thus generally estimated that 3 per cent of all oil is lost during
transport.

Disposal of ballast or bilge water and bunkering all involve
discharging a certain amount of waste oil into the sea.

In spite of recent progress, and the development of processes
for limiting such discharges (loading on residues, flushing out
tanks), the IMCO calculated that 1.38 million tonnes of oil were

spilled into the sea in connection with these operations in 1978.(8)
This insidious pollution steadily poisons the sea without enabling
compensation machinery to come into play: it is a collective process,
and sanctions against tankers discharging oil at sea, however severe,
at best can have but a limited deterrent effect.

c) Difficulties of an international kind. To these problems of
liability, which are common to all the traditional systems, must be
added those deriving from the legal regime of the sea. It is traditionally accepted that the high seas are outside the jurisdiction
of States. The seas are free, they belong to everyone and to no one.
Accordingly, under traditional law, a discharge carried out on the
high seas cannot give rise to compensation.

The only jurisdiction over this area is that which every State
individually exercises over its nationals. Owing to the present trend
in the law of the sea, this legal no-man's-land can probably be ex--
pected to shrink somewhat. Already, oil drilling on the continental
shelf, which extends continents under the sea, is subject to the laws
of the adjacent State.(9) Soon, no doubt, general recognition of an
exclusive economic zone 200 miles wide, off each adjacent State, will
cause the high seas to be reduced in area.(9a) The draft Convention
produced by the Law of the Sea Conference, in setting out the powers
which it devolves upon coastal States to protect the marine environment, urges them to prevent pollution (9b) and contamination. Nevertheless, at least for the moment, this is a serious gap. It is
rendered the more so by the fact that effluents can travel. The
limit of the high seas is an abstract concept imagined by lawyers.
And if effluent discharged on the high seas unfortunately crosses this
line and contaminates the beaches of a coastal State, no compensation
will be payable. Finally, the sea is international by its very nature
and damage caused by pollution at sea raises inextricable problems of
jurisdiction both from the legislative and the judicial standpoint,
which place a further obstacle in the way of compensation for victims.

d) Unsuitability of traditional maritime law. At the very least
one might have hoped that it would be possible to take advantage of
maritime law, which is an old system built on centuries of experience
and specially designed to regulate relations between individuals where
the sea is concerned. But it would seem that the very fact of its
special nature causes maritime law to constitute a further difficulty.

The seagoing world has always had its own laws and its own
methods. It has evolved outside the general law applicable on land
and to all intents and purposes has been uninfluenced by it. The
special conditions applicable to life at sea, with its dangers and
its isolation, explain this specific character.

However, the maritime system as a whole has been designed for
ships and adapted to their characteristics. The limitation of

liability of shipowners, which lies at the heart of the system, is
tangible evidence of this: it rests upon the notion that the victim
of damage at sea accepts a limitation on the compensation payable to
him today because he knows that he himself may reap the benefit of
such a limitation tomorrow if he should in turn cause damage.

But marine pollution has brought into being a new category of
land-based victims who are outside this circuit and for whom, in
particular, the limitation of liability of shipowners always represents a sacrifice and never an advantage. Consequently such victims claim that the general law should apply. In the same way, conventional mechanisms for marine liability, based on proof of fault,
do not seem applicable here.

The "law of marine pollution" thus lies at the meeting-point
between two legal systems, maritime law and land-based general law,
and it has to reconcile these.

This is a particularly delicate task in the case of off-shore
oil operations. The drilling risks are of special concern to the adjacent State: to begin with its coasts will be the first to be affected by any pollution; secondly, it is the State issuing the drilling licences,(10) and will therefore be directly responsible if anything goes wrong with operations. Hence it is of course purely and
simply inclined to extend its territorial legislation, particularly
its mining laws, to off-shore operations.(11)

e) Miscellaneous difficulties. To the foregoing must be added
those difficulties which stem from each national legal system; thus
in France the right of legal persons, associations or syndicates is
severely controlled; it does not enable their members to obtain compensation for personal loss.(12)

Similar difficulties can arise, for example, in the United States,
the United Kingdom and Canada (12a) (see Part III below).

In France again, a plaintiff in civil proceedings must advance
the costs of experts' reports, which can be very heavy in such cases.

Finally, once a judgement has been obtained it is necessary to
have it executed: where the polluter was a ship this involves, under
the traditional legal system, pursuing it across the seas to have it
arrested. See, for example, three judgements by the Tribunal de
Grande Instance of Saint-Nazaire, in 1974, 1975 and 1976, where
penalities of F.10,000, F.20,000 and F.100,000 were imposed by default.(19) Frequently, even this means that it will be legally impossible to have the judgement executed if the State of which the
polluter is a national affords "unofficial" protection.

3. Legislation. In the face of such lacunae, a complete over-
haul of positive law has been undertaken.

The enactments thus evolved (international conventions, regional
agreements, national legislation) are aimed primarily at preventing

marine pollution in any form (intentional discharge, accidents, dumping, incineration) and at punishing those responsible. Compensation for victims is directly guaranteed under international law only for the most spectacular forms of pollution - oil pollution - and the mose serious forms - those resulting from nuclear activities.

a) <u>International conventions</u>. International agreements on compensation for sea pollution are a recent development, and are in line with Principle 22 of the Stockholm Declaration,(13) under which the States are expected to co-operate in broadening international law covering compensation for the victims of pollution caused by activities conducted abroad. The draft Convention on the Law of the Sea takes up and develops this obligation of States, both at national and international level, to promote anti-pollution rules.(13a)

In the case of oil pollution, compensation to victims is provided for in three international conventions:

1. The Brussels Convention of 29th November 1969 on Civil Liability for Oil Pollution Damage.(14)

2. The Brussels Convention of 18th December 1971 on the Establishment of an International Fund for Compensation for Oil Pollution Damage.(15)

3. The London Convention of 17th December 1976 on Civil Liability for Pollution Damage resulting from Exploration for and Exploitation of Seabed Mineral Resources.(16) This latter Convention is in principle a regional one, since it was negotiated between nine States bordering on the North Sea; but it is wide in scope, being open to any State bordering on the North Sea or the Blatic, or the Atlantic Ocean above latitude 40°North, and so drafted as to be applicable to coastal waters adjacent to any other territories, wherever located, which are in law attached to the Contracting States.

Other agreements for the compensation of marine pollution victims, however, would appear to be purely regional, such as the Helsinki Convention of 22nd February 1974, which applies only to the Baltic (17) while the Nordic Convention on the Environment, Stockholm, 1974, concerned not only with the prevention of damage but also with compensation, exclusively relates to the Scandinavian countries.

It should be remembered that some Conventions of a deterrent kind, penalising deliberate or negligent acts of pollution, enable the victim to obtain compensation through civil proceedings. The London Convention of 12th May 1954, several times revised, was the first international enactment to make any such provision for compensating a victim of international marine pollution. The Convention for the Prevention of Marine Pollution by Dumping from Ships and Aircrafts (Oslo 1972), the Convention on the Prevention of Marine

Pollution by the Dumping of Waste (London, Mexico, Moscow 1972), the Convention for the Prevention of Pollution from Ships (London 1973) and the Convention on Land-Based Marine Pollution (Paris 1974) now offer or will later offer (17a) the same possibilities.

As regards carriage of nuclear substances, an Agreement of 19th December 1971 subjects these to the general law of nuclear liability (Paris Convention, 29th July 1960, Vienna Convention, 21st May 1963 and Brussels Supplementary Convention, 31st January 1963).

b) A large number of internal enactments have incorporated these international provisions into the national systems, sometimes supplementing or reinforcing them.(18)

The laws of France provide an example here.

Deterrent enactments made the earliest provision in law for compensation: the Act of 26th December 1964, amended by an Act of 16th May 1973 provides penalties for spillages prohibited under the London Convention of 1954. A survey of the record offices of 30 coastal tribunals in the Spring of 1977 showed that few proceedings had been initiated on the basis of this legislation up to 1979 and that they seldom succeeded, largely because there were no appropriate means of detecting infringements.(19) After the Amoco-Cadiz accident French off-shore waters were more intensively monitored, while at the same time penalties were stiffened (by two enactments of 2nd January 1969.(20)

An Act of 7th July 1976, making it an offence to discharge wastes into the sea and an Act of 11th May 1977 relating to exploration of the continental shelf and exploitation of its mineral resources, amending the previously applicable Act of 30th December 1968,(21) rounds out this set of laws.

As regards compensation itself, an Act of 26th May 1977 applies the 1969 Brussels Convention to France, and in particular requires vessels registered in French ports to show proof that they are insured for pollution liability.(22)

The official instruments, national and international, are accompanied by parallel compensation schemes organised by the industry (which finances them voluntarily) to fill in some of the gaps in the international system (see below, Compensation Machinery, II.B.).

4. Plan followed. In order to measure the progress achieved since 1967 in regard to compensation for victims of marine pollution it would seem necessary to reply to the following questions:

1. For what marine pollution damage can a victim be compensated today? Against whom must he bring proceedings and what must he prove? It is thus necessary to analyse the conditions for compensation.

2. How is such compensation guaranteed? Within what limits and subject to what reservations? How in particular do

<u>compensation funds</u> operate?  These questions will be
dealt with in Part II of the report:  Compensation
Machinery.
3. What solution is provided for the difficulties encountered
   by victims in exercising their rights of action before
   the courts, particularly in matters of jurisdiction?  See
   Part III: Compensation Procedures.

As at 30th June 1979 the position regarding ratification of the
major Conventions on marine pollution was as follows:

| Enactment | Date of Entry into Force |
|---|---|
| London Convention, 12th May 1954: | 26th May 1958 |
| 1962 amendments to above | 18th May and 28th June 1967 |
| 1969 amendments to above | 20th January 1978 |
| 1971 amendments to above | Not in force |
| | |
| Brussels Convention, 29th November 1969: Civil liability for oil pollution damage from ships | 19th June 1975 |
| | |
| Brussels Convention, 18th December 1971: Compensation Fund | In force |
| | |
| Brussels Convention, 17th December 1971: Civil liability, transport of nuclear materials by sea | |
| | |
| Oslo Convention: Prevention of Marine Pollution by Dumping | 7th April 1974 |
| | |
| London Convention: Prevention of Marine Pollution by Dumping | 20th August 1975 |
| | |
| London Convention, 2nd November 1973: Prevention of pollution by ships (MARPOL) | Not in force |
| | |
| Nordic Convention on the Prevention of the Environment, 19th February 1974 | 5th October 1976 |
| | |
| Helsinki Convention on the Protection of the Baltic Sea Environment, 22nd March 1974 | Not in force (1980?) |
| | |
| Paris Convention, 1974, on Land-based Marine Pollution | 6th May 1978 |
| | |
| Barcelona Convention, 16th February 1976 ) | |
| ) 12th February 1978 | |
| Barcelona Protocol combatting oil) pollution ) | |
| | |
| London Convention, 17th December 1976 | Not in force |

(For ratification details, see OECD document ENV(79)12, Annex II,
pp. 33 et seq.)

# I. CONDITIONS FOR COMPENSATION

## I.A. Compensable damage

(1) <u>Location of damage. Territorial jurisdiction: the various cases</u>. Where did the damage originate? Where did it occur? The fate of a victim of marine pollution depends on the reply to these two questions. If the damage occurs on the high seas outside an area within the jurisdiction of any State,(23) or else on the territory or in the territorial waters of a State not a contracting party, the victim cannot, in the present state of law, claim any compensation under the international conventions. Only the applicable ordinary law with all its shortcomings, or failing it, contributions by the industry under the voluntary Tovalop, Cristal and Opal schemes (see below), will sometimes provide compensation. The position will be the same if the State whose flag the polluting ship flies is not party to the international Convention, when victims will find that they can only claim against the value of the ship, this generally being its wreck value (see below, limitations on liability).

If the damage and the episode which gave rise to it both occurred within an area subject to the jurisdiction of a State (its coasts, territorial waters or exclusive economic zone) within the limit of the jurisdiction acknowledged to the State over the area concerned by international law,(24) the victim's compensation will depend on the internal law of that State. Compensation is provided under the conditions laid down by the law on compensation for marine pollution damage where such laws exist, as in Canada and the United States, but usually by the general law of liability in that country. There is no distinction in such case between pollution damage and any other damage, and any kind of pollution may therefore give a right to compensation if the damage meets the conditions required by the national law of the State.(24a) Again, it is the law of the coastal State which will usually be applicable to compensation for pollution caused by oil drilling off its shores.

However, in most cases the damage occurs within the waters or on the territory of a State and the event which gave rise to it occurs on the high seas. One of the contributions made by recent international conventions consists precisely in enabling the victim to obtain compensation in such a case, provided that the two States concerned - the victim State and the State to which the polluter belongs - are parties.

Aside from Conventions dealing specifically with marine pollution, mention should here be made of the Convention of 27th December 1968 on jurisdiction and the enforcement of judgements in civil and commercial matters in the European Economic Community. According to Article 53 of that Convention, as recently interpreted by the Court

of Justice of the Communities, the courts of a Member State have
jurisdiction whether the damage has been caused or been suffered in
one of the Member States.(25)

(2) Source of damage. It must first be pointed out that in
this respect international law is far from providing an exhaustive
system. Conventions aiming at preventing pollution damage of all
kinds are proliferating, but compensation for victims is really only
organised at present for the most evident form of damage, namely that
caused by oil.(26) Even that damage is far from always compensable,
as may be seen from a study of recent conventions.(27)

A distinction must be made according to whether the pollution
damage was the result of a breach of the law or an accident: in the
first case compensation for the damage is bound up with criminal proceedings and will be awarded according to the rules and conditions
laid down by each national legal system; in the second case, on the
other hand, it is international instruments which directly lay down
the conditions and terms of compensation.

Damage resulting from a breach of the law. Damage resulting
from an oil discharge which is made an offence under the London Convention of 12th May 1954 (28) may give rise to the formulation of a
civil claim by the victim in the criminal courts of the Contracting
States. However, compensation for the damage will be awarded only
if the offence is established and leads to a conviction, i.e. if it
is proved that intentional discharge took place within a prohibited
zone such as the Mediterranean or at a distance of less than 100
nautical miles from the coast, or that it was of a quantity and concentration exceeding those authorised.(29)

The 1954 Convention is due to be replaced by a new London Convention signed on 2nd November 1973, which is far more ambitious
since it prohibits discharges of all kinds: oil, but also liquid
substances carried in bulk, harmful substances carried in packaged
forms or tanks, sewage and garbage.

Similarly in the near future, victims of pollution damage resulting from dumping contrary to the provisions of the London Convention of 29th November 1972 will be able to obtain compensation.
Regional agreements with the same object have also been entered into,
prior to this Convention (Oslo 1972 for the North Sea, the Channel
and the North East Atlantic) or subsequently to it (Helsinki for the
Baltic in 1974 and Barcelona for the Mediterranean in 1976).

Damage resulting from an accident: ships carrying oil. At the
present time the only damage resulting from accidental pollution
which gives victims a right to compensation is that falling within
the Brussels Conventions of 29th November 1969 and 18th December 1971.
Such damage covers "loss or damage caused outside the ship" resulting
from an oil leak or discharge and includes the cost of measures taken

following the incident to prevent or minimise pollution damage (always provided that pollution has actually occurred). The broad formula used in the Convention would appear to make it possible to include in the damage, damage to amenities and loss of profit (de lucro captando), subject to the powers of interpretation of the court concerned.(30) However, pollution must result from an incident to a seagoing craft carrying oil in bulk and that craft must be actually carrying a cargo of "persistent" oil at the time of the incident.(31) This means that while pollution damage caused by a hovercraft carrying oil as cargo, a purely academic supposition at the moment, would be compensable, accidental pollution from a ship's bunkers would not, nor would pollution from refined oil products or from oil being shipped in drums.(32)

Oil installations. The 1976 Offshore Convention provides possibilities of compensation for victims of pollution resulting from oil prospection and exploration activities at sea. Under this Convention, any pollution damage caused by equipment used for exploration or exploitation of mineral resources shall give right to compensation. The Convention uses the definition of damage given in the 1969 Convention of Civil Liability - Oil including in particular the cost of preventive measures. The products concerned are nevertheless different: the Convention refers to crude oil and liquid natural gas.

As regards the pollution sources to which it might apply, the Convention appears to be wide in scope defining "installation" as "any well which has been used for the purpose of exploring for, producing, treating, storing or regaining control of the flow of" the product. The technical characteristics of the device hence are of little relevance: the tender and pipeline are covered, as well as the rig itself.(33) This is as it should be: the risk of pollution from offshore oil drilling is chiefly associated with the well, and the capacity of the installation or its tonnage, except for storage equipment, is only secondary.

(3) Nature of compensable damage: other obstacles to compensation. Let us now assume that some international convention does apply and a pollution victim institutes proceedings before the appropriate court: even now he cannot be certain of receiving compensation, since few among the forms of damage due to a pollution accident yet entitle the victim to redress. The requirements of civil liability account for this shortcoming. To entitle its victim to compensation, the damage must thus be certain and direct. The courts will not entertain actions based on hypothetical prejudice, or any where its occurrence is only remotely linked with the event complained of by the victim. The prejudice suffered owing to pollution seldom presents the required features: how can a fisherman establish a causal relationship between his empty nets and the noxious effluent

from a particular factory? How is the innkeeper or the fishmonger to show that the defection of his clientele is due to pollution of the shore.(34)

Case law shows that damage of an economic form which can be evaluated in money terms is virtually the only kind the courts will entertain; only exceptionally will so-called "moral" damage lacking any financial aspect attract compensation,(35) while ecological damage to fauna and flora has yet to be a concept in law.(36)

Lastly, one characteristic of compensable damage itself often makes it harder for a marine-pollution victim to obtain compensation; he must prove that the damage affected him personally; private individuals are not entitled to protect the general interest. Hence, in particular, the reason why legal persons are often awarded no compensation at all in France, since they have not personally suffered the damage for which compensation is claimed, whereas in the United States, the distinction between public nuisance and private nuisance leads to the same solution.(37)

The only form of pollution damage which at present involves no difficulty of compensation is clean-up costs. In recent international Conventions, damage for which redress is provided generally includes so-called "preventive" measures: this refers to outlays of all kinds to counter a pollution threat, from the cost of equipment and chemicals to break up and clean up the oil slick to payment for the workers employed on the job (1969 Convention, Article 5-4; 1976 Convention, Article 6-6).(38)

Compensation for preventive measures raises a number of questions, which have come up in recent accidents: to what extent, for example, should the fixed costs of a government department, army, emergency and other services, be allowed for in reckoning the cost of preventive measures? How far should the clean-up costs, paid for by the party liable for the pollution, included in the preventive measures, be taken into account on the same footing as the actual damage? Under the existing arrangements, preventive measures rank with other forms of damage, on equal terms with the victims, the latter being granted no priority.(39)

In contrast with these somewhat gloomy points, it should be noted that the courts prove fairly broadminded in determining what damage qualifies for compensation: French courts, for example, hold that the noxiousness of an effluent must be assessed from the two-fold standpoint of the conservation and consumption of fish or shellfish.(40) Loss of earnings suffered by the fisherman whose catches are ruined should also be compensated for, provided the loss has occurred beyond doubt.(41) Here the chief difficulty is in determining what sum of money a fisherman has lost.(42) The courts are also beginning to show concern in regard to "the deterioration of bordering properties, the fall-off in tourism, the taxes foregone by local authorities, diminishing returns from fishing".(43)

It is not enough for the victim of pollution to know who caused the discharge to occur. In order to obtain compensation he must also know whether that person is liable, which means knowing the basis of liability (B1) and the grounds for exoneration which the party liable may be able to invoke (B2). He must finally know exactly against whom to bring action (B3).

## B.1. Basis of liability - Determination of the party liable

If the victim had to prove the "fault" of the person who caused the occurrence of the discharge which gave rise to the damage suffered, his action would nearly always be bound to fail. In modern law two remedies are available to him:

a) The enactments making pollution a punishable offence sometimes treat prohibited discharges as offences devoid of the element of intent: the offence is committed by the mere fact of the discharge. If the damage suffered by the victim is the result of a discharge prohibited by the provisions concerned, it will therefore suffice for him to establish, through criminal proceedings, that the damage was indeed caused by that discharge (see Article 434.1 of the French Rural Code).

b) If the victim brings proceedings in the civil courts following an incident, he will still not need to prove any fault on the part of the person who caused the discharge to occur. In all legal systems today, alongside the traditional "fault liability" will be found procedures which enable the victim to avoid having to provide this difficult proof.

In some cases liability is based on the risk attaching to essentially dangerous activities, as in the United States (44) or in the Soviet Union,(45) in others a presumption of liability is connected with the custody of the object, as in the United Kingdom (46) or in France.(47) In all such cases, the advantage of the system for the victims is the same: he is relieved of the necessity of proving that the damage suffered is the result of a fault on the part of the person causing it.

International conventions. The principle of "no-fault" liability has also been adopted in the Conventions on marine pollution: Article 3-1 of the 1969 Convention on Civil Liability - Oil provides: "The owner of a ship ... shall be liable for any pollution damage caused by oil which has escaped or been discharged". Article 3-1 of the Offshore Convention contains the same provisions in connection with operators of installations. In maritime conventions, the adoption of liability mechanisms operating as of right is a noteworthy innovation: previously, maritime law used only to recognise liability

based on fault: it did not seem that ships, which are never wholly in
control of their own movements, should be made to carry any heavier
burden.(48)

Carriage of substances liable to cause radioactive pollution,
which is governed by the Paris and Vienna Conventions, on the high seas
or elsewhere is subject to a system of "no-fault" liability which is
particularly strict.(49)

New legal systems. Despite the progress achieved here and there
regarding oil and nuclear pollution, the problem of proof remains one
of the worst facing the victim of pollution damage. Accordingly, this
is a point to which lawyers should more particularly direct their
imaginative thinking.

In this respect several recent enactments deserve attention on
account of the novelty of their approach, although they do not relate
specifically to marine pollution: a Japanese Act of 5th October 1973
on compensation for damage to health associated with pollution, provides in some cases for the chain of causation between damage and discharge to be presumed: where physical injury is shown to have been
caused by the discharge of toxic substances all similar damage occurring in the same region is automatically compensated.(49a)

Of equal interest are a number of recent laws introducing compensation funds, such as the Canadian Marine Pollution Damage Act in
which the Government itself compensates the victim when the polluter
cannot be identified. An Act passed in 1971 by the Province of
Manitoba to help fishermen suffering damage from the pollution of
streams is also relevant.(50) Under that Act, fishermen who are
forced to cease their activities as a result of a pollution occurrence
are directly compensated by the Provincial Government; the latter
then has a right of recourse against the person causing the pollution.
Fishermen who suffer damage are thus relieved of the need to establish
the usual chain of causation since the Government accepts the onus of
doing so in their stead.

This, broadly, is the value of the many compensation fund schemes
appearing nowadays to cope with pollution: compensation for the victim does not necessarily depend on identifying the originator of the
damage; in an area where the origin of damage is often doubtful or
unknown, it is a considerable advantage to the victim to be relieved
of the need to show such proof.(50a)


B.2. Exoneration from liability (51)

Even in those cases where no-fault liability of the polluter may
be regarded as an established fact, the position of the victims still
depend on two factors: any limitation of liability which may be
claimed by the party liable (cf. infra II) and, above all, the conditions for such exoneration. Inasmuch as each case of exoneration

provides the party liable with a ground for escaping liability, this means one less chance for the victim to obtain compensation.

These methods of reducing liability are widely used in traditional maritime law: the party liable is thereby exonerated in a large number of cases.(52) The proof of "due diligence" on his part, i.e. reasonable diligence, is sometimes sufficient to relieve him of liability.

None of the enactments relating to marine pollution appear to adopt this system. Modern conventions exonerate the party liable only in a few specific cases:

(1) The damage resulted from an act of war, hostilities, civil war, insurrection or a natural phenomenon of an exceptional, inevitable and irresistible character /Article 3-2(a) of the 1969 Convention on Civil Liability - Oil7. In this latter case, however, the 1971 Fund exercises its subsidiary function and provides the compensation for which the shipowner is not liable. The Offshore Convention provides for the same cases, without however requiring that a natural phenomenon (cataclysm) should have been inevitable and irresistible (Article 3-3-a).(53)

The 1971 Convention also relieves the Fund of liability for discharges from public ships assigned to a non-commercial service (Article 2a).

(2) If the damage was wholly caused by an act or omission done with intent to cause damage by a third party, the 1969 Convention exonerates the shipowner but the 1971 Fund takes his place.

(3) The 1969 Convention also exonerates the owner or operator in the case of negligence of the State responsible for the maintenance of lights or other navigational aids. Here again the 1971 fund takes over from the shipowner.

(4) Finally, in all these systems an act or omission done with intent to cause damage by the person who suffers the damage, or the negligence of such a person, deprives the latter wholly or partly of the right to compensation.(55)

The above list calls for a number of comments:

a) In the first place the link should be noted between exoneration of the 1971 Fund and 1969 Convention on Civil Liability - Oil; the Fund is designed to supplement compensation of victims of pollution in case of default by owners or operators of ships.

Accordingly, it is natural that the Fund should be exempted from its liability only on stricter conditions than the ship causing the damage under the 1969 Convention. It will not be exempted, while the ship will be, if the pollution is wholly the result of the intentional act of a third party (as through a terrorist act) if the pollution has been caused by a natural disaster of an exceptional nature, or to an act or omission of the State responsible for maintaining navigational aids; and the fact that the victim is at fault only exonerates the Fund to the extent that the shipowner has been exonerated.

b) The party liable is entitled to exoneration as of right, save as regards the fault of the victim (4th case of exoneration):  in the latter case exoneration is only discretionary ("may be exonerated").

c) If the victim does not take action pursuant to the enactments mentioned above but according to the general law of the country, he will be faced with approximately the same cases of exoneration.  In French law, for instance, "force majeure", unforeseeable and unsur-mountable, is always a bar to compensation.

d) The Nuclear Conventions, which are stricter than those re-lating to marine pollution, allow exoneration of the party liable only in the case of hostilities or of a natural disaster of an exceptional nature, national legislation being moreover empowered to dispense with this latter case of exoneration.

## B.3. Status of the party liable

The person who caused the discharge to occur, from whom under the general law the victim would claim damages, may turn out to be insol-vent or worse still untraceable.  In most cases he will merely be a servant or agent.  Hence, most of the relevant enactments tend to place the burden on the owner or operator of the installation.

The owner.  Under the 1969 Convention on Civil Liability - Oil, this means "the person or persons registered as the owner of the ship, or in the absence of such registration, the person or persons owning the ship".(56)

The operator.  In the Offshore Convention it is "the person designated as operator for the purposes of the Convention by the com-petent uuthorities of the controlling State" or failing this the per-son "actually exploiting the installation".(57)

In the case of an incident involving radioactive pollution as a consequence of the carriage of radioactive substances, the party liable is the operator of the nuclear installation alone, to the ex-clusion of the carrier.(58)

The Fund.  Here it is no longer the individual operator but the whole world of operators, the oil industry as a whole, which assumes the burden of pollution damage resulting from an incident to a tanker if compensation has not been obtained from the shipowner, or if the 1969 Convention exonerates him under a case not covered in the 1971 Convention, of if he proves financially incapable of meeting his obli-gations.  Should the shipowner be insolvent or the amount of damage exceed the liability ceiling, the Fund steps in.  It is then a ques-tion not of a party liable but of a guarantor.

The State.  Can the State be held liable to the victims?  In principle, no.  An important decision of the French Conseil d'Etat

states that the State is not under any "general obligation to maintain healthy conditions".(59)   It would however seem that the State
might be held liable to victims of a pollution incident for faulty
organisation of preventive measures following such an incident.
(Thus, France has organised a system of emergency measures in such a
case:   the Polmar plan.   Delay in putting the plan into operation or
faulty application of the measures might involve the State in liability.
The Amoco-Cadiz incident again raises the question of the liability of
a coastal State for the operation of radio stations responsible for
guiding ships.

Another example of the implication of the State's liability is
supplied by the Santa Barbara case in the United States in 1969.   In
that case marine pollution of catastrophic proportions occurred in
California following a crack in the seabed, in an area where oil exploration was intense.   On the grounds that the incident had been
caused by excessive exploitation of the seabed, the State Attorney
handling the case brought proceedings against the Federal Government
which had granted the exploration and exploitation permits in the
area of the incident.(60)

Other parties liable.   The Amoco-Cadiz incident highlighted one
of the major defects in the international system of compensation for
marine pollution:   although conventions and voluntary plans settle
the position of the shipowner, they do not channel all responsibility
towards him.   There is consequently nothing to prevent other parties
from being sued on the basis of other legal remedies.   A question
which has thus come up is the system applicable to an assisting
vessel, to a shipyard, and broadly to any party whose activities might
have caused the polluting incident.   The question becomes all the more
acute in that such parties, to whom no specific provisions apply,
cannot under present law claim any limitation of liability.(61)


## II. COMPENSATION MACHINERY

In addition to the system of compensation based on traditional
third-party liability, victims of marine pollution enjoy the benefit
of two original systems:   the International Compensation Fund and
voluntary agreements entered into by the industry.   These two systems
have the same aim;   to provide compensation while limiting the liability of the parties concerned.   Moreover, both involve adherence by
the parties concerned to an ad hoc insurance system.

II.A. Supplementing the liability mechanism provided by the 1969
Convention

The Compensation Fund set up under the Brussels Convention of
18th December 1971 presents a number of points of interest:   in the

74

first place it substitutes the collective guarantee of a group for individual liability.  It acts as guarantor for default or inability to pay on the part of the ship liable for the incident, thus reducing the risk of the victims going without compensation.

The various funds. Distinction.  The same term is used to describe two institutions which differ considerably and must therefore be distinguished:

a) The Fund instituted by the 1969 Convention on Civil Liability - Oil(62) is nothing more than a system of limitation of liability for the tanker owner responsible for pollution damage.  His liability is calculated up to a ceiling in relation to the size of the ship (2,000 Poincaré francs for each ton of ship's tonnage), with an overall ceiling of 210,000 Poincaré francs.  By surrendering this Fund on the occurrence of an incident the shipowner is relieved of all liability to the victims of pollution caused by that incident.  Article 3-4 of the Convention moreover states that "no claim for compensation for pollution damage shall be made against the owner otherwise than in accordance with this Convention".

This institution belongs to traditional maritime law since it is drawn from the Convention of 10th October 1957 on limitation of shipowner's liability.

The Offshore Convention provides for a similar type of fund. However, instead of constituting a fund the owner may offer a bank or other guarantee to the satisfaction of the Court.(63)

b) The Fund instituted by the 1971 Convention is of an entirely different nature:  this brings into play a collective guarantee by the oil industry to meet a pollution incident, caused by a ship covered by the 1969 Convention.  It is funded by the oil importers. Their initial individual contribution is governed by Articles 10 and 11 of the Convention.(64)  Thereafter, an annual contribution may be demanded in order to meet payments to be made, should the existing amount of the Fund not suffice.  The Fund is managed by an Assembly consisting of all Contracting States, an Executive Committee, elected by the Assembly, a Secretariat and a Director who is the legal representative of the Fund (Convention, Articles 17, 22 and 28-2).  The role of this Fund is to supplement compensation provided by the shipowner liable and sometimes to take over if he is insolvent or exonerated from liability under the 1969 Convention.(65)

Advantages of Funds.  The system of Compensation Funds has advantages both for victims and for those liable for marine pollution incidents:

- As regards the victims, the Fund provides a guarantee of
  solvency of the party liable.  This applies to all kinds
  of fund;  set up immediately upon the occurrence of an
  incident, the Fund of the 1969 Convention type prevents

the victim from having, after a judgement has been obtained,
to hunt down the party liable in order to obtain payment.
- The party liable will be inclined to set up a type of fund
  under the 1969 Convention which enables him to limit his
  liability (cf. infra: Limitations of liability).
- The 1971 Fund offers the added advantage of spreading
  major risks - risks of disastrous proportions resulting
  from pollution incidents of the Torrey Canyon type -
  throughout the oil industry. The 1969 Convention lays
  down rules of liability, but that of 1971 institutes a system of insurance.(65)

The Compensation Fund machinery derives from conventional individual
liability concepts and is the only means of redress when the polluter
is unknown or doubtful (see above: Determination of the party liable).

## II.B. Private schemes. The Tovalop, Cristal and Opol plans

Alongside the international Conventions, industry provides victims with a number of possibilities for compensation. In 1969 a plan
known as Tovalop,(66) which now covers over 90 per cent of world
tanker tonnage provided reimbrusement for control and clean-up costs
pending the entry of the 1969 Convention into force. The plan,
voluntarily subscribed by shipowners, was financed by a mutual insurance scheme. However, apart from the fact that reimbursement de-
pended on a system of liability based on fault, the plan left two
gaps: it covered only the task of dealing with oil slicks and
cleaning the coast, and not damage caused to individuals; the amounts
of compensation provided were smaller than those laid down by the
Brussels Convention ($10 million instead of $15 million).

As a result, in 1971 a new plan called Cristal (67) was introduced to supplement Tovalop: compensation was raised from $10 to $30
million and all victims whatsoever and wheresoever were entitled to
compensation provided the damage was caused by a tanker included in
the Tovalop plan. Just as Tovalop was a prelude to the 1969 Convention,
so Cristal was to act, in principle, as a temporary substitute pending
entry of the 1971 Convention into force. A major advantage of such
plans thus is that the lengthy official international procedures
which held up application of the Conventions are avoided.

Although the Brussels Conventions of 1969 and 1977 are now in
force, Tovalop and Cristal retain some of their value because they
provide compensation whenever a member polluter belongs to a State
which has not ratified the international conventions. To enable those
schemes to perform this supporting role, substantial changes were
made to them in May 1978; now they fairly closely match the Conventions they are designed to supplement.(68)

With the same end in view, a plan called Opol (69) was signed in
1974 to provide compensation for victims in cases of pollution resulting from oil exploration or exploitation at sea.  Originally applying to the United Kingdom, it has since been extended to Denmark,
Germany, France, Ireland, Norway and the Netherlands.  It covers pollution damage caused by an installation located in waters within the
jurisdiction of a Contracting State wherever the victim may be.  The
liability thus voluntarily assumed by operators joining this group is
strict liability, and is subject to exoneration in the same cases as
the 1969 Brussels Convention on ships.  The installations concerned
include not only platforms and rigs but also storage installations,
tanks and pipelines.  Compensation also includes the cost of clean-up
operations.

Those compensation schemes established by the oil industry also
have a preventive aim;  thus in order to encourage the parties causing
pollution to take action and carry out clean-up operations themselves,
it provides compensation for the costs so incurred.

II.C. Limitations of liability

The law of marine pollution recognises two distinct forms of
limitation and liability:  the first operates in favour of the party
liable and limits the risk he assumes when undertaking an activity
involving any danger of pollution - the limitations of liability provided for in the 1969 Convention on Civil Liability - Oil, the Tovalop,
Cristal and Opol plans and the Offshore Convention.  If none of these
applies, the liability of the shipowner is usually limited to the
value of his ship, in accordance with the 1957 Convention on the limitation of shipowners' liability.  Indeed, the limitation is often
calculated according to the value of the ship after the incident
creating the claim, in which case it is limited to the value of the
wreck.(69a)  Owing to this kind of limitation, a shipowner moreover
forfeits the right to it in the event of his personal fault or
privity.  This rule appears in the conventions of 1969 (Article V.2
Conv.69) and of 1957.  The second form of limitation is altogether
different, since it is not related to the interests of the liable
entrepreneur but merely to the capacity of the insurance market:  the
1971 Fund and the limitations imposed by the nuclear conventions fall
within this class.  The difference in basis explains the difference
in amounts.  Thus the 1969 Convention limits the liability of the
shipowner carrying oil to 2,000 Poincaré francs per ton of tonnage
and imposes an absolute ceiling of 210 million Poincaré francs.  Above
that ceiling the Brussels 1971 Fund takes over and compensates victims up to 675 million Poincaré francs.(70)  The Fund Assembly may
subsequently decide to raise this ceiling to 900 million Poincaré
francs.

The private compensation schemes provide victims with compensation up to $160 per ton of tonnage, or $16.8 million (Tovalop) and $36 million (Cristal) and for oil installations $26 million of which half are allocated to clean-up costs (Opol).(71)

The nuclear conventions seem in general more generous since the ceilings of liability are, for instance, 120 million units of account under the Paris and Brussels Conventions,(72) or 1.5 billion Poincaré francs under the Convention on the liability of operators of nuclear ships.(73)

The Offshore Convention, the latest to be signed, is noteworthy in a number of respects: its limiting ceiling, at present approximating the amount provided for under the 1971 Convention, is expressed in terms of Special Drawing Rights and is to be increased automatically in five years time, from 30 million to 40 million SDRs.(74) It is thus becoming accepted international custom to make some provision for monetary erosion. The Offshore Convention also makes provision for raising the ceiling by unanimous decision of the parties.

The Offshore Convention has another unusual feature in that the ceiling it applies may be increased or even eliminated by any participating State for zones within that State's jurisdiction. Provided for under Article 7/5 of the Convention, this has been criticised as nullifying the attempt at unification represented by the Convention, while preventing the operator from covering himself against an unquantifiable risk.(75) For the victim, this mechanism seems satisfactory: the Convention guarantees him a minimum ceiling, which may be increased in areas under the jurisdiction of a State which is particularly at risk, or particularly concerned as to the cleanliness of its coastline.

National legislation. By way of comparison it may be noted that the limitation of liability is:

1. For pollution from ships:
   In the United States: $100 per gross ton or a ceiling of $14 million (control costs only). The Federal bill before Congress would impose an overall limit of $200 million. The limitation applicable to the ship would be $50 million under HR29 or $30 million under HR85.
2. For off-shore oil operations:
   - In the United States: $8 million, Water Improvement Act 1970, Section 2 F3 (clean-up costs only). Here again the bill before Congress would increase the compensation available to $200 million.
   - Canada: $10 million per oil well causing pollution with an overall ceiling of $50 million (Article 8-c, pollution of Arctic waters regulations 1972).

Traditional maritime law. No doubt some of the limits in international instruments or national laws are low, given the serious nature of potential damage, and would seem ill-adapted to ensuring full compensation for victims. /Thus the 210 million Poincaré francs fixed by the 1969 Convention and by national laws based thereon correspond approximately to the loss suffered by the French and British Governments on the occasion of the Torrey Canyon incident,(76) and this did not include damage suffered by private individuals, towns and fishing interests./

Following the Amoco-Cadiz accident, claims before the courts amount to $900 million. Whatever the outcome of the actions, clearly in this instance the scale of damage is incommensurable with the sums available for compensation. Nevertheless, these amounts constitute a considerable improvement over the limitations imposed by traditional maritime law: under the Convention of 10th October 1957 on limitation of shipowners' liability, any shipowner can escape further liability by surrendering a fund, the amount of which is calculated in relation to the size of his ship: this limitation is 1,000 Poincaré francs per register ton if the damage is to property only, and 3,000 Poincaré francs if personal injuries have been caused. Indeed, legislation in many countries limits the amount available to creditors to the value of the ship after the incident and often, therefore, to the value of the wreck.

## II.D. Guarantees

The greater the risk of insolvency of a given type of debtor, the greater the need for protection against that risk. Hence the importance of insurance of ships against pollution risks: a great number of single-ship companies, i.e. companies whose only asset is a ship, and the ease with which a ship can escape pursuit, make it the very archetype of the potential bad debtor.

Accordingly, the 1969 Convention on Civil Liability - Oil requires all ships of the Contracting States carrying more than 2,000 tons of oil in bulk as cargo to take out pollution insurance corresponding to their limit of liability. This insurance may be replaced by another form of security, e.g. a bank guarantee. A ship must carry on board a certificate, issued by the State of registry and attesting that such insurance or financial security is in force, failing which it cannot "trade".(77)

A victim of pollution damage may proceed directly against the insurer or guarantor.

The amount of damage thus covered does not correspond to the limit of liability of the ship since it is limited to F.1,500 per ton of the ship's tonnage. Beyond that amount, the 1971 Fund in turn comes into play as guarantor of the ship-owner. This assumption of

financial liability is the second function formed by the Fund set up
in 1971 (Convention, Article 5).

The risk of insolvency of the operator of an offshore installation
is considerably less.  In order to obtain an exploration permit the oil
company must establish that it has adequate financial resources.  There
is therefore less likelihood of it becoming bankrupt or disappearing.
However, the Offshore Convention provides for an ad hoc insurance, the
amount and terms of which are left to be decided by the public authorities where this exceeds a certain minimum figure laid down in the
draft.

Moreover, world oil interests have become aware of the inability
of the normal insurance market to meet the magnitude of potential
damage.  Only the major companies are in a position to assume such a
liability.  Accordingly nine oil groups have formed a pool in order to
cover their possible liability.  Cover provided for members includes
all kinds of damage to property, damage to third parties and costs of
controlling wells.  The guarantee provided is $75 million per incident
and per annum.(78)

The nuclear conventions also provide for a system of compulsory
insurance, freely organised by the States within whose jurisdiction
nuclear installations exist.  Here, however, the amount is less crucial
since the State in which the installation is located stands behind the
operator for the purpose of compensating victims in the case of an
incident.(79)


## III. COMPENSATION PROCEDURES


The difficulties facing victims in this connection are of a
special nature:  to which court should they apply?  What is the applicable law?  How can the decision be enforced?  The recent Conventions
endeavour to simplify their task both as regards exercise of the right
to bring proceedings (A) and as regards execution of the decision (B).
Nevertheless, practical application of these provisions remains a
matter of some delicacy since they have to be applied consistently
with each country's internal laws.  Finally, the mobility of most
sources of marine pollution renders the problem particularly complex.

III.A. Instituting proceedings

No double entitlement.  The victim of marine pollution damage
cannot, under the recent international Conventions, act otherwise than
on the basis of those instruments.  Article 3-4 of the 1969 Convention
on Civil Liability — Oil and Article 4-1 of the Offshore Convention
forbid all other forms of claim.  The object is to prevent victims,
in order to escape from the cases of exoneration of limitation of

liability contained in those instruments, from having resort to other legal remedies, particularly under internal law.(80)  It is a condition of the operation of the system that a party potentially liable should know with certainty the limits of the liability he may incur. Failing this, the risk should not be insured against.

It should however be borne in mind that if responsibility is not channelled onto the shipowner, then any person other than the owner, such as the ship or assisting party, may be sued under other forms of law.  Thus in the Torrey Canyon and Amoco-Cadiz incidents, the parent companies of the groups to which the shipowning companies had belonged were sued under the ordinary law of the United States.

Court of competent jurisdiction.  The question that arises is a double one of international and internal jurisdiction.  International jurisdiction is dealt with in Article 9 of the 1969 Convention:  the courts of the victim's State, e.g. the State on whose territory or in whose territorial waters the damage occurred, have sole jurisdiction to adjudicate upon claims.  (Most of the time, the shipowner will, following the incident, have constituted with a court of the victim's State a fund enabling him to limit his liability and to have his ship set free.)  The courts of that State then become exclusively competent in the matter.  The same court which has jursidiction under the 1969 Convention also has jurisdiction to entertain claims concerning the 1971 Fund (Articles 7-1 and 3).(81)

The very precision of these provisions shows the gaps that exist in international law:  the 1969 Convention on Civil Liability - Oil, for instance, covers only a limited field (cf. supra I-A).  For all other forms of pollution from other sources or other substances, questions of jurisdiction therefore remain to be solved.

The case of the "red sludge" and the Montedison Company provides an interesting illustration of this:  it concerned a substance discharged on the high seas from a ship flying the Italian flag and causing damage in France.  Should the competent court be that of the victim (French court) or that of the flag of the ship which caused the damage to occur?  The difficulty would be even greater if the ship had been loaded in a State other than that whose flag it was flying.(82)

The Offshore Convention endeavours to solve these difficulties. Under Article 10, actions for compensation based on that Convention may be brought either in the courts of the victim's State or in those of the coastal State which issued the exploration or exploitation permit (called the controlling State).  Damage occurring on the continental shelf of a State or the superjacent waters is deemed to have occurred on the territory of that State (Article 10 of the draft).

Domestic procedure. Difficulties.  Each State is required to ensure that its courts shall have jurisdiction to hear actions for compensation (1969 Convention on Civil Liability - Oil, Article 9-2). This does not mean that such actions will be successful. Numerous obstacles connected with domestic procedures will have to be surmounted. The example of France is illustrative in this connection.

(1) It is very difficult for a group of persons to bring proceedings. Only those groups which enjoy legal personality (communes, associations, syndicates) can do so. The class-action as it exists in the United States is unknown here.(83) Above all, an action brought by such legal persons can only be entertained if they show that they themselves have suffered loss. An individual person who suffers damage by marine pollution cannot therefore, in the present state of the law, achieve anything through collective action.

(2) The rules as to jurisdiction can cause the action to fail. The administrative courts can sometimes award compensation only to the State itself where the action before them is based on an offence connected with a major communications network.(84)

(3) If the damage is the result not of a breach of the law but of an accident, the victim who brings proceedings in the civil courts will have to advance the costs of experts' reports, which are particularly heavy.

France is not the only State in which victims encounter procedural difficulties. In Federal systems, the overlying powers of individual States and the Federal Government is another source of difficulty: the case of Askew v. American Waterways in the United States in 1973 on the compensation of marine pollution victims in Florida probably affords the best example: the United States Federal instrument only covered clean-up costs, and the Supreme Court recognised the Florida Act governing compensation for victims to be constitutional.(85)

Finally, on a more general plane, it is necessary to mention how difficult the multiplicity of enactments relating to pollution of the seas makes the task of the courts. The method of legislation used at present, which consists in adopting a separate enactment for each type of product, each source of pollution and even each geographical area, creates endless difficulties.

Limitation periods. For their action to be entertained, victims must institute proceedings:

(1) Under the 1969 Convention on Civil Liability - Oil and the 1971 Fund Convention, within three years of the occurrence of the damage or within six years of the occurrence of the event which gave rise to the damage (1969 Convention, Article 8, 1971 Convention, Article 6).

(2) The Offshore Convention specifies the following time limits for proceedings by a victim: within twelve months of the date on which he learned, or ought normally to have learned, of the occurrence

of the damage to him, he must either initiate legal proceedings or notify his complaint in writing to the operator. No legal proceedings can in any case be taken after a lapse of four years.(85) In regard to abandoned installations, an operator who has taken action for closing down a well in accordance with the requirements of the controlling State cannot be litigated against after five years.

Law applicable. The interpretation of international provisions or, failing these, the determination of the solution applicable to the suit depends broadly on the law of the court hearing the case, the so-called law of lex fori. Under Article 9 of the 1969 Convention, the court should be that of the place in which the damage occurred and it should apply its own law. However, in improving the prospects for pollution victims bringing proceedings before the courts, the Nordic Convention on environmental protection is exceptional. Under this enactment, claims for compensation presented by a damage victim are judged in accordance with rules which cannot be less favourable to him than those in force in the State where the source of the damage is located. This does not of course prevent the court from applying its own legislation, should the latter prove more favourable to the victim.

### III.B. Execution of judgements

The execution of foreign judgements always poses difficult problems. This is all the more so in maritime matters, where ships may avoid execution of such judgements by keeping away from the ports of those States where judgements have been given against them.

The traditional method of obtaining execution of foreign judgements is by way of "exequatur" (recognition) proceedings; the 1969 Convention on Civil Liability - Oil introduces machinery of this kind: under Article 10 any judgement given on the basis of the Convention shall be enforceable in each Contracting State, subject to the following conditions:

1. The judgement must be final (i.e. no longer subject to ordinary forms of review).
2. The court must have jurisdiction in accordance with the Convention.
3. The judgement must not have been obtained by fraud.
4. The rights of the defence must have been respected (in particular, the defendant must have been given reasonable notice).
5. The formalities required in the State where execution of the judgement is requested must have been complied with, although such formalities shall not permit the merits of the case to be re-opened.

The Offshore Convention repeats the same provisions adding that the formalities for recognition of judgements shall not include any veri ication of the applicable law (Article 11). The same concern to simplify underlies the draft Convention produced by the Law of the Sea Conference.(87)

Among international Conventions facilitating the execution of foreign judgements, mention should be made of the European Convention on Enforcement of Judgements of 27th September 1968, which includes rules regarding direct jurisdiction (European Communities Convention) and, above all, of the International Convention on the Arrest of Sea-going Ships of 10th May 1952. In order to obtain any form of security from a ship it is generally necessary to have it arrested. It is more particularly the threat of arrest, together with the desire to limit his liability, which is likely to incite the owner of a ship which has caused a pollution incident to constitute the Fund provided for under the 1969 Convention, and this Fund, constituted at the start of proceedings, is the best guarantee for the victims. Consequently, the execution and the effectiveness of judgements in this matter is linked to ratification of these Conventions by the international community in general.

The same applies, it is true, to the whole system of compensation for victims of marine pollution.

NOTES

1)  Cf. Pontavice: "La pollution des mers par les hydrocarbures" (des-
    cribes the Torrey Canyon case), 1968.  For statistics covering
    major accidental oil spills at sea, see the report based on the
    Institut Français du Pétrole data bank:  Revue de l'IFP, May-June
    1979.
2)  The rigs operating are expected to exceed the thousand mark by the
    year 2000 (see Offshore, May 1977, p. 110).  On the Santa Barbara
    accident, see A.E. Utton:  A Survey of National Law on the Control
    of Pollution from Oil and Gas Operations on the Continental Shelf,
    Columbia Journal of Transnational Law, 1970, No.5, p.331.  On the
    Ekofisk accident, and its ultimately light consequences, see
    "North Sea blow-out tamed quickly", Offshore, June 1977, p. 32,
    also "Some international aspects of the Ekofisk accident", OECD
    document ENV/TFP/77.12.
    The IFP data bank lists 11 pollution incidents due to drilling or
    production mishaps at sea between 1964 and 1978;  to these must be
    added the accident during August 1979 in the Bay of Campeche off
    Mexico, resulting in the most serious marine pollution yet ex-
    perienced (see Pétrole Informations, 5th July, p. 3; Offshore,
    August 1979, p. 43; Le Monde, 7th August: "240,000 tonnes de
    pétrole à la mer".
2a) For the Amoco-Cadiz accident, and its ecological and economic con-
    sequences, see the proceedings of the UVLOE Seminar, Brest, March
    1979.
    On international law see, D.W. Abecassis, "The Law and Practice of
    Oil Pollution by Ships", Butterworths, London, 1978.
    For the United States, see Post, "A Solution to the Problem of
    Private Compensation in Oil Discharge Situations", U. Miami L.
    Rev. 28-524.50 (1974).  For the United Kingdom see Cusine:
    "Liability for Oil Pollution under the Merchant Shipping Acts 1971,
    JMLC 1978, 105, also Abecassis, op.cit.
    For Canada: Legal remedies for existing or threatened pollution
    damage in Canada and the United States, a study by S. McCaffrey,
    OECD 1979.
    For France: Simon, La Réparation Civile des Dommages Causés en Mer
    par les Hydrocarbures.  Thesis, Paris 1976.  Remond-Gouilloud,
    Leçons d'un Naufrage, Dalloz, 1979, p. 133.
    For the Mediterranean: E. du Pontavice, Réglementation Relative à
    La Pollution des Eaux Douces et des Eaux Maritimes dans les Pays
    Méditerranéens, DMF 1972, pp. 131, 195 and 259.
3)  Poisoning due to pollution of the sea by substances containing
    mercury and cadmium respectively caused in a few years, in Japan,
    the death of 64 persons (mercury:  see Minimata case, 29th
    September 1971), and 100 persons (cadmium; see the Itai-Itai case,
    30th June 1971).  See on this subject:  "Legal systems for
    Environment Protection", FAO Legislative Studies, No. 4, p. 20,
    1972.
    Contamination of the cargoes of Japanese fishing vessels following
    the United States nuclear experiments in the Pacific gave rise, in
    1955, to payment of $2 million compensation (the Fukuryu Maru,
    see J. Balleneger, "La Pollution en Droit International", Droz.
    Paris 1975).  On the Cavtat, carrying drums of lead-tetraethyl
    which sank off the Italian coast, see the study by Peter Sand in
    "Legal Aspects of Transfrontier Pollution", OECD, Paris, 1977.  On
    23rd January 1977, the radio announced that a ship carrying ten
    500-kg drums of arsenic had sunk 700 metres down in Osaka Bay.  On
    pollution from a cargo of mercury on the Tacquari, wrecked in 1971
    In Uruguay 50 kilometres from Brazil, see Le Matin, 20th April 1978.

In April 1978, sales of fish and shellfish were prohibited in Rio Grande, Brazil, because 24 tonnes of mercury compounds had been released.

4) See as regards trends in English and American law: Avins, Absolute Liability for Oil Spillage, 36 Brooklyn L. Rev., 359, 1970, "La réparation du dommage résultant de l'exploration et de l'exploitation d'hydrocarbures en mer", B. Dubais, report to the Nice Seminar, May 1974, p. 20; as regards Swedish and Japanese law: FAO Legislative Studies, No. 4, supra. See also P. Simon, La réparation civile des dommages causés en mer par les hydro-carbures, thesis, Paris 1976.

4a) Court claims for compensation following the Amoco-Cadiz accident amounted to $900 million. In connection with the Ixtoc I accident off Mexico, it was anticipated that pollution of the Texas coast might ruin the local tourist industry, which earns Texas $300 million a year, and that if shrimp were to disappear, 1,500 shrimping boats would have to be laid up. Le Figaro, 10th August 1979.
To bring the Ixtoc I spill off Mexico under control, a directional well had to be drilled. This was expected to take at least two and a half months. Le Monde, 21st July.

5) Estimates of oil pollution due to offshore operations at present differ, but such pollution is thought to represent between 0.7 and 4 per cent of total oil pollution of the sea.
A recent study of incidents caused by oil operations at sea, for which a computerised simulation model called "Sliktrak" was used, suggests that in 90 per cent of cases the damage is not in excess of $16 million, and in no case exceeds $30 million (B.V. Dubais: The 1976 Convention on civil liability for oil pollution damage from offshore operations, Journal of Maritime Law and Commerce, 1977.
The Ixtoc I blow-out in the Bay of Campeche, in 1979, of course means that this estimate will have to be revised.
According to a further estimate, made in 1970 following the Santa Barbara accident, the damages were:
- Clean-up costs: $10.6 million
- Compensation as such: $5.8 million.
Compensation includes amounts for damage to beaches, communities, pleasure craft, the fishing industry which, including material damage, loss of wages and compensations for loss of earnings, amounted to $300,000. Legal costs were not included in this estimate (Mead and Sorrenson, 1970).

6) Regarding the case of the red sludge off Corsica and compensation for ecological damage to the marine environment, see the judgement by the Livorno Court of 27th April 1974, Gazette du Palais 1975-1, p. 182 note by C. Huglo, comment by Karsenty, and that of the Tribunal de Grande Instance of Bastia. Recueil Dalloz 1977, (p. 427, note by Rémond-Gouilloud).

7) On the sudden disappearance of Peruvian anchovy and the serious economic consequences, see La Prairie, Le Nouvel Homme et la Mer, p. 66.
It should be borne in mind that the Ekofisk accident occurred in a vital herring-spawning part of the North Sea, that the Ixtoc I spill occurred in an area whose main economic activity in recent years has been shrimping, and that the Gino, a vessel carrying carbon black, foundered on 28th April 1979 in an essential spawning area (Pétrole Informations 10th May 1979, p. 12). On the effects of an oil slick on wildlife, see in particular a report by C. Chass to the Brest seminar; also Nonov: La Pollution petrolière des Océans, La Recherche, February 1979, p. 147.

8) See the IFP report, p. 16.

9) By virtue of the Geneva Convention of 29th April 1958 on the Continental Shelf, which recognised the sovereign right of coastal States to explore their continental shelf and exploit its mineral resources.

9a) More than 100 States declared themselves in favour of the Exclusive Economic Zone at the Law of the Sea Conference. Among the declarations of the ever increasing number of the coastal states introducing exclusive economic zones, see in particular the French Act of 16th July 1976, and the Mexican Decree of 6th June 1976. On this trend see Papadakis: the International Legal Regime of Artificial Islands, Leyden, 1977.

9b) See the Informal Composite Negotiating Text, Article 56-1-b-iii, Article 145(a) and Article 193.

10) By virtue of Article 1 of the Geneva Convention of 29th April 1958 on the continental shelf, which confers sovereign rights for the purposes of exploiting mineral resources in that zone.

11) See for France, Article 5, Act of 30th December 1968 "French laws and regulations shall apply ... on installations and equipment". They also apply to the installations and equipment themselves. The difficulty can but increase with the advent of the exclusive economic zone. See Papadakis, op.cit.

12) In the United States, "class-actions" enable an individual to bring proceedings on behalf of a group of victims: Cf. "The settlement of class-actions for damages", R.F. Dole, Columbia Law Review, 1971, p. 371.

12a) See: Collective defence of the environment and admissibility of proceedings in relation to transfrontier pollution, published in Environment Protection in Frontier Regions, OECD, 1979.

13) Adopted in 1972 at the United Nations Conference on the Human Environment.

13a) Informal Composite Negotiating Text, Article 208. Pollution from land-based sources; Article 209: Pollution from seabed activities; Article 210: Pollution from activities in the area; Article 211: Dumping; Article 212: Pollution from vessels.

14) Hereinafter called the 1969 Convention on Civil Liability - Oil.

15) Hereinafter called the 1971 Convention on the Compensation Fund.

16) Hereinafter called the Offshore Convention. See Environmental Policy and Law, 2, No. 1 (1976) for particulars of the negotiations. Cf. B. Dubais, op.cit.

17) B. Dubais. The 1976 Convention ... op.cit. According to Article 17 of this enactment, bordering States undertake to introduce rules for compensation.

17a) The London Convention of 12th May 1954, amended in 1962, 1969 and 1971, provides penalties for the deliberate discharge of oil at sea. In this regard see Lucchini, "La lutte contre la pollution des mers venant du large", Revue Juridique de l'Environnement; Rapport du 2ème colloque de la Société Française pour le droit de l'environnement, 1979, p. 247.

18) In particular, see in the United States, Water Quality Improvement Act, 1970; in the United Kingdom: Oil in Navigable Waters Act, 1971; in Canada: Act on the Prevention of Pollution in Arctic Waters, 1970; and in Japan, the three acts of 25th December 1970 and more particularly Act No. 136 on the prevention of ocean pollution.
   The United States Federal Water Quality Improvement Act of 1970 covers compensation for clean-up costs only. Several coastal states have enacted supplementary legislation, particularly Florida and Maine. Federal Bills H.R. 29 and H.R. 85 before the U.S. Congress at the time of writing are designed to deal comprehensively with the issue.

19) L'application en France des règles internationales relatives à la pollution par les hydrocarbures, a report by M. Remond-Gouilloud, 3ème Congrès, Société française pour le droit de l'environnement, 7th-8th October 1977.

20) The Acts of 2nd January 1979 (J.O. 4th January) provide penalties for breaches of navigation rules and failure to follow compulsory shipping lanes, and increase the penalties for dumping in accordance with the 1954 London Convention as amended. Penalties applicable to infringers, mainly the masters of vessels, were made considerably heavier (See G. Rémond-Gouilloud, Défense d'un littoral - A propos des lois du 2 janvier 1979, Environmental Law and Policy, 1979, No. 2).

21) Act of 7th July 1976. Journal Officiel, 8th July, p. 4107, Art. 28 (new provision). Act of 11th May 1977, Journal Officiel, 12th May 1977.

22) Act of 26th May 1977 (Journal Officiel, 27th May 1977).

23) This was assumed to apply to the Gino, the ship carrying carbon black which sank off the French coast in April 1979 (see Pétrole Informations, 10th May 1979, p. 12). Regarding an instance where damage was inflicted outside territorial waters but proceedings by the victims, who were fishermen, were nevertheless entertained, see TGI, Bastia, 8th December 1976, Dalloz 1977, obs. M.R.6.
Ships not being regarded as part of a State's territory for this purpose, the only jurisdiction exercised over a ship by the State in which it is registered is of a personal kind.

24) See Article 56 of the Unofficial Composite Negotiating Text of the 3rd Conference on the Law of the Sea.

24a) Subject however to any provisions excluding other forms of compensation than those they themselves offer. See infra, provisions against simultaneous entitlement, III-A. Sums paid as damages will in any case be limited by the shipowner's limitation of liability.

25) See judgement of the Court of Justice of the European Communities: S.A. Mines de Potasse d'Alsace, Luxembourg, 30th November 1976.

26) Or the most disturbing types arising out of the transport of radioactive substances. On this question see the Pontavice Study: Reflexions sur la pollution maritime d'origine radioactive, Droit Maritime Français, 1976, pp. 643s and 707s.
The International Maritime Consultative Organisation (IMCO) plans to lay the issue of liability for the carriage of other dangerous substances before a diplomatic conference in 1982 (Journal de la Marine Marchande, 1979, p. 1387).

27) On the workings and limits of compensation ceilings see report by Rémond-Gouilloud (OECD, to be published) which shows a gap in the law resulting in lack of compensation.
In 1960 an appeal to the European Commission on Human Rights to prevent dumping of radioactive wastes in the North Sea was thus rejected, because the European Convention on Human Rights does not mention environmental damage. See "Liability for Harm to the Environment", Environmental Policy and Law, 1st January 1975, p. 17.

28) As amended in 1962, 1969 and 1971.

29) Authorised discharges must not exceed 60 litres per nautical mile travelled, or 1/15,000th of the ship's capacity, and their hydrocarbon content must be below 100 ppm.

30) See Abecassis, op.cit., p. 133 (damages recoverable). See below: Nature of compensable damage; As regards preventive measures, an example of what they can cost is supplied by the case of the Olympic Bravery, a tanker which went aground on rocks off Brittany in January 1976: according to the press, the cost of action taken by the French Navy to control the ensuing pollution, amounting to about 500 tonnes, was F.1,330,000 of which F.580,415 represented action by aircraft, F.731,000 action by ships and F.18,276 action on shore. (Le Monde, 3rd June 1976).

31) Persistent products are those which after spreading do not evaporate or dissolve in salt water. On the whole this does not apply to refined products. On the definition of persistent hydrocarbons see Abecassis, op.cit., p. 215. Simon, op.cit., pp. 22 and 23.

32) Regarding the IMCO proposals to make good these deficiencies in the next few years, see Abecassis, op.cit., p. 215.

33) See Convention, Articles 1 and 2 (which also covers abandoned installations, conferring a right to compensation for any pollution they cause within five years of shutdown, provided the closing-off operations have been carried out in accordance with the requirements of the adjoining State.

34) Precedents in the United States are relevant here: compensation has been awarded for damage to a ship itself (see among others, 1973, Oppen v. Aefua, 26 ALR Ted. 346) and to fishermen and

shellfish growers (Burgess v. Tamano, 1973 Dc. Me. 370,
F. Supp. 247) but not (in this latter case) to other local
businessmen claiming loss of custom.

35) Thus, when an oil-drilling incident polluted the coast off
California, recreational fishermen, deprived of a mere "oc-
casional Sunday piscatorial pleasure" had their claims dismissed
(Oppen v. Aetna Insurance Co.), 1973; see JMLC 1974, p. 542.

36) See however Maine v. Tamano in the United States (1970 DC. Me;
357). The State of Maine was held to be entitled to compensation
for damage to coastal waters and natural resources, in having a
quasi-sovereign interest; see 26 ALR Fed. 346, p. 342. Compensation for "ecological" damage in the real sense (see note by
Rémond-Gouilloud, Dalloz, 1977, p. 277), is however beginning to
emerge. After the Amoco-Cadiz accident, the EEC allocated
F.1.2 million especially for this purpose. At present, compensation for this form of damage involves difficulties of two
kinds: the status of the claimant qualified to ensure the protection of marine resources, and the evaluation of those resources when they have no directly quantifiable economic value
(the non-market value); see the studies by R.H. Haveman and
G. Murato, in "Environmental Damage Costs", OECD 1974, pp. 101
and 136.

37) The problem arises in French law when the damage stems from an
offence.
On the distinction in United States' Law between public nuisance
and private nuisance, see Burgess v. Tamano, 1973, AMC 1939;
see in Canada, a case where fishermen were refused compensation
for loss of earnings because the damage they had suffered was
not unique in relation to damage suffered by fishermen as a
category. See Hickey v. Electrired, 1970, cited by McCaffey,
op. cit., p. 12.

38) This was not a new approach: see decision by the Rennes Court
of Appeal as far back as 3rd November 1965 awarding damages to
seaside resorts for beach cleaning costs: F.30,173 to the
commune of La Baule and F.16,906 to Pornichet (World Mead).
See RTD Commercial 1967 - 919, No. 29, with comments by
Pontavice.

39) Unlike the solution adopted by the recent Canadian act granting
priority for compensation. See Canadian Regulation of 1972
applying the Act of 1970 on the Pollution of Arctic Waters.
Article 8c.
See Kiss: La Convention Nordique sur l'Environnement, Annuaire
Française de Droit International, 1974, p. 108.

40) Cour de Cassation, Chambre Criminelle, 18th June 1969. Semaine
juridique (1970) 16,531, with comment by Despax.

41) Thus, in connection with the Santa Barbara case in California,
American case-law recognised the right of professional fishermen
to compensation for loss of fishing time, provided that the
reduction in their earnings could be established with certainty,
and was not "remote, speculative, or conjectural". Union Oil
v. Oppen, Court of Appeal, 501 F 2nd 558, 1974.

42) On the difficulties in evaluating loss of earnings to fishermen
and oyster farmers in the Amoco-Cadiz incident, see the report
of the French National Assembly's Commission of Enquiry p. 265
et seq. Some of the problems involved in assessing loss of
earnings are mentioned in Le Monde, 4th February 1979. See
also Rémond-Gouilloud, Leçons d'un naufrage, Dalloz 1979.
On the difficulty in assessing pollution damage and distinguish-
ing between temporary and lasting damage, see New Jersey Barging
Corp., 1958, DC, NY in 26 ALR Fed. 346.

43) See Tribunal de Grande Instance of Bastia, 8th December 1976 on
sludge discharge off Corsica, Dalloz 1977, p. 427, referred to
above.

44) See Green v. General Petroleum 1928 (205 Col. 328, p. 952).
Pollution Control, by H. Williams. American Jurisprudence 2nd
Vol. 61, 1972. On the application of "res ipsa loquitur" to a
marine pollution case, see State of California v. S.S. Bournemouth,
U.S. District Court of California, 12th October 1970.

No fault liability was admitted in the United States in connection with offshore oil pollution at the beginning of the century. See Teel v. Rio Bravo Oil Co. 1907, cited by Avins, study cited in the Brooklyn Law Review, p. 365.

45) See Article 90 of the Fundamentals of USSR Civil Law, 8th December 1961 in "Fundamentals of Soviet Civil Legislation and Procedure", Soviet Legislation Series, 1968, Moscow.

46) As in the famous leading case of Rylands v. Fletcher in 1868.

47) In past decisions the French liability principle, based on custody of the object, was applied to marine pollution by ships. See, for example, Tribunal Commerce, Rouen, 3rd June 1927; Gazette Palais 18th November 1927; Tribunal Commerce d'Alger, 15th February 1928. Cor. Sup. 1928, No. 6, p. 179.

48) See Rodière: Traité de Droit Maritime: L'armement, p. 600.

49) See OECD Convention, Paris, 29th July 1960, IAEA Convention, Vienna, 21st May 1963. Nuclear liability channelled onto the operator by those Conventions is strict and absolute (see infra: cases of exoneration).

49a) See Thiem, Environmental Damage Funds, OECD, 25th October 1977, p. 18.

50) The City of Winnipeg Act, Sm 1971 c. 105, Section 653, quoted by M. Tancelin, Report on legal protection of the neighbourhood and environment in Canada, Henri Capitant, Association Conference, 1976. See Post, U. Miami L.R., 1974 (524) 548.

50a) See Thiem, Environmental Damage Funds, op.cit.

51) The basis of liability must be distinguished from the degree of liability. Among types of no-fault liability (strict liability) a sub-division may be made according to the number of cases of exoneration. Absolute liability is that which requires no proof of fault and allows the party liable no possibility of exoneration.

52) See for instance the 17 cases of exoneration of the carrier of goods by sea under the International Convention of 25th April 1924.

53) Under the Offshore Convention a party liable would thus be exonerated even where the natural phenomenon would not be regarded according to French case-law as a case of "force majeure".

54) 1969 Convention on Civil Liability - Oil, Article 3-3-b; Offshore Convention, Article 3-3-b.

55) 1969 Convention on Civil Liability - Oil, Article 3-3; Fund Convention 1971, Article 4-3; Offshore Convention, Article 3-4.

56) Convention, Article 1-2. N.B. If the ship is the property of a State, the owner means the company operating it. The charterer, apparently, cannot be. The American courts have so held in connection both with the Torrey-Canyon and with the Amoco-Cadiz; charterers are thus refused the benefit of shipowners' limitation of liabilities.

57) Convention, Article 1-3.

58) Convention, Article 1-2; OECD Paris Convention, 29th July 1960.

59) Conseil d'Etat, 21st January 1966. See Despax: "La pollution des eaux et ses problèmes juridiques", pp. 173-174. Librairies Techniques, 1968, Paris. Subsequently, however, the Nature Conservation Act of 10th July 1976 recognised "the protection of open spaces and landscapes ... and the protection of natural resources against deterioration from threats of all kinds as being in the general interest" (Act of 10th July 1976, Article 1, J.O., 13th July).

60) See "Problèmes juridiques posés par l'exploration et l'exploitation du pétrole en mer". M. Rémond, Ed. Technip, 1970.

61) The problem of the liability of an assisting ship was first raised in a matter unconnected with pollution, the Tojo Maru case of 1972, when the House of Lords ruled that an assisting ship which had caused damage to the ship it was assisting could not benefit from limitation of its liability. See 1972 AC 242 (1971) 1 All ER 1110.

62) See 1969 Convention, Article 5-3.

63) See Convention, Article 6-3.

64) The Contracting States required to contribute are those which have received total quantities of oil exceeding 150,000 tonnes during the year preceding the entry into force of the Convention.

65) The 1971 Fund also acts as the financial guarantor of ships, when the amount of the liability incurred by them exceeds 125,000 Poincaré francs per ton of the ship's tonnage. It accordingly performs a double function: it supplements the compensation and acts as guarantor for those liable (see infra, Guarantees).

66) Tanker Owners Voluntary Agreement Concerning Liability for Oil Pollution. See P. Simon, op.cit., Nos. 1972s. Abecassis, op.cit., p. 235.

67) Contract Regarding an Interim Supplement to Tanker Liability for Oil Pollution. See G. Becker: A short cruise on the good ships Tovalop and Cristal. J.M.L.C. 1974, p. 709. P. Simon, Nos. 337s. Cristal today covers about 92 per cent of world crude shipped.

68) On the remaining differences between Tovalop and the 1969 Convention, and between Cristal and the 1971 Convention, see Abecassis, op.cit., pp. 238 and 242.
Among the remaining differences between Tovalop and the 1969 Convention, the former provides compensation for pollution from tankers in ballast, and unlike the latter, covers the bare-coat charterer as well as the shipowner. However, fault or privity on the part of the owner never eliminates the limitation on compensation, and "ecological" damage is expressly excluded. Cristal differs mainly from the 1971 Convention in that it never applies in a case of exoneration under the 1969 Convention (see above: exoneration of the party liable).

69) Offshore Pollution Liability: Initially $16 million, now raised to $25 million. See E. du Pontavice, Revue Juridique de l'Environnement,.1976, No. 34, p. 4.

69a) Such is the tendency of the system of limitation based on surrender of ship and cargo in kind. This mechanism, universally adopted, was to have been replaced in 1957 by a mechanism of surrender in cash, to which many States have not adhered. The Convention of 10th October 1957 on the limitation of shipowners' liability, which came into force on 31st May 1968 will, in turn, be replaced when a new instrument, the Convention of 1976 on the limitation of maritime claims enters into force (Convention of 19th November 1976; IMCO document Leg/Conf No. 7704E).
This is notably the rule in the United States, where the courts nowadays apply the 1851 Limitation of Liability Act restrictively: thus, in the Torrey Canyon and Amoco-Cadiz cases, the status of the shipowner enabling him to avail himself of the limitation was interpreted strictly: Cf. Barracuda Tanker Corp., 2nd Cir. 1969. Amoco Transport Co. Std. Oil Co., Amoco International Oil Co., and Cl. Philipps, 17th April 1979, District Court, Illinois, Judge F.J. McGarr.

70) Originally set at 450 million Poincaré francs, the sum was increased in April 1979 after the Amoco-Cadiz accident.

70a) 210 million Poincaré francs are approximately equivalent to $15 million, 450 million Poincaré francs to $30 million and 675 million Poincaré francs to $54 million.

71) $16 million.

72) The Brussels Convention of 31st January 1963 was drawn up precisely for the purpose of raising the ceilings laid down in the Paris Convention of 29th July 1960 (a unit of account was about 1 US dollar at the time of signature).

73) Convention of 25th May 1962. But the IAEA Convention of Vienna of 21st May 1963 enables each State to limit the operator's liability to $5 million per incident.

74) On 1st May 1981, since the Convention was open for signature on 1st May 1977.

75) One Special Drawing Right (SDR) was worth $1.15 in December 1976. See B. Dubais; The 1976 Convention ... supra.

76) See R. Rodière, "Tendances contemporaines du droit privé maritime international", Hague Academy of International Law, Recueil 1972, p. 360.

77) Article 7, 1969 Convention.
    The French Act of 26th May 1977 (J.O. 27th May) complies with
    these provisions: it forbids 1) any ship registered in a French
    port and carrying more than 2,000 tons of oil to trade without
    the required security (Article 2) and 2) any ship carrying more
    than 2,000 tons of oil to enter a French port without such a
    certificate.
78) See B. Dubais, supra, p. 30.
79) At least in the system set up by the Paris and Brussels Nuclear
    Conventions: a super-guarantee is even provided on the part of
    all Contracting States, above the limit of $70 million and up to
    a ceiling of $120 million.
80) The shipwrecks of the Lamoricière and the Champollion in 1941
    and 1952 were instructive for French lawyers in this respect:
    in order to get around the limitations of liability claimed by
    the shipowners, the families of the victims based their action
    on the general law of liability for tort, under which the person
    having custody of the ship was wholly liable and could not claim
    the limitation on which he hoped to rely.
81) The proceedings initiated after the Amoco Cadiz accident high-
    lighted the ambiguities of the instrument: the French Govern-
    ment, ignoring the constitution of the Brest Fund, elected to
    claim before United States' courts since no proceedings had been
    brought in France; no court entitled to exercise the exclusive
    powers provided for under the Convention had been applied to.
82) See judgement by the Court of Justice of the European Communi-
    ties on 30th November 1976 dealing with a similar problem.
83) At least under the general law, since such an action is possible
    under French company law.
84) Private victims cannot obtain compensation under this procedure.
85) The Florida Oil Spill Prevention and Pollution Control Act of
    1970 imposed unlimited liability without fault for operators of
    ships or offshore installations with respect to private persons.
    The District Court held that since this encroached upon Federal
    law it was unconstitutional, but that judgement was reversed:
    American Water Ways Operators v. Askew, 411. US. 325. 1973.
    See 26 LAR Fed. 346.
86) Article 3 of the Convention of 22nd March 1974.
87) Following the draft discussed in May 1976 by the Third Law of
    the Sea Conference. The International Seabed Authority to be
    created under that draft would include a Tribunal, and under
    Article 59 of the draft Convention judgements and orders of the
    Tribunal shall be "enforceable in the territories of members of
    the Authority in the same way as judgements or orders of the
    highest court of that member State". (See document A/Conf. 62,
    WP.10 of 15th July 1977; Informal Composite Negotiating Text.

# COMPENSATION FOR NUCLEAR DAMAGE
## IN THE OECD MEMBER COUNTRIES

by

Patrick Reyners
OECD Nuclear Energy Agency


## I. INTRODUCTION

The present study aims to describe briefly the main features of
the system, emphasising the practical arrangements for compensating
nuclear damage, with illustrations drawn from various national legal
provisions applicable to such cases. The study will however be limited
to indicating and comparing legislative provisions which are specifically nuclear, without going into the substantive and procedural rules
of the general law, reference to which frequently occurs regarding
compensation in enactments relating to nuclear third party liability:
indeed, any such detailed analysis would go beyond the limits of this
note. The references to national nuclear legislation are intended to
illustrate the manner in which effect has been given to international
Conventions and accordingly do not seek to be exhaustive. It should
also be noted that where the legislation of a given country does not
contain a specific provision which occurs in other legislations, this
may merely signifiy that in the country concerned such a provision is
part of the general law.

Compensation for damage caused by a nuclear incident is a subject
of which we have as yet, very fortunately, only comparatively little
practical experience. Despite the growing number of nuclear installations of all kinds, and the expansion of transports of nuclear substances, there has so far been no serious nuclear incident directly
affecting members of the public, although the recent incident in the
United States has demonstrated the existence of such dangers. Therefore, and justly so, in most of the industrialised countries the legislature was concerned with introducing without delay a scheme for compensating victims of nuclear damage, the law being in advance of events
in this instance. The scheme adopted is moreover based on principles
which distinguish it from the general law of liability.

Among the considerable social upheavals which resulted from the
Industrial Revolution in the 19th century was the fact that the traditional bases of the law of civil liability were called in question.

93

A century later the appearance of a revolutionary source of energy accompanied, however, by dangers of an unprecedented type and scale, and branded in public opinion with a kind of "original sin", required in turn a new system of liability.

There is general agreement that the most remarkable feature of the system of "third party" liability applying to nuclear incidents is that it has established a notion of liability that is both strict (or "no fault") and limited. This was not created "ex nihilo" but was on the contrary the culmination of a long period of evolution in the concept of civil liability. The notion of liability for "fault" inherited from the "Lex Aquilia" of ancient Rome, under which anyone causing damage to the person or property of another through fault or negligence must pay compensation, was based on the existence of a direct link between the victim and the party causing the loss and on the idea that the latter was a free agent; at the same time it served to dissuade and even punish the offender.

With the spread of transport and industrial activity, cases of liability of principals resulting from acts of their agents (respondeat superior) are becoming more common, and the factor of personal liability is becoming less important in consequence, since the person actually causing the damage and the person liable are no longer one and the same.

Accompanying this transfer of liability is a considerable increase in the ability of human activities to cause damage, often going beyond the amount represented by the assets of the person liable; this development has resulted in the practice of insuring against liability and, in some areas like that of motor transport, of making such insurance compulsory. This development of liability insurance already represents an evolution towards some degree of socialisation of risk.

At the same time, the development of mechanisation, by increasing the number of accidents for which no individual was responsible, raised the problem of the liability of a person in charge of an inanimate object. With the passage of time, it has appeared increasingly unfair that those suffering damage which cannot be attributed to the fault or negligence of another party should for that reason have no right to compensation.

These shortcomings of the traditional doctrine of "fault" liability underlie an important change in the trend of case-law based on Article 1384(1) of the Code Napoléon, leading in France to the notion of "presumption of liability" (cf. the classic decision in the Jand' heur case in 1930) and then, in a second stage, the theory of liability for a "man-made risk" ("res ipsa loquitur").(1)  In the United Kingdom

1) The case-law of the other European States whose laws are drawn from the Code Civil has followed a comparable trend over the same period.

where, without drawing directly on Roman law, the principle of "fault"
liability was eventually recognised, the leading case of Rylands v.
Fletcher established a similar principle, in the second half of the
last century, of strict or "no fault" liability.  In the Federal
Republic of Germany, as in Austria and Switzerland and unlike in
France or the United Kingdom, it was not case-law which produced this
trend but the legislature which, in special enactments, applied the
theory of "risk liability" ("Gefährdungshaftung") to a number of activities regarded as dangerous, in regard to which the need to fix
someone with liability thus takes second place to the requirement to
pay compensation.

From the way in which legal doctrine and case-law have evolved
in the various countries, it will be seen that the system of strict
liability is intended not to replace everywhere the rule of "fault"
liability, but rather to deal with a number of exceptional situations
in which it proves necessary to go beyond the stage of "presumption
of fault" to that of acceptance of liability and waiver of the
customary grounds of defence by the operator of the activity concerned.
It would be unacceptable in practice, as the opponents of the system
fear, if its adoption in everyday life had the effect of encouraging
irresponsible behaviour by people who could be sure of (comparative)
impunity because liability for their harmful acts was automatically
covered in advance by another person.  The solution of strict liability would appear to be justified when:

- there is either a high probability of an incident, or a
  risk of very serious damage even if the probability is
  low;
- the damage is likely to affect the population directly;
- the activity concerned is nonetheless sufficiently
  important to the nation as a whole to justify its being
  undertaken.

The customary corollary of systems of strict liability is the
limitation of that liability.  Here, again, the origin of the concept
of limited liability may be sought in Roman law;  it is to be found
in the Latin term "noxae deditio", a principle under which the owner
of a good may make it over to an injured party by way of compensation,
and from which has arisen the notion of liability limited to an amount
equal to the value of the object causing the damage;  maritime law
has made wide use of this principle to limit the liability of shipowners.  In the nuclear field, however, the reason for limiting liability is the quite different one of not imposing too crushing a
burden on nuclear operators.  When the Conventions on nuclear third
party (or civil) liability were being drawn up it became clear that
to impose unlimited liability on the operator of a nuclear installation would result in dissuading industries in advance from entering

into this type of activity, and that, instead, a way had to be found of mitigating the effects of the system of strict liability by reducing the financial consequences of such liability.

To limit the liability of a nuclear operator in advance unfortunately involves the danger that claims for compensation following a nuclear incident will exceed the amount of that liability, the more so since statistical and actuarial data were and still are (for which we must be grateful) quite rare in this field. It is the desire to mitigate the social repercussions of such a situation which underlie the many forms of official intervention in this matter, and in particular the notion of subsidiary State liability. Thus, most legislative provisions guarantee that the State will take over from the operator in case of catastrophic damage.

The risk theory, limited liability, compulsory insurance, and State intervention are the principles on which nuclear third party liability is based and, as we have seen, they are not entirely new. The originality of the system of nuclear liability lies rather in the fact that for the first time these various notions have been systematically applied to a whole industry, and have been broadly accepted internationally. The existence of several international conventions on nuclear liability is a witness to the willingness of many countries, those of the OECD in particular, to harmonise their legislation in this field from the outset. This wish may be partly explained by the apocalyptic image which the Hiroshima and Nagasaki explosions gave to the peaceful uses of nuclear energy; it is also due to the need to agree in advance on uniform rules of liability and compensation in the event of a catastrophe or an incident occurring during international transport of nuclear substances causing damage outside the national frontiers; the recent increase in the number of nuclear power plants in frontier areas has provided latter-day confirmation of this need for an international legal system.

## II. INTERNATIONAL BASIS OF THE RULES OF NUCLEAR THIRD PARTY LIABILITY

One of the main characteristics of these rules is certainly the importance, from the standpoint of achieving uniformity in the law, of the various relevant international conventions and, at the same time, the leading role of the international organisations responsible for drawing up and applying those conventions. Almost all the national laws in force in this field are directly based on those conventions, or at least follow them closely. Thus most of the laws referred to in the present study are those of the countries (1) which

_____
1) With the exception of Canada, the United States and Japan.

have signed the <u>Paris Convention on Third Party Liability in the Field of Nuclear Energy</u> (1) which is regarded as the basic text in this matter. These examples do not, however, attempt to be exhaustive, and it should be noted that some of the Signatories to the Paris Convention do not have such legislation.(2)

The principles of nuclear third party liability established by the Paris Convention have frequently been described from the standpoint of the operator's liability, and it is no doubt unnecessary to revert to this question in detail.(3) It need only be mentioned that the characteristic feature of the system is the strict and exclusive liability of the nuclear operator; this means that a nuclear operator whose installation (or a transport operation) is responsible for a nuclear incident is automatically held liable to the exclusion of any other person, in particular a supplier or other Contracting Party. On the other hand, the liability is limited as to amount (4) and time. The desire to ensure effective protection for those suffering damage also resulted in the requirement laid on a nuclear operator to constitute and maintain financial security corresponding to his liability; and there is thus channelling of the operator's insurance corresponding to the channelling of his liability.

There was a second stage in which a number of the Signatories to the Paris Convention felt it necessary to improve the system of liability and financial security applying to nuclear operators by means of a system of supplementary compensation, for which, this time, governments were to be responsible in order to deal with the consequences of a catastrophic nuclear incident. It was against this background that thirteen of the sixteen Signatories to the Paris Convention adopted, in 1963, the <u>Brussels Supplementary Convention</u>,(5) under which governments undertake to meet the cost of compensation for nuclear damage in excess of the amount already covered by the financial security provided by the operator, up to a maximum of 120 million EMA units of account. The Brussels Supplementary Convention provides that a first part of the compensation, from the maximum laid down for the operator's liability up to a limit of 70 million units of account, must be covered by the government of the country in which the installation of the responsible operator is situated. The tier of compen-

---

1) This Convention, signed on 29th July 1960 by sixteen European countries, came into force on 1st April 1968; a table of ratifications of and accessions to the Convention is annexed to this document.
2) Greece, Turkey, Portugal and Luxembourg.
3) See International Co-operation in the Field of Radioactive Transfrontier Pollution, Part B - Nuclear Law Bulletin No.14, OECD 1974. See also the Study "Nuclear Third Party Liability" published by NEA in 1976.
4) 15 million units of account of the European Monetary Agreement; this unit was defined on the basis of gold was equivalent to US$ 1 when the Convention was adopted.
5) The Supplementary Convention to the Paris Convention was signed in Brussels on 31st January 1963 and came into force on 4th December 1974. The list of ratifications is annexed to this document.

sation between 70 and 120 million units of account must in turn be
paid in the form of a joint contribution from all the Contracting
Parties to the Convention in accordance with a scale of apportionment
equally based on the gross national product and the thermal power of
the reactors in the territory of each of the Contracting Parties.

Some OECD Member countries that are not signatories of these
nuclear conventions have legislation on nuclear third party liability
which is not precisely based on the principle of exclusive but limited
liability of the operator.(1)  Those countries' legislation is nonetheless drafted so as to achieve the same objectives from the point of
view of the interest of victims without infringing the principle of
fault liability.  This is what is meant by the notion of "economic
channelling".

The principles laid down in the Paris Convention were taken up
in another convention which, unlike the Paris Convention, is of worldwide application, namely the Convention on Civil Liability for Nuclear
Damage adopted in Vienna in May 1963 in the framework of the International Atomic Energy Agency.  None of the Contracting Parties to
that Convention, which came into force on 12th November 1977, is a
Member country of OECD, and most of them are developing countries.(2)
Finally, a Convention was adopted in Brussels on 25th May 1962 for the
purpose of applying rules of liability for nuclear-powered ships
similar to those applying to nuclear installations on land;  this is
the Brussels Convention on the Liability of Operators of Nuclear Ships,
which has not yet come into force.  However, several national laws
are now based on this Convention.

A revision of the Paris Convention and the Brussels Supplementary
Convention is in the process of being adopted in the framework of the
OECD Nuclear Energy Agency.  Apart from a number of amendments to improve the system established by the Conventions, which are based on
experience acquired since their application, the modifications planned
concern mainly a revaluation of the compensation amounts and a change
in the unit of account.  The monetary upheavals of recent years, together with the abolition of the official price of gold and the resulting floating rate of exchange, have led the Contracting Parties
to opt for the replacement of the present unit of account by the
Special Drawing Right of the International Monetary Fund.  As regards
the amounts, the Contracting Parties did not reach agreement on an increase of the maximum liability of the nuclear operator under the Paris
Convention;  it should be noted, however, that replacement of the unit
of account by the Special Drawing Right should in effect oblige certain countries, whose currency has been devalued as against the Special

---

1) United States, Japan,  Canada, on the other hand, although not a
   Signatory of the Paris Convention, has enacted legislation largely
   based on its principles.
2) See table of ratifications of and accessions to this Convention
   annexed to this document.

Drawing Right in recent years, to revalue accordingly the amounts laid down in their national legislation. On the other hand, agreement was reached on increasing by a factor of 2.5 - mean rate of inflation noted in all the Signatory countries of the Brussels Supplementary Convention - the liability amounts fixed by that Convention. The liability limits should therefore be raised respectively from 70 to 175 million Special Drawing Rights for the first tier and from 120 to 300 million for the last tier.

> "Accidents due to the use of atomic energy, even for peaceful purposes, take us into a world in which space is immeasurably expanded and time excessively stretched".[1]

## III. DAMAGE

### a) Nuclear incidents [2] and nuclear damage

The notions of nuclear incident and nuclear damage are closely intermingled insofar as the nuclear conventions and national legislation implementing them define nuclear damage involving the liability of an operator as any damage resulting from a nuclear incident, whether it is conventional damage or on the contrary specifically nuclear (damage to the person such as dermatosis or malignant tumours, or damage to property such as radioactive contamination). A nuclear incident is defined as any occurrence or succession of occurrences arising out of the various dangerous properties of nuclear substances. Thus these definitions do not apply to conventional damage caused by a conventional accident, and damage suffered in the course of the

---

1) "Responsabilité civile et risque atomique" by René Rodière, Aspects du Droit de l'énergie atomique, CNRS, 1965.
2) The incident at the Three Mile Island nuclear power plant, near Harrisburg, Pennsylvania, on 28th March 1979 is, to our knowledge, the first case which required implementation of the mechanism of indemnification of the population for nuclear damage on a wide scale.
It should be pointed out, however, that, despite the seriousness of the occurrence, it is not yet proven that persons in the neighbourhood of the plant have sustained nuclear damage proper. The release to the atmosphere of radioactive effluents following the incident consisted mainly of noble gases (krypton, xenon) and the mean exposure dose for persons living within a 50-mile radius is estimated at 1.5 rem. This exposure, according to certain estimates, may result in one additional case of cancer in the 2 million population in the area.
Following the recommendation by the Governor of the State to evacuate pregnant women and pre-school children within a 5-mile radius of the plant, nuclear insurers immediately paid out indemnities for evacuation expenses to the 3,000 or so persons concerned, to an amount of approximately 1.2 million dollars.
Also, a number of claims for damages have been filed against the operator on the basis of physical and emotional injury, loss of income, etc. and to date, our information is that the nuclear insurance pools intend to oppose satisfaction of these claims.

operation of a nuclear installation or the transport of nuclear substances does not automatically entitle a victim to compensation on the
basis of the special rules for nuclear third party liability; this
would be so only if the incident itself, or some of the damage, was
nuclear. In other cases the general law of liability still applies.
Some damage that is really nuclear has also been excluded from the
rules.

b) Types of nuclear damage not covered

The first type of damage to be excluded is that caused to the
installation itself, or to objects on the site of the installation and
used in conjunction with it. It would not, it was felt, be normal for
an operator's third party liability to be invoked in respect of damage
to his own property or that under his own care, if only in virtue of
the saying that "no one can be liable to himself".(1) This exclusion,
which covers other nuclear installations belonging to the same operator, is of great practical importance in view of the present tendency
to construct several units on the same nuclear power plant site or to
create "parks" for several installations for the various stages of the
fuel cycle. The main purpose here is to avoid using up in the event
of an incident, most of the available financial security to compensate
damage to industrial facilities on the site to the detriment of "real"
third parties, namely the public.

In countries whose legislation is based on the Paris Convention,
the rules for nuclear third party liability cover physical injury
suffered by the nuclear operator and his employees; on the other
hand, in Japan and the United States, which are not Parties to that
Convention, the general rules of law apply in this case.(2)

Damage to the means of transport in which nuclear substances are
being transported is a special case, as its exclusion in principle,
as provided for in the Paris Convention, can nevertheless be overridden
by national legislation provided that the share of compensation going
to other victims is not less than an amount fixed by the Convention,
or that other claims have already been met. In practice, a considerable number of countries (3) have reincluded damage to the means of
transport in the scope of the liability of a nuclear operator, and
the tendency is for this measure, whose economic incidence is clearly
important, to become more general.

There are also circumstances in which victims of nuclear damage
cannot claim against the operator of the installation concerned; this

---

1) Japanese nuclear legislation does not, however, expressly exclude
   this type of damage.
2) United States: Atomic Energy Act, 1954, as amended, Section 11(w).
   Japan: 1962 Law on compensation for nuclear damage, as amended,
   Section 2(2).
3) Austria, Denmark, Finland, France, the Federal Republic of Germany,
   Italy, the Netherlands, Norway, Sweden and the United Kingdom.

would be so in the event of damage caused by an incident which is due
to political disorders, whether internal (insurrection, civil war,
etc.) or international (armed conflict, hostilities), or a grave
natural disaster of an exceptional character. From the viewpoint of
the public interest these cases of exemption from liability, laid down
in the Paris Convention in a vastly different historical and political
context, do give rise to some reservations or difficulties, in view
especially of the increase in acts of terrorism during the last few
years in most of the industrialised countries. It is for this reason
that the Federal Republic of Germany has made no provision in its
national (1) legislation for cases of exemption from liability of nu-.
clear operators. The notion of a grave natural disaster of an exceptional nature,(2) may also give rise to divergent interpretations
depending on the special geographical situation of the country or
countries concerned.

c) Type of nuclear damage covered

While nuclear legislation attaches importance to the origin of
the damage in order to determine whether it will entitle victims to
compensation under the special rules for nuclear third party liability,
it tends not to go into detail concerning the type of damage for which
compensation is to be paid, and there is so far no real case-law in
this matter. It may be assumed, however, in the absence of limiting
provisions, that damage to property covers the loss thereof (damnum
emergens), but also temporary deprivation, loss of use, or loss of
profit (lucrum cessans). This second type of damage is especially
important in nuclear matters as it corresponds to the case of radioactive contamination.(3)

1) Atomic Energy Act, 1959, as amended, Section 25.
2) The United Kingdom legislation /Nuclear Installations Act, 1965,
   Section 13(4)7 includes nuclear damage caused by a natural disaster.
3) The laws of the Federal Republic of Germany are particularly detailed in the matter of what compensation may be paid: compensation
   for damage to property is limited to its customary value plus the
   expenditure resulting from the protective measures against dangers
   of radiation inherent in such property. In cases of fatal accidents, compensation covers reimbursement of pecuniary loss suffered
   by the victim before death, and funeral expenses. If the victim
   was required in virtue of a legal relationship to pay for the support of a third party, including a person conceived but not yet
   born at the time of the accident, such third parties may claim
   compensation for loss of financial support. In cases of bodily
   injury, compensation covers reimbursement of pecuniary loss
   suffered by the victim, taking account, where appropriate, of temporary or permanent inability to work, increased needs or impairment of promotion prospects. If the damage was caused deliberately
   or by negligence, the victim may also claim appropriate compensation for moral and physical suffering. In cases of partial or
   total inability to work, increased needs, impaired promotion prospects or loss of financial support, compensation is paid in the
   form of an annual pension. 1959 Act, Sections 28, 29, 30 and 31.

## IV. CLAIMS FOR COMPENSATION

### a) Rules of Compensation

The Paris Convention leaves the task of determining the nature, form and scope of compensation for nuclear damage to the implementing of nuclear legislation. In turn, many of the laws on nuclear third party liability preserve the application of the national rules for industrial accidents and occupational diseases to nuclear injuries suffered by workers.(1) Many countries have for this purpose a restrictive list of the complaints capable of being brought on by ionizing radiation. In these circumstances, workers suffering an accident or a disease due to radiation are subject to the same compensation scheme, whether they are employed in an installation classed as "nuclear" and subject as such to the special regime of nuclear liability or in an installation not subject to that regime (such as a gamma-ray unit in a factory or radiation equipment in a hospital). When the victim is employed in a nuclear installation the obligation of the operator, whose liability is strict, to pay compensation may be invoked indirectly by means of action brought by the organisations administering the national compensation scheme; the victim thus has no opportunity to bring an action directly against the operator unless he or she claims for damage not covered by the social insurance rules, e.g. arising out of a "fault" committed by the liable operator. Members of the public, who by definition are not covered by the rules governing industrial accidents or occupational diseases, may claim compensation directly from the operator. More generally, in many countries, the system of compensation for nuclear damage is governed on a subsidiary basis by the law on liability for tort, insofar as this does not run counter to the special rules of nuclear third party liability.

### b) Instituting claims for compensation

The liability of nuclear operators is strict and at the same time exclusive, which means that victims of nuclear damage have no alternative but to address their claims for compensation to the operator. This limitation on the rights of a victim recognised by the general law of liability is not only inherent in the logic of the system of strict liability, but is also justified by the fact that it simplifies and accelerates the compensation procedures, since all the actions are brought against a single person. The rule has another advantage, this time economic: it prevents actions being brought against the

---

1) This is the case, in particular, in the following countries: Austria, Belgium, Canada, Denmark (no recourse against the operator), France, the Netherlands, the United Kingdom (cumulative entitlement prohibited).

operator's suppliers or associates who would, in the absence of such protection, be obliged to insure themselves against nuclear risks.(1)

It remains for the victim to identify the person liable in respect of a nuclear incident. This task is made considerably easier by the fact that in all countries the operation of a nuclear installation (or transport of nuclear substances) is subject to a prior licence being issued by the authorities. The licence given to the operator (a natural or legal person) also makes him liable for any incidents that may occur in his installation or in the course of transport effected by him or on his account. While maintaining the principle of exclusive liability, the Paris Convention gives legislatures the possibility, so far as the transport of nuclear substances is concerned, of allowing the carrier to take the place of the operator who would normally be liable, on the same conditions as to liability and insurance.(2)

In many countries the victims are allowed, for reasons of convenience, to address their claims directly to the operator's insurer or to the person who has provided him with the financial security required by law.

## c) Time limits

A special feature of nuclear damage is the fact that the physical disorder it causes may come to light some time only after the actual incident. This deferred damage makes the question of the time limit for claiming compensation a very important one, and argues for comparatively long periods. At the same time, in view of the insurance requirement laid on nuclear operators, it has been found difficult to oblige them and their insurers to maintain, over a very long period, the funds needed to cover their liability, and in general it is this argument that has won the day. As a result, on the expiry of such time-limits, victims are subject to the ordinary law.

A double time limit is laid down for the barring of actions for compensation: ten years from the date of a nuclear incident, or not less than two years (3) from the day on which the victim has knowledge (or ought reasonably to have known) of both the damage and the operator liable within the above-mentioned ten-year period.

---

1) In the United States where the law differs from the nuclear conventions on this point, and admits plurality of liability, the situation for possible victims and for suppliers is nevertheless fairly similar in practice, due to "umbrella" insurance policies and indemnification agreements with the federal authorities which include a waiver of the usual means of defence on the operator's part.
2) Most national legislation implementing the Paris Convention includes such a provision; but widespread use does not so far appear to have been made of it.
3) In accordance with a recommendation of the Steering Committee for Nuclear Energy, almost all the Signatories to the Paris Convention have adopted a three-year time limit.

Only in the special case of an incident caused by substances that have been lost, stolen or abandoned can the time limit be set at a maximum of twenty years from date of the loss, etc.

Some countries (1) have preferred, however, to keep to the traditional limitation period of thirty years, as the Paris Convention allows them to do. Others (2) have allowed a special time limit for "deferred" damage; in such cases, and given the limitations of the insurance market, it is usually the State which gives a financial guarantee of compensation for damage appearing after ten years.(3)

d) Competent courts

In further pursuance of the desire to simplify the settlement of any claims for compensation of nuclear damage, the authors of the Paris Convention (like those of the Vienna Convention) laid down the principle of a single forum. This also makes it easier to see that the limitation on the operator's liability, and the other rules which derogate from the general law, are observed. This solution is also clearly useful in the event of an incident having international repercussions.

As a general rule the competent court is the court within whose area of jurisdiction the nuclear incident took place, i.e. in principle the court nearest the victims. If the site of an incident is not in the territory of any Contracting Party, namely on the high seas, or if it is impossible to determine it exactly, the competent court will then be that of the territory of the Contracting Party in which the installation of the operator liable is situated.

It is for national laws to specify the rules of jurisdiction in this matter. While in most countries the legislature has chosen the court in whose area a nuclear incident occurs, other laws refer to the rules of general law (Federal Republic of Germany) or make the administrative authorities responsible for designating the competent court for a given incident (United Kingdom). In view, however, of the special nature of the legal regime applicable, and perhaps also the possible international implications of a nuclear incident, some countries have chosen to designate in advance a single court to be competent for all nuclear incidents that may occur in their territory. In such cases it is usually a court in the capital of the country in

---

1) Federal Republic of Germany, Ibid, Section 32.
   Austria, 1964 Act on Third Party Liability for Nuclear Damage, Section 34.
2) Spain, 1964 Act on Nuclear Energy, Sections 56 to 67.
3) United Kingdom, Nuclear Installations Act, 1965, Section 16.
   Denmark, Act on Compensation for Nuclear Damage, Section 34.

question that has been selected.(1)  In the United States, jurisdiction
is in principle governed by the legislation of the State concerned;
nonetheless, in cases of "extraordinary nuclear incidents" (subject to
the special Federal regime of compensation), the Federal court for the
district in which the incident took place is the competent court of
first instance.  For instance occurring outside the United States, the
court is that of the District of Columbia.

When public funds are called upon to meet claims for compensation
(see the next Chapter) jurisdiction is usually conferred on the same
court.

If a case arose where the courts of several of the Contracting
Parties to the Paris Convention could have jurisdiction over one and
the same nuclear incident, it would be for the European Nuclear Energy
Tribunal to designate the competent court at the request of one of the
Contracting Parties concerned, so that unity of jurisdiction could be
preserved.

e) Problem of proving damage

Under a strict or "no fault" liability regime, proof of the actual
occurrence of damage and its connection with the incident would in
principle suffice to establish proof of liability.  In more precise
terms it may be stated that the three elements required to establish
nuclear third party liability are respectively proof of radiation or
contamination, occurrence of damage and existence of a chain of
causality.

The insidious nature of ionizing radiation and the fact that its
effects may be delayed for long periods is however likely to make the
proof of nuclear damage more complicated.  In particular, while some of
the physical injuries due to radiation are fairly characteristic and
hence easy to identify (e.g. radiodermatitis), other afflictions such
as cancerous tumours, leukaemia, etc. are not specifically nuclear in
origin and, since they only usually appear after a long period of time,
it is difficult to determine their cause with any certainty.  Valuable
information may be obtained by radiation monitoring equipment for
workers in nuclear industry but the equipment used for such purposes
may reveal nothing or the victim may be a member of the public and for
that reason is not subject to any preventive controls.  In the absence
of formal proof of radiation levels exceeding the safety standards
themselves set by regulations in most countries, is mere exposure to a

1) Examples:
   - Belgium, Brussels Court of First Instance, 1966 Act on Third
     Party Liability in the Field of Nuclear Energy, Section 10.
   - The Netherlands, Local Court of the Hague, Bill on liability for
     damage caused by nuclear incidents, Section 13.
   - Sweden, District Court of Stockholm, 1968 Act on Nuclear Third
     Party Liability, Section 37.

radiation hazard as part of the victim's job to be treated as proof that a disease has been caused by ionizing radiation? In their concern for victims, the courts of several countries appear to accept that a sufficient presumption exists in such cases.(1) This trend of case-law has given rise to some concern in the nuclear industry due to its far-reaching implications and insofar as it challenges the credibility of standards embodied in national and international regulations on maximum permissible doses of exposure to radiation.(2)

## V. COMPENSATION OF VICTIMS

### a) Global amounts of liability

The strict and exclusive nature of the liability of a nuclear operator is counterbalanced by its limitation. Contrary to normal practice regarding industrial accidents or accidents in the course of transport, this limitation is global rather than individual. The fact that the number of victims of a major nuclear incident cannot be foreseen no doubt made the adoption of such a solution inevitable. Apart from catastrophic nuclear incidents with vast numbers of casualties, a less serious incident could nevertheless injure a large number of people, e.g. by radioactive contamination.

The Paris Convention introduced a "bracket" (minimum 5 million units of account and maximum 15 million) within which each Contracting Party had to fix the maximum amount of the nuclear operator's liability under its national legislation. The idea behind the Convention was to fix a maximum amount (15 million) in principle while permitting national legislation to fix higher or lower amounts to allow for the nature of hazards, local insurance capacity or other considerations. In most cases, Contracting Parties have opted for intermediate amounts

---

1) See, for example, the decision of 10th February 1966 by the Chambre Sociale of the French Cour de Cassation in the case of Dame Majoni v. the Commissariat à l'Energie Atomique (Notes in Nuclear Law Bulletin Nos. 1, 3 and 6).
2) It is recalled in this respect that radiation protection specialists make a distinction between the "stochastic" effects of ionizing radiations regarding which the probability of an effect occurring, rather than its gravity, is considered as a function of the radiation dose without a threshold for the latter (this applies, e.g. to hereditary effects or to certain somatic risks such as cancerogenesis and "non-stochastic" effects regarding which the gravity of the effect varies according to the dose intensity and concerning which a threshold can therefore be of consequence). This distinction helps to explain the frequent controversies in scientific circles concerning the potential or actual harmful effects of the public's exposure to very low radiation doses due to experiments or to radioactive materials released to the environment - thus making the courts' task by no means an easy one.

in their legislation, i.e. equivalent to about (initially) 10 million units of account.(1)

Most countries have laid down one single liability amount, expressed in their national currency, for all nuclear installations. Legislation in several countries, however, authorises the appropriate public authorities to prescribe different liability amounts according to the size of installations or the degree of risk involved in a particular activity or transport. Some countries,(2) following the Paris Convention have introduced a similar system of brackets. Others have chosen to lay down different amounts for each category of nuclear installation.(3) Another possibility involves fixing a single liability amount but requiring differing amounts of financial security to cover the operator's liability;  this approach pre-supposes that the State will undertake where necessary to cover the difference between the amount of financial security and the amount of liability.(4)

In view of the high rate of inflation in Western countries over the last few years, national liability amounts are undoubtedly threatened by depreciation in the relatively short term. Only rarely does legislation make provision for increases (5) or, by delegation of parliamentary powers, enable amounts to be increased by regulations. In such conditions amendments to national laws solely for the purpose of increasing liability amounts have been few (6) and far between and were in most cases designed to correct the effects of a devaluation of the national currency rather than those of inflation. It is true that the system set up by the Paris Convention does not expressly forbid the Contracting Parties to let the nuclear operator's liability amount "stray" from the original amount so long as it does not fall below the "floor" specified in the Convention;  however, this practice is undoubtedly contrary to the spirit of the Convention.

It should also be noted that with the present system of floating exchange rates, variations in the value of national compensation figures are likely to be magnified by the diverging changes in national currencies. The fact that since the de facto abandonment of an official gold price, the value of the unit of account in the Paris and Brussels Conventions, which is indirectly based on gold, has been

---

1) The Vienna Convention lays down a minimum amount for the operator's nuclear liability (US$ 5 million, 1963) and Contracting Parties are thus free to fix higher amounts. The number of States whose national laws are based on the Vienna Convention is still at present too small to define a tendency in the Contracting Parties.
2) Norway, Atomic Energy Act of 1972, Section 30.
   Sweden, Ibid, Section 17.
3) Austria, Ibid, Sections 15 and 29.
4) Federal Republic of Germany, Ibid, Sections 13 and 31.
5) Spain, Ibid, Section 57.
6) The Netherlands, Spain, Switzerland, the United Kingdom.

queried, adds even more to the confusion and militates even more in
favour of a speedy implementation of the revision of the Conventions
referred to above.

These considerations raise the question of whether liability
amounts as at present laid down in national laws are capable of coping
with the consequences of a serious nuclear disaster should one take
place today. Between the beginning of the 1960s, when the Conventions
on nuclear third party liability were adopted, and 1977, the number
of nuclear installations has not only enormously increased but the
thermal power of commercial reactors has increased approximately ten-
fold as compared to the reactors which then existed. Over the same
period, the average consumer price index in the Signatory countries
of the Paris Convention has increased from 100 in 1960 to about 390
in 1979. Even if account is taken of the fact that nuclear safety
technology has also made great progress over this period, the virtual
stagnation of liability amounts in most countries' legislation throughout the period clearly shows that in real terms there have been significant falls. In practice, as it is to be expected that courts, in
considering claims for compensation, will allow for the consequences
of inflation on purchasing power, it follows that where incidents require the commitment of all the available financial cover, the number
of victims who can be compensated will diminish over the years or,
more probably, that the compensation awarded to each victim will be
progressively reduced. Here again, it is to be hoped that adoption
of the revision of the Conventions will encourage countries to substantially increase the liability limits for nuclear damage in their
national laws.

A table of the present liability amounts of nuclear operators
expressed in national currencies appears as an annex to this study.

b) <u>Limitation of individual amounts of compensation</u>

In general the Paris Convention leaves it to national legislation to determine the nature, form and extent of compensation and
in particular makes no provision for the limitation of individual
amounts of compensation. With two exceptions (1) national legislation does not contain any such limitation either; however, to the
extent that victims of a nuclear incident receive compensation under
schemes for industrial accidents or occupational diseases, it follows
that the scales and limits of compensation in such schemes are applicable to them. As already mentioned, individuals covered by such
schemes may, if the legislation permits, invoke the liability of the
nuclear operator on the basis of a serious or inexcusable fault. In

_____

1) <u>Austria</u>, <u>Ibid</u>, Sections 15 and 29. <u>Sweden</u>, <u>Ibid</u>, Section 17.

some countries, moreover, nuclear law expressly confers on the victims the right to claim compensation (pretium doloris).(1)

There is one case where the court may wholly or partially refuse
to award compensation to the victim.  This occurs when the operator
proves that the victim was responsible for or contributed to the
damage or she has suffered following an act which was unlawful or
intentional.(2)  In such cases, nuclear legislation conforms to the
law on industrial accidents whereby the "fault" of a victim does not
exonerate an employer from liability or even reduce it except where
such fault is intentional.

c) Apportionment of damages

Liability amounts for damage due to a nuclear incident have been
calculated so as to cover the foreseeable consequences of such events.
The law shows no less concern, in many countries, with ensuring that
compensation for personal injury is given priority over compensation
for damage to property.  In most cases national legislation merely
lays down such priority in principle.(3)  Austrian law goes further
by specifying different liability amounts for the various types of
installations, depending on whether the case involves physical injury
or damage to property;(4)  it also provides as a protective measure
for the payment to victims of prescribed percentages of the total
amount of financial security available, on the basis of a timetable
which takes account of the way in which the damage becomes apparent
over time.  This approach, which enables proceedings to be delayed
until a complete schedule of damage requiring compensation is available, has moreover been adopted by several other countries.

Swiss law (5) is noeworthy in that it authorises the court
having jurisdiction to reduce the amount of compensation in an equitable manner in cases where the victim was in receipt of an exceptionally large income at the time the damage occurred.  Elsewhere,
in Japan,(6) victims of nuclear damage are in general given priority
as concerns their claims for compensation as against the ordinary

---

1) E.g. Federal Republic of Germany, Ibid, Section 29.
2) E.g. Canada, Act of 1970 on nuclear third party liability,
   Section 12.  Austria, Ibid, Section 7.  Denmark, Ibid, Section 15.
   Norway, Ibid, Section 26.  United Kingdom, Section 13.
3) E.g. Spain, Ibid, Section 51.  France, Ibid, Section 13.
   Norway, Ibid, Section 32.
4) Ibid, Section 15: On the basis of the liability amount for large
   nuclear installations (500 million schillings), the apportionment
   is 375 million schillings for personal injuries and 125 million
   schillings for damage to property.  These amounts may nevertheless be wholly or partially transferred to the other category
   where the first one does not fully use them up.
5) Act of 1959 on the Peaceful Uses of Atomic Energy and Protection
   against Radiation, Section 15.
6) Act No. 147 (Ibid), Section 9.

creditors of a nuclear operator. It may also be noted that legislation in the Federal Republic of Germany (1) makes a distinction
between those who suffer damage to property by giving priority to
compensation for "true third parties" as against persons representing
industrial undertakings which in one way or another are associated
with or profit from the nuclear installation in question, for example,
by the direct use of its energy by virtue of their location.

In the event of a major nuclear disaster, it is unfortunately
impossible to exclude the possibility that, irrespective of whether
or not the compensation scheme under the Brussels Supplementary
Convention comes into play, the funds available for the payment of
compensation may be insufficient to provide total redress for all
victims. In such circumstances, it is generally provided that compensation, without prejudice to the priority measures referred to
above, would be distributed among victims in proportion to the damage
suffered.(2) Responsibility for carrying out this procedure may lie
either with the competent court (3) or may be dealt with directly by
the public authorities (see "State Intervention"). The competent
authorities may first take protective steps and pay out on a pro-
visional basis a predetermined percentage of the compensation to
which victims are entitled.(4) Such apportionment may also be designed to hold back funds for the purpose of compensating deferred
damage.

## VI. STATE INTERVENTION

Under a legal regime deliberately at variance with the normal
principles of law governing compensation and which covers activities
for which governments have considerable responsibilities (if not in
some cases a monopoly) it is not surprising to find that the State
concerns itself with the insurance of nuclear installations and is
very active in making sure that victims receive satisfactory compensation, either by itself assuming responsibility should the need
arise, or by organising and supervising the compensation procedure.

a) Insurance for nuclear damage

The first way of ensuring compensation for victims of a nuclear
incident is to ascertain that the financial security to be provided
by the nuclear operator meets the conditions laid down by the public

---

1) Ibid, Section 15(c).
2) E.g. Denmark, Ibid, Section 23. France, Ibid, Section 13.
   The Netherlands, Ibid, Section 15. Sweden, Ibid, Section 19.
3) Italy, Act of 1962 on the Peaceful Uses of Nuclear Energy, as
   amended, Section 25.
4) Austria, Ibid, Section 16.

authorities.  Although some governments follow the policy of providing
coverage themselves for their own nuclear installations, as a general
rule the latter are covered by liability insurance for a sum equal to
that of the third party liability of their operator or in some cases
a fraction of that liability as laid down by the law, where it has
been fixed at a level exceeding the capacity of the local insurance
market.(1)  Although the Paris Convention states that the security
for the operator's liability is intended exclusively for the purpose
of covering damage caused by a nuclear incident, for practical reasons
insurance is usually taken out for each installation and for a specific period of time.  In such cases the legislation of some countries,
in order to provide greater protection, requires the nuclear operator
to take out insurance for a sum somewhat greater than his maximum
liability (in general one-fifth) and to restore this insurance without
delay under supervision of the public authorities in case of incident.
The authorities must moreover be notified of any cancellation of liability insurance policies.

## b) Guaranteed payment of compensation

Although the Paris Convention does not so provide (unlike the
Vienna Convention) the law of most countries, including Canada, the
United States and Japan which are not signatories, stipulates that
the State must intervene up to the amount of the operator's liability
in cases where the operator or his insurer are for one reason or
another unable to meet their commitments.  The population is thus re-
assured that in no case will it have to bear the consequences of the
insolvency of the nuclear operator liable.

The fact that the State has assumed beforehand the responsibility
of granting an operatig licence for the nuclear installation or a
licence for the transport at the source of the incident is in itself
an argument in favour of its intervention in case of default by the
operator liable.  In most cases, the government directly commits
itself to pay compensation to victims of a nuclear incident;  however,
in some countries (2) the necessary funds must be voted by parliament
in line with the procedure generally followed for natural catastrophies
or disasters of an exceptional nature.  Another example already mentioned of intervention by the State in a subsidiary capacity occurs
where nuclear damage only becomes apparent after the expiry of limitation periods for bringing compensation proceedings.  In this

1) It may be noted in passing that the present-day capacity of nuclear
   insurance pools of the Signatory countries of the Paris Convention
   as regards third party liability is on average some $30 million due
   to re-insurance and co-insurance mechanisms.  It is nevertheless
   very much higher in some countries such as the Federal Republic of
   Germany or the United States (DM 200 million and US$ 140 million
   respectively).
2) This is so in Japan, Law of 1942 on compensation for nuclear damage,
   Section 16, and in the United Kingdom, Ibid, Section 16.

connection, the possibility offered by Swiss law will be noted which provides that, after the end of the ten years following a nuclear incident, victims may submit claims to a Fund for Deferred Nuclear Damage. This fund is a public law body comparable to an old age insurance fund.

As pointed out in the Introduction, in countries which are Parties to the Brussels Supplementary Convention, the State does not limit its action to this secondary role but itself takes responsibility for payment of compensation for nuclear damage for amounts exceeding the maximum liability of the operator up to the amount fixed in the Convention. If compensation to be paid exceeds the amount of compensation which falls to be paid by the State of the nuclear operator liable (cf. Chapter II) it will then be up to such State to request the contribution of other Contracting Parties in accordance with the Convention. It follows that in such a case, claims for compensation would continue to be directed to the same State and victims would not have to resort to the excessively complex procedures involved in direct approaches to the other Contracting Parties.

In countries not covered by the nuclear conventions, the Government (or a body representing it) can provide a similar guarantee by concluding an indemnification agreement with each nuclear operator whereby the Government assumes responsibility for providing compensation for victims for damage exceeding the amount of financial security prescribed up to a specified figure.(1)

c) Organisation of compensation

The growing awareness of public opinion to the nuclear hazard and the magnitude of the funds involved have in many countries led the State to give itself the means of exercising detailed control over the procedure for settling claims arising from nuclear damage. Such control may simply take the form of an obligation on the part of the operator concerned and his insurer to notify the appropriate public authority for compensation which are submitted to them.(2) In other countries, the State takes a more active part either according to a

---

1) In the United States, for example, the Nuclear Regulatory Commission is empowered to enter into indemnification agreements whereby it undertakes to provide compensation for nuclear damage for which the operator is held liable to to a maximum of $500 million - 1954 Atomic Energy Act, as amended, Section 170. Japanese law contains similar provisions - Law of 1962 on indemnity agreements for compensation of nuclear damage.
2) Italy, Ibid, Section 25. The Netherlands, Ibid, Section 10. United Kingdom, Ibid, Section 20.

fairly systematic procedure as in Canada,(1) or especially in cases
where there is reason to believe that the funds available will be insufficient.(2)  Thus in Norway the Government may issue special regulations for the purpose of deciding the apportionment of funds.(3)
It must however be noted that in many Member countries, it is up to
the competent court to decide on claims and take any necessary steps
in this connection.  This is the case notably in the United States.(4)

In some countries, it is provided that settlement of claims
arising from major nuclear disasters may be preceded by a public enquiry designed to establish the number of victims and inviting them
to make themselves known as soon as possible so as to facilitate and
speed up the settlement of their claims.(5)  As this procedure is in
effect likely to take some time, it is provided in some countries
that loans or advances may be made to victims in need.(6)  Such advances are subsequently deducted from the amount of compensation
actually paid.

---

1) In case of a serious nuclear incident in Canada, the Executive may
   initiate a special procedure, the first effect of which is to suspend the settlement of compensation claims and substitute the
   State for the nuclear operator for this purpose.  A Nuclear Damage
   Claims Commission is then set up;  this Commission is given exclusive jurisdiction to hear and decide any claim for compensation
   submitted to it which arises from the nuclear incident in relation
   to which it has been set up.  Compensation is awarded by orders
   issued by the Commission and directed to the appropriate Minister
   (Minister for Energy, Mines and Resources), who pays them out of a
   special fund.
2) E.g. Denmark, Ibid, Section 23.  Spain, Ibid, Section 51.
   Finland, Nuclear Liability Act, 1972, Section 20.
3) Ibid, Section 41.  This is also the case in France, Ibid,
   Section 20.
4) Whenever the competent court concludes, on the application of an
   insurer, nuclear operator or of the NRC or DOE (where these bodies
   have concluded indemnification agreements) that third party liability resulting from a single nuclear incident may exceed the
   liability ceiling, the following provisions are applicable:
   - total payments shall not exceed 15 per cent of the maximum
     amount without prior approval of the competent court;
   - the court shall not authorise payments in excess of such 15 per
     cent unless these payments are in accordance with a distribution
     plan approved by the court or do not prejudice the adoption and
     implementation of such a plan;
   - the NRC or the DOE shall, and other interested persons may, sub-
     mit a distribution plan to the competent court.  The plan shall
     include an allocation of appropriate amounts for personal injury
     claims, property damage claims and possible latent injury claims
     which may not be discovered until a later time.  It shall further
     contain an establishment of priorities between claimants and
     classes of claims as necessary to ensure the most equitable
     allocation of available funds.  The court has the power to
     approve, disapprove or modify plans proposed or to adopt another
     plan, and to make all orders to implement and enforce the appor-
     tionment of claims;
   - within 90 days after the court has finally determined the total
     claim, the NRC or DOE shall report to the Congress of the United
     States on the estimated requirements for full compensation and
     relief of all claimants.
5) France, Ibid, Section 13. Switzerland, Ibid, Section 15.
6) Canada, Ibid, Section 31. The Netherlands, Ibid, Section 31.

In spite of the measures taken to guarantee payment of compensation for nuclear damage, it may nevertheless happen that some claims cannot be met, either exceptionally because no operator can be held liable for the damage, or because victims for valid reasons only became aware of it after the end of the period within which claims had to be made, or alternatively due to the exhaustion of funds available under the relevant legislation. In such a case, national solidarity is nevertheless likely to play a part and legislation in several countries expressly provides that the State shall take various steps, or shall approach parliament, with a view to providing compensation for such damage.(1)  Such action is nevertheless frequently only available in relation to physical injuries.


## VII. INTERNATIONAL ASPECTS

a) <u>Territorial scope</u>

The Paris Convention lays down the principle that it does not apply either to nuclear incidents or to damage caused on the territory of non-Contracting States, except where otherwise provided by the national law of the Contracting State where the installation concerned is situated.  Moreover, the Steering Committee for Nuclear Energy has successively recommended to Member countries that the Convention be applied to nuclear incidents on the high seas and to damage occurring on the high seas, and that its scope of application should be extended to damage occurring in a Contracting State or on a ship registered in such State, even where the nuclear incident causing the damage occurred in a non-Contracting State.(2)

In practice, national legislation is far from being uniform in this field.  Although in some cases no special rule exists, in others damage occurring on the territory of States which are Parties to the Convention and caused by a nuclear incident occurring in a non-Contracting State is covered.  A non-Contracting State may even be entitled to take advantage of the national system of nuclear third

---

1) This is the case in particular in the following countries: <u>United Kingdom, Ibid</u>, Section 18.  <u>Sweden, Ibid</u>, Section 32. <u>Switzerland, Ibid</u>, Section 18.  <u>Denmark, Ibid</u>, Section 34. <u>Spain, Ibid</u>, Sections 51 and 68.  <u>Finland, Ibid</u>, Section 33. <u>Federal Republic of Germany, Ibid</u>, Section 35(1).
2) The Paris Convention, aside from such extensions, has itself introduced an exception to the limitation of its scope of application:  where, in the case of a nuclear incident occurring in a non-Contracting State or damage suffered in such State, a person (other than the operator concerned), being a national of a Contracting Party, has been obliged to pay compensation to victims, such person has a right of recourse in turn against the nuclear operator even though the latter would not in the normal course of events be liable for the incident or the damage in question.

party liability, subject to the condition of reciprocity.(1)  Legislation of the Federal Republic of Germany (2) deserves a special mention in this respect since the operator of a nuclear installation in that country is held liable irrespective of the place where the incident occurred or where the damage was suffered.  However, compensation in excess of 15 million units of account of the European Monetary Agreement is only paid on condition of reciprocity where the damage occurred in other States.

In fact, no country, apart from the Federal Republic of Germany, awards compensation for nuclear damage occurring in States which are not Parties to the Paris Convention, except in some cases subject to a condition of reciprocity.  This rule also complicates insurance cover for the transport of nuclear materials across non-Contracting countries.  Since the Paris Convention reserves the operator's financial security exclusively for compensation of damage covered by the Convention, insurers must provide duplicate cover in such cases.  As regards the Brussels Supplementary Convention, the very nature of that instrument as an expression of international solidarity means that only Contracting Parties can benefit from it and any alteration to its scope of application by national law would require the prior unanimous consent of the Contracting Parties.

As regards countries which are not Parties to the nuclear Conventions, bilateral arrangements may be entered into.  This is notably the case for Canada and the United States which have settled the problems arising from their vicinity on this basis.(3)

## b) International carriage

The need for a uniform liability regime was felt to be particularly acute at the time of drafting the Paris Convention in relation to the carriage of nuclear substances, due to its international implications. The international carriage of nuclear materials has grown at a rapid rate over recent years.

The first exception to the normal rules which is made in this area entails the nuclear operator rather than the carrier being held liable, unless otherwise provided, for damage caused by the nuclear substances being transported.  As a general rule the operator despatching the substances is deemed to be liable up until the time when the substances are taken in charge by the operator of another installation. The consignor operator and the consignee operator may however provide otherwise by written contract.  In case of incident, the identity of

---

1) This is the case in particular under legislation in the Scandinavian countries.
2) Ibid, Sections 25 and 31.
3) Canada - USA nuclear liability rules - October 1976.

the operator liable may be immediately determined by reference to a certificate of financial security handed over to the carrier. This certificate (1) specifies the name of the operator liable and the substances transported, the route to be taken and the amount and type of security.

Transportation from or to a non-Contracting State poses a special problem since it is not certain that an operator who is a national of that State will be covered by appropriate security. The Paris Convention, with a view to the protection of victims, therefore provides that the operator who despatches nuclear substances to a non-Contracting State must assume liability for them until they are unloaded from the means of transport which has brought them to the territory of that State. Conversely, a consignee operator subject to the Paris Convention must assume liability for substances from the time they are loaded onto the means of transport by which they are to leave the non-Contracting State.

c) Power plants close to frontiers

In the same way as the international carriage of nuclear substances, nuclear power plants which are being set up in increasing numbers in frontier regions are likely to affect the population of one or more neighbouring States should an incident occur. These installations are not the subject of special arrangements as regards nuclear third party liability and provisions of national legislation concerning the scope of application of domestic law are consequently applicable as mentioned above.

d) Enforcement of judgements

The preceding paragraph raises the question of how victims of a nuclear incident for which an operator who is a national of a foreign country is liable, could obtain redress for damage suffered - this is in the first place dealt with by rules on jurisdiction which it has been seen /see Chapter IV(c)7 give jurisdiction to one single court which is in principle that of the place of the incident. The Convention provides, moreover, that judgements given on this basis may be enforced in the territory of any other Contracting Party on fulfilment of the formalities prescribed by that Party. No further consideration of the substance of the case is permitted. If proceedings for compensation were to be brought against a Contracting Party under the Convention, that Party could not invoke its immunity from proceedings,

---

1) Transport certificates, issued by insurers under the control of the appropriate authorities, are in practice used mainly for international transport. They are drawn up in accordance with a model document prepared by NEA.

116

except of course as concerns measures of execution. Procedural rules concerning the confirmation of foreign judgements are normally part of the ordinary law; however, the law of some countries (1) provides for example that the original judgement, or a certified copy, must be forwarded to the competent national authority, together with a translation, where necessary, and with a declaration by the public authority of the country where the judgement was delivered confirming that the judgement was based on the Paris Convention and is enforceable in that country.

The nuclear Conventions also lay down that their provisions (like those of national legislation) shall be applied without any discrimination based on nationality or permanent or temporary residence. Thus, any person who is a national of a foreign country (including a non-Contracting country) and who is the victim of nuclear damage in a country Party to the Paris Convention, will receive compensation on identical terms to those governing compensation for victims who are nationals of that country.

e) Applicable law

Bearing in mind the extreme complexity of this private international law problem, the observations which follow have been deliberately simplified. As a general rule, the Paris Convention provides that for any question of substance or procedure not governed by the Convention the court having jurisdiction must apply its own national law (lex fori). For example, where an incident occurs in an installation situated in Contracting Party A and damage is suffered in the territory of another Contracting Party B (i.e. nuclear power plant in a frontier region) the court having jurisdiction (normally that of the place of the incident) will apply its own national law to claims for cmmpensation from victims who are nationals of the other Contracting Party. The position is nevertheless more complicated where, in the course of international carriage, nuclear materials which are being transported under the responsibility of an operator of Contracting Party A cause a nuclear incident in the territory of another Contracting Party B. In such a case, the court with jurisdiction will be that of Party B and will apply its national nuclear law to claims for compensation and its apportionment and regarding time limits for submitting claims. On the other hand, the Paris Convention, which makes possible, by the use of contractual arrangements /see Chapter VI(b)7 the determination of the operator liable, also provides that the liability ceiling of the operator is that specified by the national law of the operator liable. This rule is designed to avoid a situation where an operator could, in the course of carriage, be held liable for different amounts according to the country being crossed.

1) Finland, Ibid, Section 38.

If, in the two cases set out above, country B was on the contrary not a Party to the Paris Convention, the position of victims in such country would be very different. They could no doubt bring proceedings before a court in their own country (within whose jurisdiction the damage had occurred) and that court could award compensation under its national law, but in such a case country A would probably (contrary to the previous cases) refuse to enforce such judgement as being contrary to its own public order (the judgement in country B is based on the unlimited liability of the operator or because a judgement had already been delivered in country A). The situation is somewhat more favourable from the insurance angle; insurance policies stipulate that the funds are to be paid according to the law applicable in the location where victims have suffered the damage. There would probably be no problem if all the damage were suffered (and compensated) on the territory of a non-Contracting country (international transport case); on the other hand, there might be difficulties if the incident has occurred in a Contracting country and the insurance funds have already been totally earmarked for compensation of damage caused in that country. Were victims in country B to take proceedings against the operator liable before a court in country A, they would be likely to run up against the provisions of the law of country A restricting the scope of application of the operator's liability /see Chapter VII(a)7 unless provision had been made under that law for its extension.(1) One last possibility, mentioned for the record, would be for victims in country B, after exhausting their domestic remedies, to ask their government to approach country A on the basis of its responsibility as the State having licensed the operator liable.

f) Differences between the various compensation regimes from the standpoint of victims

It is quite clear that victims of a nuclear incident will be subject to different compensation regimes depending on whether they are in a country not party to any Convention, in a country party to the Paris Convention alone or in a country party to both the Paris Convention and the Brussels Supplementary Convention. This is also true in the case of a nuclear incident with effects in countries other than that of the operator's nationality, except where the victims are able

---

1) In this respect, it should be specified that in addition to the provisions on the limitation of its scope /see Chapter VII(a)7, the Paris Convention lays down that the nuclear operator cannot be held liable outside the Convention for damage caused by a nuclear incident, and also, that no person other than the operator is obliged to pay compensation for such damage (except under an international agreement in the field of transport prior to the Convention). The question here is to know whether these provisions could be invoked against victims in a non-Contracting country to stop them from taking proceedings against the operator concerned on the basis of ordinary law on liability, without involving the international liability of the Contracting State in question on that occasion.

to benefit from the national law of countries which provide for an extension of the scope of application of their nuclear third party liability system.

Thus nationals of countries such as Austria and Switzerland (not party to any convention) could not obtain compensation under the Paris Convention for damage due to an incident in a nuclear installation in Italy. Similarly, nationals of Belgium (party to the Paris Convention alone) would not obtain the benefit of the international contribution introduced by the Brussels Supplementary Convention, in relation to damage caused by an incident in an installation in France (or in the course of carriage on behalf of and under the responsibility of a French nuclear operator).

On the other hand, it must be repeated once more that, in accordance with the prnnciples laid down by the Paris Convention, national law of the Contracting Parties must be applied without any discrimination of nationality or residence. It follows that a national of a non-Contracting country who suffered from nuclear damage within the territory of a State Party to the Paris Convention, would be entitled to the same compensation and the same treatment as nationals of that State. The same absence of discrimination is to be found in the application of the Brussels Supplementary Convention with one minor exception concerning damage suffered by nationals of a non-Contracting country aboard a ship on the high seas or an aircraft flying over them. This exception may moreover be excluded by Contracting Parties by a declaration treating such persons in the same way as their own nationals where they habitually reside in their territories.

As has already been stressed, the rules of nuclear third party liability have been designed to cover the exceptional hazards attached to certain types of nuclear installations and not to cover all activities in this field without distinction. Another possible source of differences between national systems therefore consists in the definition of those installations and transport of nuclear materials which are subject to this special liability regime. Having regard to the undisputed complexity of the definitions appearing in this connection in the Paris Convention, several Contracting Parties have drawn up exclusive lists of installations covered by that regime (1) or have laid down certain classification criteria. It follows that installations covered by the Paris Convention in one country are not necessarily so covered in another.


VIII. FINAL OBSERVATIONS


The purpose of this Note has not been to praise the virtues of the compensation regime for nuclear damage but simply to try to

1) Spain, Ibid, Section 2, France, Ibid, Decree of 11th December 1963 as amended in 1973.

clarify its general workings with particular reference to the way in which it transcends national frontiers and the principles of private law.

It would moreover be difficult to give a final verdict on a compensation regime which has not as yet been put to the test on a large scale. Practical difficulties involved in its application have so far been encountered principally in the field of insuring nuclear risks - and attempts are being made to overcome these difficulties at international level within the NEA Group of Governmental Experts on nuclear third part liability.

On the other hand, it may be noted that in spite of the remarkable efforts which have been made to achieve international harmonisation, the as yet insufficient number of ratifications of the nuclear Conventions results in the continuance of disturbing disparities between national compensation systems within the OECD area. In this connection, it may be noted that the "public debate on nuclear energy" in some countries has had the effect, paradoxically, of delaying or even blocking the procedure for ratification of the Conventions, thus detracting from the uniformity of the international system of nuclear third party liability. This setback is likely to be particularly noticeable in the event of an incident with international repercussions since, at national level, most countries have not waited for ratification of the nuclear Conventions before introducing legislation based on the principles contained in them.

The regime can still be criticised in one respect: by its very conception its scope is limited to incidents likely to occur in large nuclear installations. This means that cases not involving such installations are governed by the ordinary law of liability and, whatever may be the weight of arguments to the effect that it is not economically justifiable to maintain substantial insurance for minor nuclear hazards, it may be regretted from the standpoint of possible victims of radiation from a radioactive source outside the special nuclear third party liability regime, that the latter are not covered by strict and exclusive rules of liability, especially having regard to the problems of proving nuclear damage. This discrimination may seem somewhat unjust even though, in practice, nuclear liability insurance has been inclined to go beyond the narrow limits established by the Conventions, and case-law is emerging which tends to strengthen the presumption of liability of the user of such sources.

Another criticism which is sometimes made in relation to the Paris Convention is that it is far more detailed in relation to the liability and insurance regime of the nuclear operator than it is for conditions of compensation of potential victims. From a similar standpoint and based on the principle that the "polluter pays", it may be thought odd that at a time when nuclear energy has reached maturity, the nuclear industry should continue to receive substantial State assistance in the provision of financial security to cover possible nuclear incidents and should also be exempted from liability in certain cases. In this respect, a trend now seems to be emerging to limit State intervention in this area to categories of damage which cannot be insured specifically and to increase the insurance obligations of operators, either by increasing the insurance required (Federal Republic of Germany, Switzerland) or in the context of a mutual fund system supported by nuclear operators (United States).

To conclude, the question might possibly be asked whether the very nature of the limitation of liability might not in extreme cases influence the behaviour of the nuclear operator who to some extent sees himself relieved from liability to penalties imposed by the ordinary law on any entrepreneur who fails in his duty not to commit a fault causing damage. But this would be to ignore the extremely strict controls imposed on the operator at the time of construction and during operation of the installation and which, in case of his default, may lead to the imposition of severe economic consequences. There does not therefore appear to be any reason, on condition that controls continue to be strictly enforced in the future, to fear that the regime will lead to any form of slackness on the part of nuclear operators or to a "dilution" of their liability.

In any event, the compensation regime for nuclear damage cannot claim to be faultless or immutable and this Note has set out in its different chapters the points where improvements are required in the light of practical experience and economic developments. Work at present being carried out within the NEA Group of Governmental Experts, whose mandate is to study the problems of interpretation of the Paris and Brussels Convention, pursues this very objective.

Table I

STATE OF RATIFICATIONS

Paris Convention

| Country | Convention | Additional Protocol |
|---------|-----------|---------------------|
| Turkey | 10th October 1961 | 5th April 1968 |
| Spain | 31st October 1961 | 30th April 1965 |
| United Kingdom | 23rd February 1966 | 23rd February 1966 |
| France | 9th March 1966 | 9th March 1966 |
| Belgium | 3rd August 1966 | 3rd August 1966 |
| Sweden | 1st April 1968 | 1st April 1968 |
| Greece | 12th May 1970 | 12th May 1970 |
| Finland (accession) | 16th June 1972 | 16th June 1972 |
| Norway | 2nd July 1973 | 2nd July 1973 |
| Denmark | 4th September 1974 | 4th September 1974 |
| Italy | 17th September 1975 | 17th September 1975 |
| Germany | 30th September 1975 | 30th September 1975 |
| Portugal | 29th September 1977 | 29th September 1977 |
| The Netherlands | 28th December 1979 | 28th December 1979 |

Brussels Supplementary Convention

| Country | Convention | Additional Protocol |
|---------|-----------|---------------------|
| United Kingdom | 24th March 1966 | 24th March 1966 |
| France | 30th March 1966 | 30th March 1966 |
| Spain | 27th July 1966 | 27th July 1966 |
| Sweden | 3rd April 1968 | 3rd April 1968 |
| Norway | 7th July 1973 | 7th July 1973 |
| Denmark | 4th September 1974 | 4th September 1974 |
| Germany | 1st October 1975 | 1st October 1975 |
| Italy | 3rd February 1976 | 3rd February 1976 |
| Finland (accession) | 14th January 1977 | 14th January 1977 |
| The Netherlands | 28th September 1979 | 28th September 1979 |

Vienna Convention

| | |
|---|---|
| Ratifications | |
| Cuba | 25th November 1965 |
| Arab Republic of Egypt | 5th November 1965 |
| Philippine | 15th November 1965 |
| Argentine | 25th April 1964 |
| Yugoslavia | 12th August 1977 |
| Accessions | |
| Cameroons | 6th March 1964 |
| Trinidad and Tobago | 31st January 1966 |
| Bolivia | 10th April 1968 |
| Republic of Niger | 24th July 1979 |
| Peru | 26th April 1980 |

Table II

MAXIMUM AMOUNTS OF INDEMNIFICATION
FOR LARGE NUCLEAR INSTALLATIONS
(in millions of national monetary units)
or EMA u/a

| Country | Nuclear Operator | | | Ceiling of additional State intervention |
| --- | --- | --- | --- | --- |
| | Maximum (basic) | Approximate equivalent in millions of US dollars 1979 value | Other lower amounts (minimum) | |
| Austria (schillings) | 500 (1964)* | 38.3 | 3 (particle accelerators) | |
| Belgium (BF) | 1,000 (1980) | 28.2 | | |
| Canada (C$) | 75 (1970) | 64.4 | any other amount fixed by the Government | To be decided by Parliament |
| Denmark (krona) | 75 (1974) | 14.4 | 5 EMA u/a minimum | 120 EMA u/a |
| Finland (marks) | 42 (1972) | 11 | 21 | 120 EMA u/a |
| France (FF) | 50 (1968) | 11.8 | | 600 |
| Germany, F.R. (DM) | 500 (1975) (financial coverage) | 276 | | 1,000 ($442) |
| Italy (lira) | 7,500 (1975) | 9.2 | | 43,750/75,000 |
| Japan (yen) | 10,000 (1980) | 48.1 | between 1 billion and 100 million yen | To be decided by Parliament |
| Netherlands (guilder) | 100 (1979) (financial security) | 50.2 | To be decided by Government | 1,000 (1979) |
| Norway (krona) | 70 (1972) | 13.9 | 35 | 120 EMA u/a |
| Spain (pesetas) | 350 (1968) | 5.3 | 1** | Appropriate measures to be taken by the State |
| Sweden (krona) | 50 (1968) | 11.7 | 25 | 120 EMA u/a |
| Switzerland (SF) | 200 (1977) | 122.6 | 40 | 1,000 (Bill) |
| United Kingdom (£) | 5 (1969) | 10.7 | | 50 |
| United States ($) | 140 (1975)**** | 140 | | 560*** |

* Year amounts were fixed.
** Installations classified as "radioactive".
*** 100 million dollars for damage caused by an incident outside the United States.
**** Additional guarantee being constituted to reach 560 M$ in the 1980s.

COMPENSATION FOR POLLUTION DAMAGE AND INSURANCE

by

Jean Bigot
Professor at the University of Paris I,
Panthéon-Sorbonne
Director of the "Institut des Assurances de Paris"
Member of the "Conseil National des Assurances"

## 1. PURPOSE OF THE REPORT

This report forms part of the OECD programmes of study on the making good of damage caused by pollution, particularly transfrontier pollution.

In the context of these programmes its purpose is to study:

- the present situation in various Western European countries regarding insurance cover for damage caused by pollution;
- possible future measures for improving such a form of compensation.

## 2. AMBIT OF THE REPORT

The ambit of the report is insurance against damage caused by pollution proper, i.e. "the introduction by man, directly or indirectly, of substances or energy into the environment resulting in deleterious effects of such a nature as to endanger human health, harm living resources and ecosystems, and impair or interfere with amenities and other legitimate uses of the environment" $\overline{/C}(74)224\overline{7}$. This definition refers to pollution in the etymological sense of the term and leaves aside the other forms of environmental impairment (such as the deterioration of natural surroundings by the construction of unaesthetic or poorly integrated buildings), which are problems of town planning.

The report deals with insurance against industrial pollution and excludes pollution caused by individuals.

Pollution will be considered in its various aspects and manifestations (pollution of water, air and soil), but radioactive and marine oil pollution, which comes under special compensation procedures, will not be included. The report deals solely with the provision of

compensation for damage by means of insurance. This matter was dis-
cussed in 1978 at the meeting of the International Association for
Insurance Law in Madrid (proceedings published by MAFFRE in Madrid)
and was the subject of an investigation by the European Insurance
Committee covering 12 European countries (Austria, Belgium, Denmark,
France, Germany, Italy, the Netherlands, Norway, Spain, Sweden,
Switzerland and the United Kingdom).


## I. THE PRESENT SITUATION

A. Under-insurance

This appears to be due to a combination of two factors:

- the absence of any system of compulsory insurance;
- the very limited number of industrial firms insured
  against the pollution risk.


1. The absence of compulsory insurance

Whereas insurance is commonly compulsory for certain types of
activity (driving, transport, building and construction and certain
other occupations), it is striking to find that there is no obligation for reputedly polluting industries to insure against the risk
of pollution. It will accordingly be necessary to consider the question of the expediency of instituting compulsory insurance (see
Part II).


2. The limited number of firms insured against the pollution
   risk

Small and medium-sized firms are, to all intents and purposes,
without insurance against the pollution risk. Only major industrial
firms deemed to be polluters cover themselves against it. This
state of affairs is mainly due to the fact that once insurers appreciated the magnitude of the pollution risk, they systematically
excluded it from their general policies (see B below). At the same
time, they began to write policies covering third-party liability of
polluters. In view of their cost, these policies seem at present to
be attractive only to those industrial firms which pollute most. We
are thus confronted with the phenomenon which insurers call risk
selection operating against the insurer, i.e. they cover only the
most serious risks and are unable to offset them against the good
risks. For want of enough policy-holders, pollution insurance continues to be insurance with fairly limited cover. Its cost could be
reduced and its content improved, if it were capable of embracing a
larger number of insurable firms potentially in need of it (see
Part II).

B. The development of the attitude of insurers to the pollution risk

In most West European countries the attitude of insurers to the pollution risk seems to have gone through three successive phases.

Initially, neither the public, manufacturers nor insurers appreciated the magnitude and gravity of the pollution phenomenon. Consequently there were no exclusion conditions for pollution and whenever it occurred accidentally, it was automatically covered by the general third-party liability "public liability") for the activities of the firm insured.

In the second phase, and in the light of experience of spectacular loss-causing incidents (in particular radioactive pollution as in the Palomares case in Spain, and marine pollution as in the Torrey Canyon case) insurers became fully aware of the seriousness of potential damage and systematically excluded the risk of pollution or environmental damage from their general third-party liability policies. As a result, all industrial firms which had not taken out any special insurance for the pollution risk found themselves without any cover against it. The following paragraphs sum up the situation in various countries.

- In Germany, general third-party insurance normally excludes damage to persons or property caused by water pollution, but covers bodily injury or physical damage to property caused by pollution of the air or soil or by the action of waste water. Insurance against pollution risks is available to operators of polluting plant (third-party environmental damage insurance, 1978).

- The situation in Austria is much the same, but the extended cover for plant operators does not seem to be provided at present.

- In Belgium, most of the older policies which are still in force do not mention pollution as being either included or excluded, but some policies are beginning to be issued which specifically cover it.

- In Denmark, policies issued to industrialists other than reputed polluters usually cover the pollution risk, while those industries deemed to pollute have the possibility of taking out special insurance.

- In Spain, general policies normally cover the pollution risk. Owners of installations for storing polluting products can obtain special cover against the risk of leakage and infiltration.

- In France, general policies exclude the pollution risk, but a special policy issued by an insurers' pool (the GARPOL) covers this class of risk.

- In Italy, general policies exclude damage from pollution and other forms of disamenity. Insurers have recently devised a special pollution policy which is issued by a consortium of insurance companies.

- In Norway, all pollution damage is normally excluded from general policies.

- In the Netherlands, general policies cover pollution of the soil, air and water.

- In the United Kingdom, building contractors' insurance covers damage caused by dust, fumes, noise and vibration. Other industries' policies cover all kinds of pollution damage.

- In Sweden, the pollution risk is excluded from general policies, except when it is accidental or due to failure by the insured party to comply with a law unknown to him.

- In Switzerland, general policies cover damage caused by waste water or other industrial waste. On the other hand, a special policy is required to cover the risk of leakage from underground tanks or pipes for storing or transporting polluting substances.

In the third phase, insurers devised special cover for pollution risks.

C. Forms of insurance cover

Insurers have shown themselves to be very cautious, not to say reluctant, in dealing with the risk that pollution represents. They are aware of its magnitude and growth. They are above all concerned because of the way in which the law on third-party liability in the field of environmental damage has been developing, and in particular owing to:

- the tendency towards the "strict" liability which may be incurred even in the absence of any fault on the part of the polluter by reason of the sole fact of damage's occurrence (e.g. the German Act on water management of 23rd January 1970; the Swiss Federal Act on the protection of waters of 1st July 1970; the Belgian Act on toxic wastes of 22nd July 1974; English case-law based on a judgement of the House of Lords of 1869 (Rylands v. Fletcher); French judicial decisions based on disturbance going beyond the normal inconveniences of neighbourship, and on the automatic liability of a person having charge of a source of pollution or a polluting substance);

- the variety and extent of damage which may, in law, be attributed to a polluter: bodily injury, property damage (deterioration of physical property), cost of depollution, non-physical damage (economic damage), ecological damage, etc.

## Analysis of forms of insurance cover

### 1. Insurance for polluters remains a form of third party liability insurance

#### Consequences

a) It does not cover the consequences of pollution which are of a penal or administrative nature (fines inflicted on the polluter, suspension of work, cessation of operations, closure of the establishment, cost of pollution control facilities officially ordered to be provided).

b) It does not directly cover damage caused by pollution, but only damage attributable to an insured party whose liability is established.

A claim remains unsettled as long as the polluter's liability is not established, and this is subject to proof, which is extremely difficult to provide, that three conditions are satisfied:

- That the pollution is attributable to the party insured; in areas of high industrial density such proof is difficult to furnish owing to the presence of a number of polluters.

- That the party insured disregarded the administrative regulations or trade rules and customs, or criminally infringed environmental protection regulations.

- That there is a causal relationship between the fact of pollution attributable to the party insured and the whole of the damage. This is a particularly thorny problem in the case of synergic pollution (as when a river becomes polluted owing to a combination of substances which individually are not polluting). In most cases, liability will be established only after lengthy, complicated, costly and indeterminate surveys and procedures. In addition, the rules as to third-party liability are sometimes unsuited for making good damage of a public nature, which is frequently the kind caused by pollution. The present aim of legislation in most countries is however to facilitate action by environmental protection associations.

### 2. Criteria of insurability

For insurers the main criteria of the insurability of a pollution risk are:

- The fortuitous character of the event causing the pollution. They insist that the harmful event must be abnormal, unexpected and not in the normal course of things. They want to avoid the risk of having to cover inevitable or foreseeable damage caused by the insured party's customary activities or by a risk he has accepted.

- Compliance by the insured party with the standards prescribed for protecting the environment. They refuse to insure against conscious and wilful failure of the insured party to comply with these standards on the ground that the cause of damage by pollution is then no longer of a sufficiently fortuitous nature.

- The suddenness of the cause of the damage. While not all insurers share this point of view, some agree to cover only sudden events, a criterion which implies that the latter must be of a fortuitous and unforeseeable nature.

Mention should, however, be made of the constructive attitude of the French insurance companies in the pollution insurance pool /GARPOL/,(1) as marked by:

- their increasing the range of causes of pollution insured against. These are no longer only emissions, discharges or deposits of polluting substances, but also the production of odours, noise, vibrations, waves, radiation or changes in temperature exceeding the extent permitted by neighbourship obligations;

- their covering recurring or prolonged cases of pollution by departing from the previous restrictive principle whereby only such pollution damage was covered as was caused by an accident, i.e. an isolated and sudden event. Insurers as a whole consider that the unforeseeable character of the event causing the pollution is a fundamental condition for the risk to be insurable. This moreover is in accordance with the nature of the contract of insurance, which is necessarily aleatory. There are however different ways of expressing an unforeseeable character, and the concept needs to be clarified.

It is not the intention of insurers to decline to undertake liability in respect of the harmful consequences of incidents which are "conceivable"; otherwise the contract would be to no purpose. It is conceivable a priori that the piping of a sedimentation tank may break, or that an agent of the party insured may make an operational error. On the other hand, insurers will undertake liability only in respect of damage or injury arising from a fortuitous cause (even if attributable to an error or omission on the part of the insured party or his agents), and they decline to undertake liability in respect of damage or injury arising from a willful, deliberate and conscious action on the part of the insured. As regards whether a risk is insurable, a distinction may be drawn between different types of pollution.

a) Intentional pollution. This is pollution deliberately caused by a polluter with the wilful intent of polluting the environment. Such behaviour is to all intents and purposes a purely academic assumption and is manifestly not insurable, since insurance cannot cover an intentional wrong.

1) See J. Deprimoz, "Les nouvelles voies prises par l'assurance responsabilité civile pollution en France" (new developments in third party liability insurance against pollution in France). Revue Générale des Assurances Terrestres, 1978, p. 481 and ff.

b) <u>Reckless pollution</u>. Without actually intending to pollute, the polluter knowingly and deliberately fails to comply with the environmental protection regulations and through his recklessness causes pollution. If such recklessness is due to the actions of the insured party (and not, unbeknown to him, of one of his subordinates), insurers consider that its harmful consequences are not insurable.

c) <u>Accidental pollution</u>. Even today some insurers limit their cover to pollution arising from an <u>accidental cause</u>, an accident being defined as a circumstance or event which is <u>sudden</u> and <u>unforeseeable</u> from the point of view of the insured. The condition of suddenness may be found inappropriate. As one author points out (J. Deprimoz): "While in the case of pollution by harmful agents discharged into rivers or into the air it is relatively easy to determine whether the discharge stems from an isolated or continuous cause, on the other hand it is seldom possible to attribute a sudden cause to emissions of dust, noise, odours, vibration or radiation, which constitute the other most characteristic forms of environmental impairment".

d) <u>Residual pollution</u>. This is pollution caused by the emission in a quantity deemed tolerable, and actually tolerated, of pollutants which cannot be totally eliminated even if control and prevention standards are strictly observed, and which may fortuitously cause damage or injury. It will be observed that the assumption here is that the discharge of waste is wilful, deliberate and foreseen (<u>hence not accidental</u>). What is not foreseen is that it will give rise to pollution capable of causing damage to the environment. In other words, the occurrence giving rise to the pollution is wilful, while the damage is unintentional, fortuitous and unforeseen. <u>The pollution is neither accidental nor reckless</u>. According to the traditional doctrine, residual pollution would not be insurable because it would not result from an accident (e.g. the breakage of a part), but from the wilful discharge of polluting substances by the party insured. This situation, which is <u>extremely frequent in practice</u>, has led insurers to cover residual pollution <u>as long as it is not reckless</u>, i.e. as long as the insured complies with safety standards and regulations. In other words, the insurer withholds his cover only from the time when the management of the firm insured has knowledge of the disamenity caused by its operations, and if it does not immediately take the necessary remedial measures. This is an appreciable extension of cover as compared with that limited to the accident concept.

e) <u>Synergic pollution</u>. By synergic pollution is meant pollution resulting from the addition or combination of effluents discharged from several industrial establishments which individually are not of a polluting character and which but for such addition or combination would not have any polluting effect on the environment (water, air, or soil). This is a situation often met with in areas of high industrial density. The various polluters are usually held liable, either jointly and severally or "in solidum". So far insurers do not seem to have introduced any restrictions on their cover in the event their policy-holder is held liable jointly and severally with other potential polluters. But if courts of law should end by systematically holding liable all "potential" or presumably "potential" polluters, in the case of synergic pollution, it may well be that in future insurers will consider taking measures to limit their liability in such a case.

f) Potential pollution. This is pollution which, owing to the state of the art and technology at some given time, has not yet become apparent, but which may well become evident under conditions which were unforeseeable at that particular time. For the moment, while insurers do not formally exclude potential pollution from their policies, they have the means of escaping liability for this risk either by making use of the right to terminate the insurance contract at given intervals, by not renewing it on the anniversary date, by terminating it following a claim, or by declining to write this type of risk in the future.

### 3. Risks excluded

The risks excluded from insurance are fairly numerous. A first instance is where exclusions are not specific to pollution insurance and are based on the frequency or magnitude of the uninsurable risk, e.g.:

- damage or injury by pollution occasioned by foreign war, civil war, riot and civil commotion, strikes and lockouts, etc.;
- pollution damage or injury caused by such disastrous events as hurricanes, waterspouts, cyclones, floods, earthquakes, etc.;
- damage or injury from nuclear pollution (specific cover for this risk is provided by atomic insurance syndicates).

Exclusions due to the foreseeable nature of the harmful event are also found. Policies thus generally exclude:

- intentional or malicious pollution;
- reckless pollution: for example when the reasons of economy or convenience a manufacturer gets rid of harmful effluents by discharging them into a river while fully aware that he will cause the destruction of plant and animal life in the watercourse; or when the party insured deliberately, consciously and persistently infringes the environmental protection regulations;
- pollution caused by the poor condition, inadequacy or insufficient maintenance by the party insured, of equipment intended to prevent environmental damage;

- pollution caused by the deliberately negligent or inappropriate utilisation of the insured party's installations, as
when a manufacturer, while aware that certain weather conditions (fog) such as to cause a chemical reaction with
the result that normally harmless emanations produced by
his factory become toxic, nevertheless continues to operate
the latter without taking any precautions. "The insurer
is unable to cover the consequences of damage or injury
which, from the point of view of the insured, is <u>very likely</u>
to occur, or whose likelihood the insured has deliberately
accepted by choosing a certain method of work in order to
reduce his costs or increase or maintain production".*(1)

The techniques used by insurance companies for limiting cover to
aleatory risks vary from country to country.

- In the Federal Republic of Germany, general policies cover
only accidental events. Pollution insurance policies exclude damage
or injury attributable to conscious non-compliance with environmental
regulations, or deliberate disregard of the directions given by the
builder of the installations regarding their regular inspection, or
the deliberate failure by the insured party to carry out necessary
repairs. In Austria, the situation is very similar.

- In Belgium, the general tendency of insurers is to reject the
concept of accident, which they deem too restrictive, in favour of
that of damage or injury, but not in the case of pollution risks.
"Pollution" policies normally stipulate compliance with the regulations
and withhold cover if the latter are breached either deliberately or
unintentionally.

- In Denmark, insurers cover only "fortuitous incidents" and exclude failure to comply with an instruction from the authorities.

- In Spain also, policies normally stipulate compliance with the
laws and regulations.

- In France, general third party liability policies until recently
limited cover to accidental damage and injury, but they now exclude
the pollution risk. GARPOL's new "pollution" insurance policy no
longer refers to the concept of accident and its suddenness, but to
the concept of a fortuitous, harmful event. There is no cover, if a
regulation is broken consciously and deliberately, or if the installations are in poor condition, inadequate or improperly maintained.

- In Italy, the new pollution policies exclude damage and injury
due to non-compliance with the law, to the repeated overshooting of
permitted emission levels when the excess pollution was foreseeable,

---

* Unofficial translation by OECD Secretariat.
1) Report by the European Insurance Committee on Pollution Insurance.

to the absence or inadequacy of preventive measures and when defective
installations failed to be repaired.

- In the Netherlands, cover is obtainable for non-accidental pollution depending on the case, but it excludes failure to comply with
the regulations in force.

- The situation is very similar in the United Kingdom and Sweden.

- In Switzerland, general third-party liability policies exclude
damage and injury which are made highly probable by the behaviour of
an insured party who seeks to keep down his operating costs or speed
up his operations.  On the other hand, they do not appear to exclude
failure to comply with the law.  However, cover is only continued if
plant and equipment for storing or transporting polluting substances
are properly maintained, cleaned and periodically inspected.

A study of the situation in these various countries shows:

- that while some countries no longer limit cover to the
  risk of accidental pollution, which they find too restrictive (e.g. France and Italy), such extended cover is not
  the general practice;
- that most countries exclude deliberate breaches of the
  regulations in force.

4. Damage and injury covered by insurance

Damage to persons (bodily injury, disablement and death) are
covered without restriction.  The same applies to injury to property
(damage to physical assets and cost of depollution) and non-physical
damage (economic loss, loss of profits and operating losses) resulting
from it.  The insurance cover for such damage and injury calls for no
special comment, but the insurance of some other kinds of damage and
injury raises certain problems.

a. Indirect economic damage

Hotel keepers, restaurant keepers and shop keepers at a tourist
resort which has been deserted because the neighbourhood is polluted
suffer serious economic damage certainly as a consequence of the pollution, although their actual installations may not necessarily have
been polluted, i.e. not have suffered physical damage by pollution.
This is a case of non-physical damage which does not result from physical damage to insured property.  Insurers are usually unwilling to
cover this type of damage, although it often occurs in practice (the
wreck of the Amoco Cadiz caused the most affected seaside resorts to
lose their tourist business.

Some countries, however, have made efforts to cover such damage.

In the Federal Republic of Germany and in France, the new "environmental liability" policies cover it with an excess clause which

varies with the case. In Italy also it is covered in case industrial, commercial, agricultural or service activities are interrupted or suspended, and in general when the property in the polluted place becomes unusable.

In Sweden, it is covered if it involves liability due to an offence by the polluter under the Swedish law of torts, but it is apparently excluded in cases of strict, no fault liability.

### b. Genetic damage and injury

Pollution of the water, air or soil may cause genetic damage or injury to plant or animal species and even to mankind, either before birth or development, or in the second or subsequent generations. This is a serious problem of which insurance companies have recently become aware. In most countries such damage or injury is not the subject of specific exclusions, so that it would seem to be covered by insurance policies. In Italy, however, policies exclude damage and injury resulting from deterioration of a genetic character. It will be remembered that on the occasion of the Seveso disaster it was feared that the pollution of the air by chemicals might have caused practical and genetic damage.

### c. Cost of neutralising damage

The cost of neutralising the damage or injury affecting the property of third-party victims is non-physical damage which is normally covered when it results from physical damage to their property and is sometimes covered when it does not (see a. above).

The cost of neutralising damage or injury affecting the property of the insured party himself should be distinguished from the preventive expenditure he incurs in order to prevent the damage from occurring (see above). In fact this means salvage expenses incurred by the insured party after an accident in order to prevent the damage from spreading. Most policies do not expressly cover such expenses. In the Federal Republic of Germany, however, they may be covered by pollution insurance, and in the United Kingdom by extended cover known as "clean up". In France and Switzerland salvage expenses are covered in the case of fortuitous events.

Generally speaking, it may be supposed that salvage expenses should be covered when they are useful and reasonable. By minimising the consequences of an accident, the insured party is taking care of the interests of the insurer and, in accordance with the general principles of law, should be compensated for doing so.

Following a case of pollution, the polluting establishment may be temporarily or permanently closed by a decision of the authorities. This involves an operational loss to the insured party himself, which insurers are unwilling to cover under liability insurance provided against damage or injury to third parties, but not against damage or injury to the insured party.

### d. Ecological damage

This is damage caused to the environment itself, affecting plant or animal life which is not private property. Most insurers do not regard such damage as insurable, since nobody's possessions are damaged. In other words, "the right to the quality of life" is not covered. This question deserves to be investigated, because the attitude of insurers seems contrary to the general tendency, which is to allow environmental protection associations or public authorities to seek legal redress for such public ecological damage.

### e. Persistent damage

In cases of persistent and lasting pollution which it is technically impossible to arrest without closing the polluting establishment, the courts sometimes make the polluter pay repeated periodical compensation, sometimes subject to revision. It is a kind of allowance payable as long as the damage lasts, but insurance companies usually are unwilling to cover this form of compensation.

### f. Preventive expenditure

This is expenditure incurred by the party insured in order to prevent an accident from happening. Most insurance companies are unwilling to cover it, except the GARPOL in France. In 1976, the Belgian Supreme Court of Appeal,[1] by virtue of the law on insurance contracts, included it under liability insurance cover when it is useful and the risk is certain and imminent. In 1977 the French Supreme Court of Appeal took the same line and pointed out in its annual report that insurance cover must include preventive expenditure. Moreover, it may be argued that an insured party, by averting an imminent risk by suitable measures, is defending the interests of the insurer and should be compensated for doing so, if such action is useful and reasonable.

### 5. Limitations on cover

### a. Maximum insurable value

Damage, even including bodily injury, is not covered without limit as to amount but is subject to a ceiling (which is sometimes

---

1) In its decision of 28th April 1978 the Belgian Supreme Court of Appeal stated that expenses incurred by the plaintiff when complying with a legal obligation (e.g. cleaning up roads, removal of shipwrecks) could not be recovered as damage. See H. Bocken report "Réparation des dommages à l'environnement en droit belge", 1979.

fairly high in the case of major polluting industries) and to substantial excess clauses.   Some firms insure only against major risks.
This means that with regard to amounts falling outside his insurance
cover the polluter remains his own insurer.   If he has only taken out
insurance up to a small amount and the cost of the damage or injury is
substantial, he will experience difficulty in meeting it and the persons who have suffered the pollution may well find themselves without
any compensation.   This poses the problems of minimum compulsory insurance and the assumption, by the State or by a guarantee or compensation fund, of liability for pollution damage or injury not covered
by insurance or compensation (see below).   The cover granted by insurers may be increased considerably through co-insurance or, better
still, an insurance pool (see below).   It should be noted that cover
is usually limited in amount, both per incident and per insurance
year.   If a single incident reaches or exceeds the amount of the
cover, the latter will be exhausted for that particular year and the
party insured will remain without cover unless he is able to reinstate
it.   The same applies if during an insurance year a series of claims
relating to one or more incidents exceeds the total yearly amount of
cover.

### b. Time limit to cover

Most policies run for one year and are renewable unless termin-
ated by the insurer or the insured.   In addition, the insurer has the
option of unilaterally terminating the contract following a claim.

Policies usually cover damage and injury occurring during their
currency (loss occurrence basis), even if a claim from a third party
is made after the contract has expired.   Some countries add a further
condition regarding the date of claims (claims made basis).   In the
Netherlands and the United Kingdom, claims must be made during the
period covered.   French and Italian policies grant a year's grace
following expiry of the contract for claims to be presented.

### c. Territorial limits to cover

Some countries (Scandinavian countries) do not state the territorial limits of cover, which is liable to create problems unless
cover is taken to be worldwide.

Other countries (including Germany, the Netherlands, Spain and
the United Kingdom) normally restrict cover to damage and injury occurring on their soil, thus leaving transfrontier pollution uninsured
unless cover is specially extended.

The other countries (including Belgium, France and Italy) cover
transfrontier pollution whenever the insured establishment is located
on their soil.   It is important in the eyes of the insurer to know the

regulations in force at the place where the establishment is operated
and to be able to inspect installations on the spot.

### d. How insurance is organised

In most countries insurance is not institutionalised. Insurance
companies cover pollution risks either individually or by means of
traditional co-insurance. In France, however, in order to increase
underwriting capacity and the amount of insurance provided, insurance
companies have formed a joint reinsurance participation pool (the
GARPOL) in which pollution risks are pooled and the members insure and
reinsure each other. Italy seems to be moving towards a system based
on a consortium of insurance companies.

### e. Prevention

By prevention is meant any and all measures making it in the
interest of the party insured that a risk should fail to materialise.
In this regard, the whole of the penal and administrative regulations
concerning environmental protection constitute a general measure of
prevention. Apart from this legal framework, prevention methods exist
which are specific to insurance, in particular technical supervision
and the inclusion of an excess clause in the policy.

### 1) Technical supervision of installations

The pollution risk mainly depends on the type of activity carried
on by the insured, the operating methods and pollution control equipment used.

Hence insurers reserve the right to supervise the insured's installations (those used for production and those used for pollution
control) at the time when the insurance is written and throughout the
term of the policy, in order to satisfy themselves that these are
properly maintained and are still suited to the production operations
of the insured. They also reserve the right to terminate the contract
if the insured fails to comply with the insurer's injunctions to adopt
such measures of prevention as are objectively necessary. The French
system is somewhat sophisticated and is as follows:

- the insurer has a permanent right of supervision (including
  the right to inspect installations);
- if a defect is found which affords grounds for foreseeing
  the occurrence of damage or injury, the insurer asks the
  party insured what measures he proposes to take;
- if the insured does not comply with this request, the
  insurer may suspend cover after thirty days. If the
  parties do not reach agreement, the insurer reserves the
  right to terminate the contract.

2) Excess clauses

These also constitute effective measures of prevention. If in the event of an incident the polluter is required to bear personally a large proportion of the liability, such a measure can be an incentive to take the greatest care. The excess should however not be so large as to reduce the insurance to cover for risks of a diastrous nature only.

Such are the present general characteristics of pollution insurance.


CONCLUSIONS OF PART I


Examination of the present situation in the various countries of Western Europe shows that:

- the pollution risk is usually excluded from general "accident third-party liability" policies;
- it is covered only in consideration of a surcharge under such policies or of a premium for special insurance;
- since only major manufacturers have so far taken out such insurance, industry has very little insurance cover against pollution risks;
- when it exists, pollution insurance usually still provides fairly limited cover;
- in any event, such insurance continues to be a liability insurance, with all the attendant constraints;
- insurers are quite entitled to terminate their commitments if they find the yearly frequency and degree of risk excessive, either when the contract expires or following a claim.


II. POSSIBLE FUTURE MEASURES


In view of the complex and technical nature of the problems involved, this part of the report does not contain any actual suggestions, but a proposal that a study be made of a certain number of questions, in particular:

- Should compulsory insurance be introduced?
- How can major risks be insured?
- Can the cover provided by third-party liability policies be improved?
- Is another form of insurance conceivable?
- Can prevention be improved?

A. Compulsory insurance

The institution of compulsory insurance for polluting enterprises would offer at least two advantages:

- Within the limit of the insurance cover provided, it would not leave without compensation persons who had suffered damage or injury by pollution.
- It would increase the number of parties insured, all bearing one another's risks under this compulsory insurance, with the attendant improved risk disperson.

Compulsory insurance however raises many technical problems, some of which are discussed below.

1. How might the firms required to effect such insurance be defined?

As matters now stand, it would seem out of the question to make insurance compulsory for all industry, an important part of which is not of a polluting nature (but which may accidentally be exposed to a pollution incident). It would appear reasonable to bring under compulsory insurance those branches of industry which are reputed to be polluting (notably cement works, the manufacture of chemicals, petrochemicals and synthetic chemicals, paper pulp mills, metal foundries, chemical fertilizer factories, dye-works, certain agricultural operations of an industrial character (pig farming, aerosol crop-spraying) and even public authorities operating establishments or services involving a specific pollution risk (e.g. slaughterhouses, waste-water and refuse disposal plants). One might thus consider making insurance compulsory for so-called "classified" establishments which the regulations in force treat as polluting.

2. When the public authorities institute compulsory insurance, they at the same time prescribe minimum amounts of cover. How might the minimum cover threshold be fixed, more particularly the amount of the coverage having regard to the variety of industries and diversity of potential accidents?

3. The institution of any compulsory insurance is generally accompanied by the establishment of an agency responsible for rating risks refused by insurers or relinquished by them following an incident. If at any given time an insured manufacturer does not comply with the prescribed safety and prevention standards, he can then no longer be covered by insurance and it becomes necessary to establish a Rating Bureau.

4. If an uninsured incident occurs, the insurance company will not meet any claims arising out of it. Should then a guarantee fund be set up to meet claims not covered by insurance, as has been done for motor vehicle insurance? A Guarantee Fund exists in the

Netherlands for air pollution but only in a subsidiary capacity.
Setting up a Guarantee Fund itself presents formidable problems:

- If such a Fund is set up without there being any compulsory
  insurance, the Fund has to meet all pollution claims that
  are not covered by insurance (which are likely to be
  numerous in the absence of any compulsory insurance). The
  Fund may well promptly become insolvent.
- If neither compulsory insurance is instituted nor any Fund
  set up, those suffering damage or injury from pollution
  will be left without compensation if the party responsible
  for the pollution is not insured (as is now frequently the
  case), is insolvent, or if the amount of the claim is much
  more than any insurance cover available.
- If both compulsory insurance and a Guarantee Fund were
  instituted, new problems would arise:
  - Who would finance the Fund? It would be legitimate to
    expect the polluting industrial firms themselves to
    finance the Fund in part. But would there be a sufficient
    number of them to meet all the liabilities of the Fund?
    Could not the Fund be financed by a tax or fee on the
    polluting products? (Examples: the oil fee financing
    the Trans-Alaska Pipeline Fund in the United States, and
    the tax on fuel oils in Japan and the Netherlands).
  - With regard to what magnitude of incident should the Fund
    be liable? It would be well to see that the Fund was made
    liable only with regard to major incidents.
  - What would be the limits on the liability of the Fund?
  - If the pollution were to be caused by the State itself or
    by public authorities (public corporations, municipalities,
    etc.) and if they were exempted from compulsory insurance,
    it would be legitimate for the cost of compensation to be
    borne by the State or the public authority concerned.

5. In certain countries - particularly in France - there are
agencies responsible for collecting charges from polluters to finance
the study and installation of pollution control systems (Agences
Financières de Bassin). These charges are not in the nature of insurance premiums, the agencies concerned are not insurance companies
and do not meet the cost of damage or injury caused by pollution. The
Act governing them makes no provision for this type of action. They
are not technically equipped to deal with compensation, and in any
case this is not their function, which should mainly be one for
insurance.

## B. Insurance of major risks

The Seveso case in Italy (accidental contamination of the environment by a toxic substance) has brought home yet again to public opinion the disastrous dimensions which pollution can assume. How may such risks be insured against? At individual level the insurers grant cover only up to a certain amount, even if it may be substantial. How are major risks to be covered? The solution seems likely to consist in establishing a joint reinsurance participation pool, of which there is now one in France (the GARPOL). By this technique insurers pool the risks which they have written, each assuming a share of these risks, and they apportion among themselves the premiums and the cost of claims in proportion to their shares. This technique enables the risk to be better spread, raises the underwriting limit (maximum limit of liability in respect of a risk) and is often the basis of a rating agreement. At international level a conceivable step would be co-operation or even joint reinsurance between national pools. The most heavily polluting industries might moreover band together in order to finance a compensation fund for damage or injury exceeding the insurance cover available in the event of disasters as already exists for marine pollution.

## C. Improving insurance cover

The problem is still how to extend cover to risks of non-accidental pollution (it being established that insurers will not cover reckless pollution). Insurers are still divided over this matter. A legitimate expectation is that once the extended cover is offered on some particular national market the other markets will be constrained to follow suit. In any event, it is highly desirable that cover should no longer be limited to accidental pollution, which is too restrictive.

## D. Introduction of "environmental damage policies"

Whatever improvements may be made to polluters' insurance policies, these will continue to be liability policies which will not avail until after the polluter's third-party liability has been established. This is a lengthy, uncertain and costly procedure which creates a climate of contention between the polluter and his victims, both with regard to establishing the responsibility of the party insured and with regard to recognition and assessment of the damage or injury. The idea naturally comes to mind of replacing third-party liability policies by insurance policies directly covering risks of environmental pollution, regardless of any normal third-party liability on the part of the polluter (and hence even in fortuitous cases or cases of "force majeure" such as to exonerate the polluter from all liability under the general law). Such policies would no longer be

141

third party liability policies, but "direct" policies. It may be noted
that certain pollution risks are already covered under direct policies:

- Life assurance or insurance against personal accident or
  disease covering the risk of death or disability of the
  insured, even if caused by pollution.
- Fire insurance and water-damage insurance may cover certain
  kinds of pollution due to the occurrence of a fire or of
  damage by water.

Such policies however leave outside their ambit a great many
risks connected with pollution. Might one not give consideration to
a "pollution" policy covering the environment (water, air, soil)
against pollution risks? Such a policy would be taken out by the polluter (on his own behalf and on behalf of his immediate neighbours).
It might even be taken out by the "pollutee", i.e. anyone fearing
damage or injury by pollution (manufacturers, traders, municipalities,
tourist resorts, farmers, individuals with regard to their dwellings,
etc.). This would be a last resort, as by virtue of the "Polluter-
Pays Principle" it is anomalous that the victims should be the ones
who have to pay premiums for insurance against pollution risks; this
is a cost which should normally be borne by the polluter. The formulation of such an insurance policy no doubt would give rise to many
technical problems (especially definition of the environment insured).

Should this type of insurance be expected to promote incompetence
and negligence on the part of polluters, the personal liability of
polluters could be maintained through recourse by the environment's
insurer against the polluter responsible for the incident and against
his third-party liability insurer. Such a policy would considerably
simplify the settlement of claims, since the insurer would admit the
latter upon the occurrence of an incident, making any subsequent recourse against the polluter his personal matter. It would be desirable
if all such direct policies taken out by the "pollutees" were to include such a clause providing for legal defence and recourse on their
behalf in cases where the incident is such that the amount covered is
exceeded. Such insurance must however be expected to meet with some
opposition from persons exposed to a pollution risk; individuals
living in the vicinity of a polluting industrial establishment would
probably find it more equitable that the polluter should bear the
cost of their insurance.

E. Prevention

It would seem highly desirable that preventive measures designed
to avoid incidents be strengthened, and in particular:
- that insurers should grant cover only to firms provided with
adequate prevention facilities (thereby putting pressure on the others

to obtain equivalent equipment) and that such facilities should be strictly supervised by insurers. Such provisions are included in French pollution insurance policies;

- that substantial excesses should apply in the event of an incident. In this connection, the question arises as to whether an excess clause would avail against third parties who had suffered injury or damage. If it were to be stated that an excess clause would so avail, then the third party would be left to proceed on his own behalf to recover the amount from the polluter, if the latter was liable (and would be entitled to recover none of the excess if the polluter was not liable). If the excess clause were not to avail against third parties who had suffered damage or injury, it would then fall on the insurer to recover the amount from the polluter for his own account. This second solution seems preferable;

- that a system of no-claims bonuses and claims penalties applicable to premiums should be set up to reward manufacturers who have been diligent and to penalise those who have been negligent, on the basis of the number of incidents recorded during the insurance year. This system already operates in certain countries in the case of motor-vehicle insurance and building contractors' insurance.


## CONCLUSIONS OF PART II

Insurance should become the main source of compensation for damage or injury caused by pollution.

Compulsory insurance for polluters is socially and economically desirable, but raises serious technical problems.

The cover afforded by third-party liability insurance against pollution could be further improved. To avoid the constraints of liability insurance, a system of "environmental damage" insurance might be worked out to facilitate compensation.

At the same time, measures for prevention and control should be strengthened.

<u>ENVIRONMENTAL DAMAGE FUNDS</u>

by

Volker Thiem*

Former fellow, Max-Planck-Institute for
Foreign and International Law, Hamburg

INTRODUCTION

In the context of increasing pollution, the question has arisen,
to what extent private tort liability, directed as it is towards the
resolution of disputes between individuals, can be considered effective in dealing with the particular phenomenon of pollution damage.
In view of the vast areas affected by pollution and the multiplicity
of polluters and injured parties, and in consideration of multiple-
source pollution and the consequent difficulties in claiming damages
from any one particular polluter, there exists doubt as to whether
current liability in tort can adequately provide for an effective
compensation settlement other than in cases of obvious local nuisance.
Furthermore, there is an inherent limitation in only allowing damages
to the individual, which hinders the extraction of full compensation
for the deterioration in the environment, the pollution of air, water
and land.

The following investigation aims to examine an alternative to
traditional civil-law damages, which has, so far not been the subject
of a comparative law analysis:  compensation funds.  In particular,
the experience derived from the functioning of existing funds will be
considered.

A. THE PROBLEM: INADEQUACIES IN ACTIONS BASED ON THE
TRADITIONAL CONCEPT OF TORT LIABILITY

The traditional right to compensation is based in all countries
fundamentally on liability for negligence (faute; Verschulden), strict
liability (ultrahazardous activities; risque; Gefährdungshaftung) and

_____

* Formerly legal officer, Federal Environmental Agency, Berlin, now
  with the Ministry of Interior, Bonn.

144

nuisance (neighbour law;  trouble de voisinage; Nachbarrecht).  A
further basis is state responsibility for negligence or taking (in-
verse condemnation; enteignender Eingriff).

The inadequacies of this general basis of action are many.  Both
content and scope of the claim as well as enforcement against an individual polluter are affected.  The textual framing of a claim is also
affected, though to a lesser extent:  relevant inadequacies are -
the difficulties in proving negligence, the limitation of claims by
the requirement for public-law authorisation, the broad interpretation
of the assumption of risk (Mitverschulden; fait de la victime) and
limitations on the awarding of nominal damages.  The chief difficulties
in enforcing a claim are that:

- in many cases, although a polluter can be found, there are
  difficulties relating to the establishing of a chain of
  causality between the act of pollution and the damage that
  has occurred;
- in many cases it is impossible to trace an individual
  polluter;
- where many polluters are involved, the question as to
  their proportional responsibility arises;
- if a polluter is ordered to pay damages, the plaintiff
  may still end up with a financial loss if the polluter
  is unable to pay (a problem especially relevant to
  instances of extensive damage).

Problems in proving a case have been eased by relaxation in the
standards of evidence, reversals of the burden of proof and even certain presumptions of causality.  Also important is the concept of
joint responsibility applicable in most countries.  Despite all this,
numerous problems remain unsolved:

- much pollution is caused by small-scale emitters, ruling
  out individual actions from the outset;
- most relaxations of the standards of evidence scarcely
  aid the detection of polluters (cf. the cases of long-
  distance pollution and furtive discharge of oil at sea);
- even in cases, in which the polluter is apparently conclusively identified, there remain problems:  many
  pollution victims are reluctant to bring an action to court.
  Uncertainty as to the outcome of the trial, the awarding of
  costs and the duration of proceedings often has the effect
  that victims are afraid to press a claim, especially if
  the polluter voluntarily offers to pay - albeit frequently
  insufficient - compensation.

Many suggestions have been made as to how the inadequacies of
compensation for pollution damage can be overcome.  Virtually all of

them concern only points of detail (liability, burden of proof).
Practically no-one has attempted to supply a comprehensive solution.
However, such a comprehensive "most tempting and promising alternative"
is available: compensation funds. This solution overcomes the fundamental drawback of the traditional liability in tort - its concern
only for individual conflicts. It achieves this by combining the
raising of an emission levy with the direct compensation of individuals,
a system analogous to that of social insurance.

## B. AN ALTERNATIVE: COMPENSATION FUNDS

### I. General description

The fundamental idea underlying the concept of the compensation
fund is to provide a party harmed in any way by pollution with a right
to compensation from the fund, as well as, or instead of, his right
to claim against the individual polluter. The fund is financed by a
levy placed on potential polluters, the amount of which is assessed
according to the risk of damage they impose. In certain respects,
such a fund resembles a form of compulsory insurance. A right of redress ensures that individual responsibility for damages remains exis-
tant, so that a preventative function is preserved independent of that
exercised by the levy. By this means, compensation for damages can
be arranged in a simple, comprehensive and effective fashion.

### II. Fields of use

#### 1. Instances in which an individual polluter cannot be identi-
fied, or in which a claim cannot be enforced for some other
reason

It is in the improved enforcement of claims that the compensation fund is of decisive value. This is especially important in
those instances in which the inadequacies of individual liability in
tort are most apparent: the cases in which a particular polluter
cannot be detected, or an individual compensation claim cannot be enforced for other reasons.

The Dutch Air Pollution Fund,(1) for example, can deal with such
cases. Other countries, too, have set up funds with this thought in
mind, for example, Japan, the United States and Canada.(2)  In France
and the Federal Republic of Germany, there has been much support
amongst writers for the establishment of a compensation fund for those

---

1) Art. 64 wet inzake de luchtverontreiniging, Stb 1970, p. 580.  For
   the exact wording, see p. 10a.
2) For details, see below.

cases in which the polluter cannot be identified. The main fields under consideration in France are water pollution,(1) air traffic noise (2) and radioactive pollution.(3) German literature concerns itself predominantly with air pollution.(4)

Environmental protection law apart, damage caused by an unidentified party is covered by a form of compensation fund in car insurance. In several countries, there exist compensation funds run by car insurance companies, to cover those instances when the vehicle that caused the damage cannot be identified, or when the other party has no insurance cover.(5) The basic problem is the same as that in environmental control. If a legitimate claim cannot be enforced, then the community of potential causers of damage must bear the cost of compensation.

## 2. Right to compensation from the fund in all cases of pollution damage

The possible field of application of a compensation fund is, however, wider. Even if the individual polluter is identified, intervention on the part of the fund could be desirable and the prescribing of at least a preliminary obligation to intervene could be justified in that it would help the victim in the enforcement of his claim. As is stated above, even if the polluter is identified, there still

---

1) Cf. Malafosse, p. 245.
2) Goy, Rév. gén. air 1960, 379, Derrida, D. 1965, J. 222 (232: "fonds de garantie aéronautique"); Kiss, A.F.D.I. 1970, 769; Girod, Rév. de Droit rural 1972, 483 (492); Girod, La Réparation du Dommage Ecologique 124 and 259.
3) Nonnenmacher, Vers un Droit Atomique, 1956, 44, State liability instead of private liability; Rodière, Rév. de Droit Comparé 1959, 10, also in favour of collective liability.
4) Cf. Bullinger VersR 1972, 599 (605, 606); Simitis VersR 1972, 1087 (1090); Landau in: Gerechtigkeit in der Industriegesellschaft, Materialien zum Rechtspolitischen Kongress der SPD 1972 in Braunschweig, 1973, 117 ff; H. Westermann, Welche gesetzlichen Massnahmen zur Luftreinhaltung und zur Verbesserung des Nachbarrechts sind erforderlich, 1958, 67 ff.
5) Federal Republic of Germany: paras.12-14 PflichtversG i.d.F. v. 5.4.1965 (BGBl. I 213); Claims are raised directly with the fund. The claimant will receive compensation as far as he is eligible for such. Compensation for pain and suffering will only be made if its refusal would amount to serious injustice (para. 35, sect.2, sub-sect. 1 PflichtversG). Damage to property is only compensated in the absence of insurance cover (para. 12, sect. 2, sub-sect.2 PflichtversG). Liability is restricted to claims of more than DM 1,000.
France: fonds de garantie, loi du 31 déc. 1951 mod. 7 janv. 1959; Cf. also Schneider, Der Fonds de Garantie Automobile im Rahmen des Schutzes der Verkehrsopfer, 1967; Cf. also Mazeaud-Tunc I no. 269; Goy, Rév. gén. air 1960, 379 (the suggestion that the idea could be applied to emission control);
United States: Unsatisfied Judgement Funds in some States and in some Canadian provinces; ct. Schneider 126;
Sweden: Garantiefonds since the Act of 10.5.1929.

exist problems in enforcement. Legal uncertainty, difficulties in
establishing causality, the greater resources of the polluter and the
danger of losing the case not only make enforcement more difficult,
but thwart it altogether in some cases.(1)  The fully realisable
social task of the State in such instances would be to pay in anticipation and to ensure correct assessment of compensation through the
right of redress or through levies.  Also it would be advantageous if
uniform rules for apportionment could be fixed even for the cases
where the polluter is known, thus overcoming loopholes in substantive
liability.  Negligence, Act of God, limited liability, compliance with
standards, etc. should no longer be allowed as defences to an individual claim for damages by a pollution victim.

Some collective compensation systems are already heading in the
right direction.  The Japanese Law for the Compensation of Pollution-
related Health Damage permits claims against the compensation fund,
whether or not the polluter is known.(2)  The same applies to the
Maine Coastal Protection Fund, which pays compensation for oil pollution damage in the American State, Maine.(3)

Examples from fields of law other than environment control make
it clear that collective responsibility for compensation payments can
be highly successful.  Workeen's compensation insurance (4) is a prime
example.  This system of collective responsibility for compensation
has brought to an end the confrontation between the injured party and
the party liable in law.  It links a claim for comppnsation against
the working community with precondition that it is based on injuries
or illness related to employment.  It has been seen to give extremely
satisfactory results in all industrialised nations in the world (5)
and is now regarded as a model for the development of similar systems
in other fields, for example, for a general traffic accident compensation fund (6) or, still more progressive, a general industrial insurance.(7)  In terms of its basic principle, it could just as easily

---

1) It is because of this that in many cases victims agree with low
   lump sums paid by the polluter.
2) Law No. 111 of 5.10.1973, as amended by law No. 85 of 1974; a
   German translation is to be found in "Umweltschutz in Japan"
   edited by M. Bothe, in the series "Beiträge zur Umweltgestaltung",
   published by E. Schmidt-Verlag, Berlin 1975.
3) Oil-Discharge Prevention and Pollution Control Act of 1970, ME.
   Rev. STAT. Ann. tit. 38, paras. 551-557 (supp. 1973).
4) Federal Republic of Germany:  The first workmen's compensation insurance law (Unfallversicherungsgesetz of 6.7.1884, RGBI 1884, 69)
   came into force on 1.10.1885.
   United States: Cf. Friedmann/Ladinsky, Social Change and the Law of
   Industrial Accidents, Col. L. Rev. 67 (1967) 50 (65 ff.).
5) Cf. v. Hippel, Schadensausgleich bei Verkerhsunfallschäden, 1968,
   52.
6) Cf. v. Hippel, 53 ff. (With a survey of foreign solutions to the
   problem); Cf. also A. Tunc, Traffic Accident Compensation Law and
   Proposals, in: Int. Encyclopedia of Comparative Law, vol. XI,
   chapter 14, 1971.
7) Schäfer, Soziale Schäden, soziale Kosten und soziale Sicherung,
   1972; Cf. v. Hippel Zeitschrift für Rechtspolitik 1976, 252.

act as a model for the creation of an "environment damage fund".(1)
There are even closer analogies with environmental protection: workmen's compensation insurance for industrial accidents and occupational
illnesses was established when it was realised that in an age of increasing industrialisation and developing technology, industrial liability in tort was no longer able to deal equitably with the numeri-
cally increasing and even more difficult cases of accident and illness.(2)

To a certain extent, the French regulations governing compensation for crop damage caused by big game (Art. 14 de la Loi de
finances pour 1969 relative à la réparation des dommages aux récoltes
par le grand gibier) could be taken as a model, as suggested in the
French literature by Malafosse.(3)  The regulations provide agricultural concerns with a direct claim for compensation against the
national department responsible for hunting (l'Office nationale de la
chasse) for crop damage caused by big game.  The department has built
up a fund financed by a levy charged on hunting permits (permis de
chasse).  It pays compensation for 95 per cent of the material damage.
If the department provides compensation, this can be recovered from
the party actually liable for the damage.

### 3. Particular fields of use:  financing of preventive measures and the total cost of compensation for pollution victims

A further possible function of a compensation fund is to support
and finance preventive measures to aid individuals (e.g. with sound
insulation or with removal costs) living in affected areas (e.g. near
airports, highways and industrial installations).  In these instances,
claims would, in fact, be comparatively simple to enforce, with, for
example, an action against the airport owner based on the nuisance of
air traffic noise, or against those responsible for having the high-
way built, on account of traffic noise.  In many respects, however,
this is not the perfect solution and the question of compensation
could be more adequately dealt with in a system similar to a compensation fund.  The fact that the State (and thus ultimately the general
public) finances compensation for traffic noise from normal taxation
sources, for example, is less than satisfactory.  It would be more
appropriate economically if the "polluter must pay principle" were
followed, i.e. the cost of compensation should be placed on the
shoulders of the parties causing the injury concerned, in the case of
motor vehicles, manufacturers, dealers and owners should bear the cost,

---

1) Cf. Schäfer, who refers to the indeterminable ecological risk as
   the basis for his system of industrial insurance for personal
   injury.
2) Cf. footnote 1), page 7.
3) Malafosse, 245.

and in the case of aeroplanes, it should be the manufacturers, air companies and passengers that pay.

Such a system of passing on the costs of compensation is currently to be found in connection with the Paris airports (1) and more recently in Japan.(2)

Furthermore, claims to date have never been optimal from the point of view of content. For financial reasons, the tolerance levels have been set high and there are no compensation rules to make an escape from the affected area possible, i.e. by the financing of removals, or by an offer to purchase property. In this field, a fund could intervene and make more generous financial provisions, because the compensation measures would be financed by a levy raised on all polluters. The State, whether or not liable from a legal point of view, would not, according to this economic approach, carry the burden of compensation, but would rather act as mediator between injured party and compensator. To this extent, State organs would fulfil precisely the same function as those funds that intervene in the event of an unidentified polluter: on the one hand, they would constitute an organisatory framework making for easier enforcement of claims, and on the other hand, they would undertake the co-ordination of compensation costs by collecting levies.

Standardisation of the requirements for a claim for compensation (e.g. reimbursement of the cost of fitting double glazing in areas with a continuous sound level of more than 75 dB) would make enforcement much easier. Compensation claims can, in general, be regulated administratively. The courts need not be resorted to. From this type of compensation system, it would be possible to develop a generally applicable compensation model for typical pollution cases, and which could intervene on behalf of all those living in particularly hazardous areas.

In order to be able to assess the possibilities and the limitations of compensation funds more accurately, an evaluation of experience with existing funds would not be out of place. In this context, the Dutch Air Pollution Fund, the Japanese Law for the Compensation of Pollution-related Health Damage, the funds for oil pollution damage in the American State, Maine, and in Canada as well as the French compensation fund for nuisance caused by air traffic noise will be considered.

---

1) Décret no. 73-193 of 13.2.1973, printed in Lamarque at p. 329.
2) Since 1975, air companies have been charged a special landing fee assessed according to weight and noise level of the aircraft.

## C. EXPERIENCE WITH EXISTING FUNDS

## I. The Dutch Air Pollution Fund

Since 18th September 1972 there has existed in the Netherlands a fund to compensate victims of air pollution (het fonds Luchtverontreiniging).(1)  Its legal basis is the Law on Air Pollution (wet inzake de Luchtverontreiniging) (2) and it thus falls under environmental administration law.  The fund is administered by the Ministry for Public Health and Environmental Hygiene.(3)  Compensation is paid in cases where there is no other course of redress, or if enforcement of existing claims fails (4) i.e. chiefly in cases where damage is attributable to multiple-source pollution.(5)

---

1) Art. 64 wet inzake de Luchtverontreiniging, Stb 1970, 580; cf. Langelaar, Milieu en recht 1974, 69;  Stroink, Milieu en recht 1974, 121.
2) Art. 64 wet inzake de Luchtverontreiniging:
   (1) There shall be an Air Pollution Fund, from which anyone who, as a result of air pollution occurring above Netherlands territory, has suffered damage for which he cannot reasonably be expected to pay, can on request be granted such compensation as is considered fair, insofar as reasonable compensation has not been or cannot be obtained from other sources.
   (2) If prior establishment of the absence of compensation from other sources as referred to at the end of paragraph (1) should result in unreasonable delay or costs that cannot be charged to the interested party, compensation can be awarded from the Fund in consideration of the assignment to the Fund of any rights with respect to the damage which the interested party may have against third parties.
   (3) The Fund shall be a body corporate and have its offices in The Hague.
   (4) Our Minister shall be responsible for the administration of the Fund.
   (5) The Fund shall receive annually:
       a) a share, to be determined each year by our Minister, of the proceeds from the levies imposed under Section 65.
       b) the proceeds from rights assigned to the Fund in accordance with paragraph (2).
       c) the credit balance from the Fund's previous accounting period.
       d) other income.
   (6) Regulations shall be laid down by General Administrative Order as to the submission of applications for compensation, the manner of dealing with them and the appropriate decision to be taken.
   (7) Regulations shall be laid down by General Administrative Order concerning the administration of the Fund and the auditing.
   (8) The General Chamber of Audit shall, if it so desires, be allowed to inspect the books and documents and be given all the information it considers necessary to obtain a good understanding of the administration of the Fund.
   (9) Our Minister shall report annually to the States-General on the administration of the Fund.
3) Art. 64, Sect. 4.
4) Art. 64, Sects. 1 and 2.
5) Information on content and effectiveness of the fund was given by Ms M.E. Van Os-Hendrikse and Mr. M.P. van Wessem of the Ministry for Volksgezondheit and Milieuhygiene (Public Health and Environmental Hygiene) on 6th October 1976.

The fund is financed by a levy on various materials and products
such as light and heavy fuel oil, heating oil, petrol, coal, natural
gas and town gas.(1)  It was the incidence of smog in Rijnmond area
that prompted the creation of the fund.  In 1965, in particular, smog
had been the cause of serious agricultural damage, yet it had proved
impossible to identify specific polluters, from whom compensation
could be claimed.(2)

## 1. Legal basis and entitlement to claim

The fund is incorporated in chapter 7 of the Law on Air Pollution
under the heading of "finance provisions".  The legal character of the
regulations is disputed.(3)  The basis of the dispute is the question
whether claims should be allowed against the fund for damages that
could have been covered by an insurance policy.  The fund has so far
refused to pay out compensation for damage to car paintwork, taking
the view that such damage could have been covered by an all-risks
insurance policy (fully comprehensive insurance).(4)

The various conditions on which compensation is made are out-
lined in Art. 64, sections 1 and 2.  Art. 64 states:

"1. There shall be an Air Pollution Fund, from which anyone
    who, as a result of air pollution occurring above
    Netherlands territory, has suffered damage for which he
    cannot reasonably be expected to pay, can on request be
    granted such compensation as is considered fair, insofar
    as reasonable compensation has not been or cannot be
    obtained from other sources.

 2. If prior establishment of the absence of compensation
    from other sources as referred to at the end of para-
    graph 1. should result in unreasonable delay or costs
    that cannot be charged to the interested party, compen-
    sation can be awarded from the Fund in consideration of
    the assignment to the Fund of any rights with respect
    to the damage which the interested party may have against
    third parties."

As has already been mentioned, the term "other sources" refers
to insurance, or insurance that could have been taken out.  This section is chiefly designed to cover damage that cannot be attributed to

---

1) Article 64, Section 5; Cf. also Economist Intelligence Mint (Europe),
   Survey of the Practical Advantages and Disadvantages of the Instruments of Environmental Policy used in the Member States-case study
   on the Netherlands (unpublished) referred to in future as EIU.
2) Interview with Ms. van Os-Hendrikse, op.cit. (note 5);  cf. also
   EIU, 39.
3) Second progress report from the Ministry (for Volksgezondheid and
   Milieuhygiene) for the period 1st January 1974 to 31st December 1975.
4) First ministerial report;  cf. also second report.

a particular polluter. If the polluter can be identified the claimant will be referred directly to him. Four cases of copper-poisoning in sheep were rejected, because the polluter could be traced and the claims could be pressed against him directly.(1)

Compensation can, however, be made if it were theoretically possible to trace the polluter responsible, but detection would be inordinately time-consuming or expensive. Article 64, Section 2 states:

> "If prior establishment of the absence of compensation from other sources as referred to at the end of paragraph (1) should result in unreasonable delay or costs that cannot be charged to the interested party, compensation can be awarded from the Fund in consideration of the assignment to the Fund of any rights with respect to the damage which the interested party may have against third parties."

The conditions prescribed in this alternative were considered by the Fund administration to have been fulfilled by a case of trans-frontier pollution that caused damage on a Dutch farm. The probable polluters were three Belgian companies, which, of course, disputed their causal contribution. In this instance, the Fund paid compensation in return for the assignment to the Fund of the right of redress. No assigned right of redress has yet been made use of.(2) In another case, the Fund denied liability. A municipality in Vlardingen pressed for compensation for damage to a building, caused probably by a nearby factor y.

It was considered inappropriate to pay compensation under Article 64, Section 2 in this case. Amongst other thoughts uppermost in the reaching of this decision was the view that municipal authorities are in a much better position than a private individual to trace a polluter.(3)

The net result has been that the Fund acts in a subsidiary capacity and that in the first instance civil law claims should be pressed against the actual polluter. There is no exact definition of the damage for which compensation may be made. So far, both health and property damage have been compensated. Although compensation is only made on an equitable basis, as yet no upper limit has been set on the amount that can be paid. All accepted claims for damage have to date been met with full compensation.

Compensation is paid irrespective of whether the conduct causing the damage is in contravention of the law or fully legal.(4)(There are no restrictions on liability or exclusions of any kind (e.g. limits on the amount that may be claimed or non-liability in the

1) Second progress report.
2) Interview with Ms. van Os-Hendrikse (note 5, p. 10a).
3) Ibid.
4) Prevailing view; cf. Langelaar, "Milieu en Recht", 1974, p.73; this attitude is also taken by the Fund administration.

instance of an Act of God). No consideration has yet been taken of assumption of risk.(1) Anyone may register a claim, even the State itself,(1) although such a case has not yet occurred.

The question of proof of causality is raised: it has to be established that the damage was caused by air pollution. The criteria for the appreciation of evidence are not specially regulated. In practice, the rules of evidence are very lenient.

The mere probability that the damage was caused by a form of air pollution is sufficient to establish a claim.(2) Local factory inspectors assist the fund in the investigation of the facts of a case, or if need be, experts are called in. The processing of such claims is, however, a lengthy matter, taking up to two years to complete.(2) In the case of damage to health, if no causal relationship to air pollution can be proved the application to the fund will fail.(3)

So far, remarkably few claims have been registered. Since the Fund came into being on 18th September 1972, only 108 applications have been made (up to 1st October 1976). The majority of these cases involved damage to the paintwork of cars (72 cases, of which 63 were related to a single incident of pollution); claims for crop damage (22 cases), injury to animals (5 cases), damage to health (5 cases), damage to buildings (2 cases), damage to clothing (1 case) as well as for miscellaneous damage (1 case) have been made.(4)

The first compensation payment was made in 1974. A woman cyclist rode into a cloud of soot, with the result that her suede jacket, which cost 300 florins new, was ruined. A compensation payment of 250 florins was made, corresponding to the value of the jacket at the time.(5)

In 1975, compensation was awarded in two cases. One case concerned damages arising from a deposit of cement dust on greenhouses belonging to a nursery gardener in Eijsten (province Limburg). The polluter was, in all probability, a Belgian firm. On assignment of the right of redress, compensation totalling 7,446 florins was awarded. The amount of compensation was determined on the basis of two expert appraisals, for which the fund paid fees amounting to 986 florins.(6)

The second instance in which compensation was paid in 1975 concerned damage to a crop of brussel sprouts in Vlaardingen. A powder-fine dust had settled on the crop and no polluter could be identified. 2,454.79 florins was paid in compensation.(7)

---

1) As note 1, p. 13.
2) As note 2, p. 13.
3) Cf. second progress report.
4) Cf. first and second progress report.
5) Cf. first progress report.
6) Second progress report.
7) Cf. first progress report.

In 1976, up until 1st October, compensation of between 2,000 and 34,000 florins was paid in each of eight cases of crop damage.(1)

Compensation was refused chiefly in the already mentioned cases of damage to car paintwork.(2)  In other cases, it proved possible to trace the polluter,(2) in one case there was no causal relationship between air pollution and the damage and in another case no compensation was applied for after the damage had been reported.(2)

## 2. Allocation of cost

In order to encompass all potential polluters (industry, motor-vehicles, domestic heating) a tax has been placed on sales of light and heavy fuel oil, petrol, coal, natural gas and town gas.  The tax has been progressively increased and finds its ultimate expression in increased prices to the consumer.(3)  The levy is not merely used to finance compensation payments.  It also finances public and private pollution prevention measures.  For example, the owner of a firm registered as a polluting concern can, subject to certain conditions, demand a grant towards, or even the total cost in some cases, of pollution control measures.(4)  In 1974, 55 million florins were raised.  In 1973 and 1974 together, the Fund received 1,300,000 florins from the levy on fuels.(5)  Since this sum is considerably greater than the total actually paid out in compensation the Fund has already been put to other uses.(6)  Whether the levy has a deterrent effect, encouraging the polluter to take preventive measures in future rather than pay so much in tax cannot be conclusively determined on the basis of results to date.(7)  It can however be said with some certainty that although a settlement, in accordance with the polluter pays principle places the burden of costs for damages on the potential polluter, this is not usually sufficient to have a preventive effect. The right of the Fund to redress tends, however, to preserve this function.(8)

## 3. Evaluation

Points of criticism raised by the administration itself are the inexplicit drafting of the law and the numerous undefined legal terms that have led to difficulties in interpretation and offer little legal

---

1) Interview with Ms van Os-Hendrikse, op.cit. (note 5, page
2) Second progress report.
3) EIU, op.cit. (note 6, p.
4) Surprisingly enough, in practice, this possibility has been little
   utilised;  cf. interview with Ms van Os-Hendrikse.
5) First progress report;  cf. also EIU, op.cit. (note 6, p.
6) EIU, op.cit.
7) Interview with the Fund administration, 6th October 1976.
8) Cf. Article 64, Section 2.

clarity. Injured parties are, in certain cases, scarcely in a position to judge whether their claims should be directed to the Fund or to the polluter. Another criticism is that the Fund has been very little publicised.(1) The general public is practically unaware of the existence of the Fund. This may be ascribed to the fact that the Fund has only been announced by the Minister of Public Health and Hygiene in governmental papers (in the Staatsblatt) and has not been made known to the general public. An article in the consumers journal "Konsumengids" failed to raise any great reaction.(1) The third field of criticism takes the form of a degree of self-critique by the Fund's administration. Initially, the preconditions for liability were construed narrowly in order to avoid excessive demand on the Fund. Now a more generous application, that would even cover the cases of paintwork damage, is under consideration.(1)

To conclude, the principles behind the compensation fund are on the whole viewed positively, although its little practical effect is regrettable and there seems to be no real scope for a significant extension in its field of operation. To accomplish this would entail quite some effort: summary estimations undertaken by Amsterdam University indicate that the annual cost of air pollution damage (to health, buildings,ccrops, etc.) is currently around 2 million florins.(1) When one compares this figure with the amount of compensation - less than 100,000 florins - paid out in over three years, it becomes apparent, even taking individual settlements into account, that the social cost of air pollution damage is nowhere near covered. This situation could be altered to a certain extent, if damages currently covered by health insurance were in future referred to the Fund.

II. The Japanese Law for the Compensation of Pollution-related Health Damage

A comprehensive system for the compensation of injury to health caused by pollution came into force with the enactment of the "Law for the Compensation of Pollution-related Health Damage".(2) The law contains administrative rules for the compensation of damage to health, not, however, for damage to property. The victims of specific pollution-related diseases designated in the act (mostly respiratory diseases and chronic metal-poisoning), after their case has been examined by a board of doctors, lawyers and administrative officials, receive compensation that covers medical expenses, disablement

1) Interview with the Fund administration, 6th October 1976.
2) Law No. 111 of 5th October 1973, amended by Law No. 85 of 1974; a German translation is to be found in "Umweltschutz in Japan" edited by M. Bothe, appearing in the series "Beiträge zur Umweltgestaltung", magazine No. 38, published by E. Schmidt-Verlag, 1975; (in future referred to as the Compensation Law).

benefits, dependants' allowances, educational grants, assistance with
the costs of medical treatment and funeral costs.(1)  The problem of
proving that the health damage is attributable to air or water pollution is overcome by a procedure allowing standardised epidemological
evidence.  Certain individually determined areas in which research has
shown a definite causal relationship between health damage and pollution are designated as high-risk zones.  Anyone contracting one of the
designated diseases in a high-risk zone can, on application to the local
prefecture, obtain a certificate identifying him as a "State-recognised
pollution victim", as it were.  This certificate is sufficient to claim
free medical treatment and reimbursement of other medical expenses.(2)
The compensation scheme is financed by emission charges levied on individual concerns operating within the officially designated high-risk
zones.(3)  Also a proportion of the motor-vehicle tax is channelled
into the fund.(4)

## 1. Origins of the Fund

The occurrence of a considerable number of instances of serious
pollution-related health damage, which an inadequate social security
system was unable to compensate properly was the factor underlying the
creation of the compensation fund for health damage.  Four serious
pollution cases (Itai-itai, Kuamoto Minamata, Niigata Minamata and
Yokkaichi) emphasised the ned for comprehensive regulations governing
compensation settlements.(4)  Many serious pollution-related illnesses
demanded immediate support.  The delay in waiting for a judicial
decision could only worsen the victims' situation in various ways.
Administrative rules to obviate the problems of judicial enforcement
(identification of the polluter, proof of causality, proof of negligence) also seemed to be urgently required.(5)  At the time, civil
law remedies were only available to a limited category of victims.
The rest could only resort to individual or collective negotiations
with the polluters (6) or take their case into arbitration.(7)  There
was, however, no overall answer to the problem.

1) Paras. 3 and 4 of the Compensation Law.
2) Paras. 19 ff of the Compensation Law.
3) Law No. 85 of 11th June 1974, cf. Gresser, p. 93.
4) Cf. Nomura, Environmental Policy and Law 1975, 179; Environment
   Agency (1974) 171 ff; Gresser 102.
5) Environment Agency (1974), 167.
6) Environment Agency (1974), 167; an agreement was reached in the
   first Minamata case setting compensation at 100,000 dollars (800
   dollars per death), the sick received 280 dollars and children 80
   dollars per annum.  Part of the agreement was that all further
   rights against the Chisso concern were to be waived, even if negligence on the part of the company proved to be the cause.
7) Cf. law No. 108 of 1st June 1970 for the settlement of disputes
   relating to pollution damage, amended by law 101 of 1974.  A
   German translation of the act is to be found in "Umweltschutz in
   Japan", edited by M. Bothe, 1975.

In 1969, the Law on Special Measures for the Relief of Pollution-related Injury to Health was enacted.(1)  The aim of the act was to institute administrative measures to assist in cases of pollution-related illness.  The question of civil law responsibility was to remain a secondary consideration.  The law provided for the designation of specific toxic substances and pollution diseases, as well as specific high-risk areas in the same way as the 1973 act.(2)  14,186 people received assistance on the basis of this law.(3)  The costs of compensation were met equally by State and industry.  This was certainly a flaw in the act and an obvious departure from the "polluter pays principle", which was also propagated in Japan, but this is explicable in terms of the distressed situation of the pollution victim at the time the law was conceived.  A fast intervention was required and an assumption by the State of 50 per cent of the financial burden seemed the simplest solution and offered the best chance of a swift passage through Parliament.  A second inadequacy of the law was its limitation to the reimbursement of medical expenses.(3)

The new compensation system came into effect in 1974.  It conformed in many respects with the 1969 act and continued the system of compensation for illnesses designated in the earlier act (chiefly respiratory illnesses, such as chronic bronchitis and asthma) as well as, to some extent, metal poisonings (from cadmium, quicksilver, arsenic lead, etc.) although they were a considerably more distressing manifestation.(4)

## 2. Legal basis and entitlement to claim

Basically, the Japanese Compensation Law in its present form, just as the Netherlands Air Pollution Fund, conforms with the fundamental idea that the community of polluters should be collectively responsible for making good the damage they cause.  The Japanese system,

---

1) Cf. Environment Agency, 167; Law No.90 of 15th December 1969; the law basically took over a compensation system already established at the regional level;  cf. Sand, 21; the forerunner of compensation for "victims of technology" was the legislation relating to radiation damage, cf. law No. 147 of 1961 and law No. 148 of the same year concerning compensation agreements; cf. also Gresser, 106.
2) Cf. Environment Agency (1974), 167.
3) Cf. Environment Agency (1974), 168.
4) Regional bodies had in part already set forth their own regulations for compensation in the years between 1969 and 1973, prior to the enactment of the law.  These regulations provided for a better settlement than the nationally applicable legislation of 1969. After the 1973 law had come into effect, the regional regulations lapsed;  cf. S. Nakashin, Nomura Research Institute, Comparative Pollution Compensation System, A Discussion of Damage to Property and Loss of Income, 1975 (a project study).

too, should be seen in the context of the enforcement problem of individual civil liability and may be regarded as an attempt to circumvent
the dilemma of proving causality.  There are also further reasons
behind the Fund - the inadequate social security for injured parties
combined with the appearance of a great number of very serious cases
of pollution-related health damage, requiring assistance fast.  Also,
the State perceived its own special liability in that it not only
tolerated a policy of economic and industrial development at any cost,
it positively encouraged it.(1)  Moreover, the availability of State
systems for the settling of disputes has for many years been a dominant
element in the Japanese legal set-up.(1)

As with the Dutch Air Pollution Fund, the Compensation Law dis-
plays no definite legal character.  Beyond dispute is the fact that
claims may be brought against the fund independent of existing claims
for compensation filed against the individual polluter.  The claim
against the fund is in no way dependent upon the existence or the
raising of a civil law claim for compensation.  In some respects, the
Compensation Law is regarded as a development from the strict liability
for water and air pollution imposed by a law passed shortly before.
That the word "support" (kyūasi) in the 1969 law was replaced by compensation (hoshō) seems to support this suggestion, making the intention to progress from administrative measures of support to a right
to compensation clearly discernible.(2) A claim against the Fund is
reviewed irrespective of the actual conduct of the individual polluter.
Whether the act causing the damage was lawful or not is totally ir-
relevant.  Nor is the existence of a justifiable excuse - limited
liability or Act of God - relevant.  The only precondition to be fulfilled in order to establish liability is that health damage, as defined in the act, is evidence.

These designated illnesses constitute a certain limiting factor
so that other forms of health damage, although they may be related to
pollution, are excluded.  In fact, it is the designation of pollution-
related illnesses in defined pollution zones and the consequent considerable relaxing in the proof of causality that lend the Japanese
Compensation Law its essential individuality.  The designation of illnesses and pollution zones was based on extensive epidemological research into the causal relationship between pollution and health
damage.(3)  Clinical and experimental studies were undertaken, death
rates and other statistics were carefully analysed.(3) In particular,
the relationship between emissions prevalent in certain areas and a
comparative increase in specific diseases was investigated and

---

1) Nomura, Environmental Policy and Law (1975) 179.
2) Gresser.
3) Gresser, 110.

registered.  In order to allow for "natural" causes of illness, details of age, sex and smoking and eating habits were also included in the investigation (1) as were other known causes of illness.  It should, however, be mentioned that the basis for the determination of causal relationships between certain emissions and health damage is not necessarily scientifically conclusive.  Although as yet unchallenged by pollution victims or industry, the statutory determination of illnesses and pollution zones constitutes a problem factor that should not be under-estimated.(2)

It remains only to state that the individual, in order to realise his claim for compensation must report his injury and undergo the relevant medical examination.  Also at this stage, it is possible for mistakes to be made in an individual case and injustice may result.(3)  In spite of everything, simpler conditions of liability are scarcely conceivable.  Assumption of risk on the part of the claimant is not even considered.

The practical effectiveness of the compensation system is witnessed by the fact that up until the end of 1975, 35,733 people were awarded damages or were certified for compensation.(4)

## 3. Allocation of cost

As has already been indicated, the fund is financed by levies raised on individual industrial emissions and by the allocation of a part of the motor-vehicle tax.(5)  The costs are ascribed differently in the different zones.  In a class 2 zone, specific pollutants are included and individual concerns pay, e.g. the Chisso concern pays for the emission of effluent with a mercury content.(6)  These concerns have to pay all compensation for damage attributable to them.(6)  In class one zones, all pollutants are included except those already in class 2.  The amount of the levy is assessed according to the predicted needs of the Fund, and with regard to the existing emission standards.  Firms in these zones that emit certain closely-defined pollutants, are taxed according to the volume of the emission.(7)  In addition, there is the estimated role of motor-vehicles in pollution damage.  20 per cent of the Fund's income is derived from motor-vehicle tax.  The fundamental principle behind the system of levies in the

1) Gresser, 113.
2) Gresser Morishima/Fijikura, The Law for the Compensation of Pollution-related Disease, An Assessment of the First Two Years of Implementation, Interim Report (1975) 13.
3) Cf. e.g. Gresser, 3.
4) Cf. e.g. Gresser, 1.
5) Paras. 42ff of the Compensation Law, law No. 85 of 11th June 1974.
6) Gresser, 116.
7) Paras. 52ff of the Compensation Law, Gresser, 116.

"polluter pays principle", which has also found recognition in Japan.(1)

## 4. Evaluation

Criticism of the Japanese Compensation Law has been made in view of its restriction to specific health-damage. Also damage to property still goes without remedy.(2) However, the overwhelmingly positive contribution that the Japanese law makes in compensating health-damage remains unaffected by this criticism. Without this law, there would be no compensation available in many cases and in others only limited compensation, and that a great delay, would be obtainable.

The system of levies is criticised inasmuch as it differs according to zone. Firms that are active outside the statutory-determined zones are not burdened with levies, although they may be emitting similar amounts of pollution as enterprises within the zones. This leads to competitive advantages for concerns operating outside the designated zones and is a defect in this otherwise environmentally equitable system of taxing emissions.(3)

The deterrent effect of the levies is judged cautiously. The basic principle of a levy that varies according to the noxiousness and the volume of the emission is admittedly suited to the obtaining of a deterrent effect. In general however, the levy is not high enough to incite the polluter to take steps to reduce the volume of his pollution. This is largely due to the fact that the levy is determined according to the needs of the fund. There can be no deterrent effect as long as the cost of compensation for designated health-damage is less than the cost of pollution control. A deterrent effect could be assured if the levy, instead of being dictated by the actual amount paid out in compensation, were to cover compensation for "ecological damage" and cover risk of future damage.(4)

## III. The North American water pollution funds

### 1. The Maine Coastal Protection Fund

The most progressive use of a compensation fund, restricted though it is to water pollution, has been made by the American federal State of Maine.(5)

---

1) Cf. Environment Agency, Japan (1973) and (1974).
2) Nakashin (project study); amongst others Gresser, 3ff, 21.
3) E.g. Gresser, 11.
4) E.g. Gresser, 27ff, and 159.
5) Oil-Discharge Prevention and Pollution Control Act of 1970, ME. Rev. STAT. Ann. tit. 38, paras. 551-557 (supp. 1973), cf. Pedrick, Earth Law Journal, 1975 301 (310); Post, XXVIII Univ. of Miami Law Review (1974), 524 (547).

The Maine Coastal Protection Fund has in fact completely replaced common law remedies.(1)  It guarantees compensation to individuals and State organs for damage occasioned by oil pollution, irrespective of the person and conduct of the polluter.  The cost of compensation is covered by a levy that is assessed according to the amount of oil transported.

The application of the Fund is described in a report from the Department of Environmental Protection of the State of Maine dated 5th October 1976.  It states that since the Fund came into being in 1970, twenty claims for compensation have been raised.  Eight of these claims were related to a tanker mishap in 1972 and have not yet been resolved, chiefly because the rules for the processing claims were not laid down until after the spill.

Five claims were dismissed because of lack of substantiation.  A further five claims were accepted and the remaining two applications to the Fund were settled outside, before processing had begun.  The majority of claims concerned damage to pleasure boats.  Two cases related to the death of harvested marine resources.  Proof of causality becomes a problem when claims are brought relatively late, resulting in considerable difficulties in investigating the particular incident.

The chief application of the Fund lies in the financing of State environmental protection measures.  Not only are State clean-up costs financed by the fund.  Research projects are also paid for.  In this way, the financing of a $100,000 research project was possible and $200,000 has been spent on pollution control equipment.  The fact that the reimbursement of State clean-up costs and expenditure on precautionary measures is not dependent on the incident or the person of the particular polluter has had the effect that immediate action can be taken on a large scale, as there are no longer any financial problems.

The $4 million non-lapsing, revolving Fund is raised by a levy placed on terminal oil facilities of $\frac{1}{2}$ cent per barrel of transported oil, or oil products.(2)  Once the 4 million limit is reached, the levy is reduced to a level that covers the day-to-day running costs of the Fund, the cost of cleaning up mystery spills (where it is impossible to assign liability) and the expense of research and development projects.(2)  The Fund is regarded as being particularly effective.(3)  The claimant has no trouble in enforcing his claim.  It can be seen that the total actual cost of pollution control (damage not only to individuals, but also to the general public) is borne by the

---

1) Information received by the author from the Department of Environmental Protection, Maine, dated 5th October 1976; cf. also para.551 (3) Oil Discharge Prevention and Pollution Control Act.
2) Para. 551.
3) Information rendered by the Department of Environmental Protection, Maine, 5th October 1976.

polluters, and even research and development programmes related to the form of pollution involved is financed by the relevant branch of industry. The Fund is again an integral part of administrative law, or, to be more precise, of the Oil Discharge Prevention and Pollution Control Act of 1970.(1) Although the legal character of the regulations cannot be determined in detail, it does in fact replace traditional common law legal remedies.

Furthermore, it embodies a processing system similar to that of a court of arbitration as well as comprehensive for the financing of State precautionary and prevention measures.(2)

Claims must be raised with the State administration of the Fund (Department of Environmental Protection, Division of Oil Conveyance Services for the Department of Environmental Protection) within six months of the incidence of damage.(2) The Fund is liable to pay compensation whether the polluter is identifiable or not. The only condition that a claim must fulfil is the presentation of evidence of damage caused by oil pollution.(3)

The deterrent effect of the Fund is ensured by a right to redress which is exercised in every case of an identifiable polluter.(4)

Alongside the Maine Coastal Protection Fund, funds exist in other States (Florida), as well as at the national level. These funds are

---

1) v. Westermann, Welche gesetzlichen Massnahmen zur Luftreinhaltung und zur Verbesserung des Nachbarrechts sind erforderlich, 1958, 67 ff; Bullinger, Versicherungsrecht 1972, 599 (606); Langelaar, Milieu en Recht 1974, 69; Post, University of Miami Law and Commerce 7 (1975) 1, 45 ff; Environment Agency, Japan (1974) 184; Malafosse 245; Girod, Rev. de Droit Rural 1972, 483, 492; Girod, La réparation du dommage écologique (1974), 252 f.
2) Para. 551.
3) Para. 551: Third party damages: Anyone claiming to have suffered damages to real estate or personal property or loss of income directly or indirectly as a result of a "prohibited) discharge of oil petroleum products or their by-products ... may apply within six months after the occurrence of such a discharge to the commission stating the amount of damage he claims to have suffered as a result of such discharge.
   A. If the claimant, the board and the person causing the discharge can agree to the damage claim, the board shall certify the amount of the claim and the name of the claimant to the Treasurer of State and the Treasurer of State shall pay the same from the Maine Coastal Petroleum Fund.
   B. If the claimant, the commission and the person causing the discharge cannot agree as to the amount of the damage claim, the claim shall forthwith be transmitted for action to the Board of Arbitration as provided in this sub-chapter.
   C. Third party damage claims shall be stated in their entirety in one application. Damages omitted from any claim at the time the award is made shall be deemed waived.
   D. Damage claims arising under the provisions of this sub-chapter shall be recoverable only in the manner provided under this sub-chapter, it being the intent of the Legislature that the remedies provided in this sub-chapter are exclusive.
4) Information given by the Department of Environmental Protection, Maine, 5th October 1976.

considerably more restricted in their field of application. They
serve either to accommodate State pollution control measures, and exclude private claims,(1) or they are limited to the covering of damage where financial limits of liability exist in certain cases of
strict liability.(2)  A national fund for water pollution damage en-
compassing both private and public claims has been repeatedly ad-
vocated, but has not, as yet, materialised.(3)

## 2. The Canadian Maritime Pollution Claims Fund

The Canadian Maritime Pollution Claims Fund (4) is a Fund on the
national level for water pollution.  The Fund is part of the Canadian
Shipping Act, which contains a special section devoted to the regulation of water pollution, chiefly by oil.  This section also introduces strict liability for water pollution originating from shipping.(5)
The Fund supplements this liability in those cases in which the claimant cannot identify the polluter, or if his claim fails owing to
limited liability on the part of the polluter.(6)  As such, the Fund
acts only in a subsidiary capacity.

The practical relevance of the Fund is described by a report
from the Fund administrator:(7)  only two cases of oil pollution have
necessitated intervention on the part of the Fund.  This is largely
because the oil companies are, in relevant cases, sued directly.
Also, only ships transporting more than 1,000 tons of oil come within
the scope of the regulations.

Although the claimant is in general obliged to seek redress
directly from the polluter, the fishery industry can, in the case of
loss of earnings, claim from the Fund.(8)  The Fund is financed by
levies on the volume of oil transported.(9)

---

1) As the Florida oil-spill-prevention and pollution control act of
   1970 (14 110 Stat. Ann., 376).  It established a $5,000,000 Florida
   Coastal Protection Fund to finance State pollution control (pollution abatement, wild-life clean-up-costs).  The Fund is made up
   by license fees, fines and compensation claims against individual
   polluters (377 ll (1)); cf. Pedrick, 310.
2) As the funds set up by the Trans-Alaska-Pipeline Act and the Deep-
   water-Post Act (P.L. 93-627 33 U.S.C. sec. 1301 of seg. (1974);
   Post XVIII Univ. of Miami Law Rev. (1974), 524 (547).
3) Thus President Ford before Congress, reported in the New York
   Times, 10th July 1975; cf. Wood, 7 Journal of Maritime Law and
   Commerce (1975) 1 (67).
4) Canadian Shipping Act (as amended) Can. Rev. Stat. c.27 2d Supp.
   1970 paras. 737 ff; cf. Post, XXVIII University of Miami Law
   Review (1974) 525 (548).
5) Para. 734.
6) Paras. 737 ff.
7) Information given by the Ministry of Transport, 19th October 1976
   (Transports Canada, Public Affairs Liaison Officer, Marine).
8) Para. 746.
9) 15 cent/t; Canada Gazette, Part II, Vol. 106, No. 4, 3rd February
   1972. P.C. 1972-185, SPR/72-73, Reg. 3.

Similar regulations to those found in the Canadian Shipping Act
exist in the Provinces. For example, the Fisherman's Assistance and
Polluters' Liability Act, 1970, enacted in Manitoba provides financial
support for fishermen who suffer damage as a result of river water
pollution. Aid from the State Assistance Fund is afforded to the
claimant should the enforcement of his own claim prove to be probem-
atic or indeed impossible. The claim is enforced by the Province by
right of redress.(1) The wide effect of such a fund becomes apparent
when one considers that in one claim for redress reimbursement for
support rendered to 1,590 persons was sought.(2)

IV. European Water Pollution Funds

The ground basis for actions on damage is laid by the IMCO Convention on Civil Liability for Oil Pollution Damage, 1969.(3) This
Convention does not afford full compensation for victims of oil pollution damage in all cases while it imposes an additional burden on
shipowners. The International Convention on the Establishment of an
International Fund for Oil Pollution Damage, 1971, ensures full compensation and gives relief to the shipowners by imposing the financial burdens on the cargo interests.(4) Full compensation is paid to
any person suffering from oil pollution damage if such person has
been unable to obtain adequate compensation under the terms of the
Liability Convention.

No compensation is granted in cases of mystery spills.

As oil pollution by offshore facilities increases, a Convention
on Civil Liability for Oil Pollution Damage from Offshore Installations
was adopted in London on 17th December 1976 and opened for signature
in London on 4th May 1977.(5)

Scandinavian States have considered additional measures including
the establishment of funds.(6) Such a fund has recently been set up

---

1) Cf. the case of Interprovincial Co-operatives Limited and Pryden
   Chemicals Limited c. Her Majesty The Queen in right of the Province
   of Manitoba/1976; The defendants, "Chlor-alkali plants" in
   Saskatchewan and Ontario were accused of discharging mercury.
2) As note.
3) 9 Int. Legal Mat. 45 (1970).
4) 9 Int. Legal Mat. 45 (1970); until the Fund comes into force,
   Cristal, a voluntary insurance system by the oil companies remains
   effective.
5) So far exists a voluntary insurance system for offshore operators,
   the so-called OPOL. Until the international convention comes into
   force, this system can pay compensation up to a maximum of $16
   million per pollution incident.
6) For example, Norway; Cf. Aftenposten of 3rd June 1976: a fund to
   compensate damage to fishery vessels and fishing equipment; the
   Fund is to amount to 8,000,000 Nkr; cf. also Aftenposten 2nd May
   1976 about a fund that would extend liability to oil damage caused
   by ships (Pollution report of 30th April 1974, which would also
   provide for oil pollution control measures).

in Finland – the Oil Protection Fund.(1)  It covers particularly those
cases in which no causal link can be traced between victim and polluter.

## V. The French compensation system for air traffic noise

A decree of 13th February 1973 introduced an administrative compensation system for airports in Paris.  This is an example of a fund
as an equitable solution to the question of compensation arising from
a collision of interests (airport/residents).(2)

The content of the compensation system is as follows:  zones were
designated around the airports in Paris according to the continuous
noise level.(3)  Those living in the most affected zones could claim
compensation for the installation of double-glazing or could, by way
of choice, apply for their property to be purchased or for resettle-
ment.  Schools, hospitals, nursing homes and similar institutions
could claim reimbursement for outlay on soundproofing even if they
fell within the less affected zone B.  Claims are directed against the
airport administration (Aéroport de Paris).  This body administers the
Fund, which is financed by levies (taxe parafiscale) on the individual
air companies.(4)

### 1. Origins of the Fund

The Fund originated as a result of the considerable air traffic
noise from the Paris airport, Orly.  More recently, the new air ter-
minal at Roissy (Charles de Gaulle) has also added to the problem.
Orly airport was built in 1946 in a built-up suburb of Paris.  The
rapid increase in air traffic had already led to serious noise pollution.  In 1966, local residents formed an interest group, in which the
majority of the neighbouring communities (150,000 inhabitants) were
represented.(5)  In 1967, recourse was made to the civil courts and a
series of judgements followed which all recognised the accountability
of the defendant air companies, Air France, Pan Am and TWA.(6) Experts

1) Cf. International Protection of Environment, Vol. 3.
2) Décret No.73-193 of 13th February 1973 printed in Lamarque, p.329;
   cf. Goy, La lutte contre les nuisances aux abords des Aérodromes
   en France, extract of Rev. Gén. Air (1974).
3) Zone A: more than 96 PN dB; zone B: more than 89 PN dB; zone C:
   more than 84 PN dB (PN dB is approx. 12-13 units higher than dB(A)).
4) Cf. décret of 13th February 1973;  cf. also Arrêté of 27th March
   1973 (amended 10th May 1974) printed in Lamarque, 336.
5) Goy, para. 2, note 1, p.33 and notes 3 and 4, p. 33.
6) The following judgements have been given (basis for claim: art.
   141-2 Code de l'Aviation Civile: T.G.I. Paris 10th July 1968, ICP,
   1968, II, 1595;  Cour Paris 9th July 1969; ICP, 1969, II, 16143,
   Trib. confl. 2nd March 1970, Rec. Lebon 970 and 1221; T.G.I. Pans
   4th November 1970 RGAE 1970, 417; Cour Paris 6th July 1971,
   D. Sanm., 166;  T.G.I. Paris, 9th May 1973 in Lamarque 249;  Cour
   Paris 12th April 1972;  Cass. civ. 17th December 1974, D.S. 1975,
   J., 441;  Cass. civ. 17th December 1974, D.S. 1975, J., 462.

appointed by the Cour d'Appel de Paris in 1971 proposed the establishing of a fund to compensate the communities and individuals affected,
financed by a levy on the air companies.(1)  The decree of 13th
February 1973 follows this proposal in essence, after numerous parliamentary initiatives had shown support for the idea.(2)

## 2. Legal basis and entitlement to claim

The compensation fund, which is of an unambiguous public law
character, runs concurrent to other civil law or public law compensation claims.  It can only be regarded as a discriminatory administrative measure (available to local residents) and its function is certainly not to provide wholesale compensation in settlement of existing
claims against the State or the air companies.(3)  In the administration of justice, there is the tendency to deny the existence of damage
in view of the possibility of obtaining reimbursement of expenditure
(for soundproofing) or the takeover of property.(4)  The preconditions
for compensation are quite simple.  Anyone possessing a building or
land in zone A can apply for reimbursement for the cost of soundproofing or to have his property purchased.(5)  Contributory responsibility is taken into account inasmuch as anyone moving into the present
zones after 1st July 1970 is barred from claiming.(6)

A special department of the State airport company is commissioned
with the running of the Fund.  It has taken up contact with the communities and the local residents and with their co-operation individual
properties are examined and registered.  The residents are then ten-
dered an offer for their property.  In general, sale has so far been
preferred to soundproofing.  Surrounding schools and hospitals are
practically all soundproofed.  One school has been moved.(7)

---

1) Cour de Paris of 6th July 1971, D. somm. 166, Goy, note 4, p. 31.
2) cf. Goy, note 3, p. 33.
3) Lamarque, 248, Goy, para. 3c.
4) T.G.I. Paris of 9th May 1971, printed in part in Lamarque, 248;
   cf. also Goy, para. 2c.
5) Cf. arts. 3 and 4 of the decree of 13th February 1973 and the
   directive issued in conjunction with it (arrêté of 27th March 1973);
   at first residents in Orly were denied compensation in the directive.  Not until the decisions of the C.E. of 21st April 1975 and
   7th May 1975 (D.S. 1976, J., 587 in Ann. Moderne) was equality with
   residents in Roissy re-established.
6) Art. 4 of the arrêté of 27th March 1973.
7) Cf. the progress report of the Aéroport de Paris, note sur l'usage
   de riverains des aérodromes d'Orly et Roissy - Charles-de-Gaulle,
   July 1976;  cf. also Lamarque, p. 97;  until the end of 1976, the
   Fund paid out F.85 million in compensation.  Eighty schools have
   been provided with soundproofing as have hospitals and nursing
   homes, etc.;  compensation for private persons has only just begun:
   of 150 house-owners in Goussainville, 109 reacted to the offer of
   purchase and 101 actually agreed to sell (information from M.H.
   Bigot, Aéroport de Paris).

## 3. Allocation of cost

The system of finance is uncomplicated. All the air companies pay a levy of F.1 per passenger on an internal flight and F.3 per passenger on flights abroad into the Fund.(1)

## 4. Evaluation

Despite certain imperfections, the compensation scheme is considered to be the correct start to an adequate model for the compensation of residents in particularly affected zones. Its basic principles could also be applied in other fields, for example, the compensation of people living near to motorways, railways and large industrial complexes where, for planning, technical or economic reasons, the prevention of noise pollution is not possible.(2)

Of particular value is the effective form of the compensation, which achieves a rectification of the traffic noise - residential area relationship, a desirable development from the point of view of environmental policy. Also the ease with which a claim can be enforced is a strong point of the Fund. The standardisation of claims and administrative support make recourse to the courts unnecessary. The compensation system can aid all those affected, which is never the case in the enforcement of civil law claims. Above all, the compensation costs are not met by the general public, but are quite rightly borne by the branch of industry causing the problem.

A significant imperfection in the Fund is the method of raising the levy. Admittedly, it conforms with the "polluter pays principle" by burdening the polluter with the financing of the Fund, but the objective that lies behind this principle, i.e. to encourage the development of environment-conscious technology by the use of economic sanctions, has not been attained. Instead of linking the levy to the extent of traffic noise, a passenger levy was chosen and it is not clear why a passenger on an internal flight should pay less than one flying abroad. In terms of establishing a preventive effect, it would have seemed sensible to have fixed the levy according to the noise level of the particular type of aeroplane.(3) The current situation is that, for example, 300 passengers on the relatively quiet Airbus pay F.900 whereas 100 passengers on the much noisier Concorde pay only F.300. It has also been criticised that expenditure on soundproofing is only reimbursed with two-thirds of the actual cost.(3) Even the restriction on compensation as only being available to residents of zone A has been faulted.(4)

---

1) Art. 4 of the decree of 13th February 1973.
2) In France similar funds have been proposed for dams, for damage to agriculture and for damage from air pollution, Le Monde, 19th June 1976.
3) Goy, para. 2b.
4) Cf. Moderne, annotation regarding C.E. of 7th April 1975, D.S. 1976, J. 587.

## D. BASIC TRACES OF A FUND MODEL

Although experience with compensation funds to date has not met
all expectations, the general impression is positive. The protection
of the individual is more adequate. Gaps in substantive law and difficulties in enforcement are overcome. Compensation funds have proved
particularly successful in providing damages in cases where traditional
civil law liability offers no remedy: i.e. cases of multiple-source
pollution. Also very important is that where a compensation fund is
available, the claimant no longer has to run the risks involved in enforcing his claim in the courts. The burden of compensation is
covered by levies placed on potential polluters (industry, motor-
vehicles, domestic fuels, etc.), a system which is at the same time
both just and economically efficient.

An essential task of damage funds could in the first place be
the compensation of health damage, for most environmental damages concern human health. It may however be surprising that particularly in
this field there is no marked need for compensation by funds. In
nearly all industrial States pollution-related health damage is compensated by system of health insurances (mostly compulsory insurance
financed by contributions of employers or employees or by State subsidies). Therefore, only where the social security system is particularly insufficient does a need for other kinds of compensation become obvious.

This is proven by the fact that in Japan, numerous pollution
victims presented claims under the Japanese law for pollution-related
health damage, while no sufficient social security comparable to those
of Western industrial States exists.

In contrast hereto, the Dutch example shows that if a comprehensive health insurance system does exist, an environmental fund for the
compensation of health damage is hardly used (five cases up to 1976).

This result must not necessarily be unsatisfying. In a system
of comprehensive social security it is even easier for the victim to
turn to his health insurance than to a fund where any demand for compensation would have to be examined as regards its causal relation to
pollution.

But although in most countries there is no absolute need for
special "pollution claims" related to health damage, the question
arises to allocate damage costs - now paid by health insurances - to
the real polluters.

Up to now damages are covered by insurances and/or by the State
and thus ultimately by the victims' contributions. This, however,
does not represent a just and economically reasonable allocation of
social costs. Therefore, damage funds should pay a certain part of
the money raised to the insurances (health insurances).

Finding a satisfying method for measuring pollution-related health damages may be complicated but the Japanese system shows how to distinguish pollution-related damage from other damage by means of epidemological proof. An allocation of damage costs to the circles of polluters concerned (certain industries, cars, heatings) would not only relieve those who pay high premiums for personal insurance, but also mean the consistent application of the polluter-pays-principle on which environmental policy of nearly all States is based.

Apart from compensation of health damage a vast field of application of funds will continue to consist in the compensation of material damages and pecuniary losses, a task which has played the most important part in the previous practice of the funds described above.

## I.    Entitlement to claim, content and extent of compensation

A compensation fund for the payment of individual damages has to deal with claims that were previously based on various forms of liability, e.g. negligence, strict liability and nuisance/neighbour law. Correspondingly, the conditions for and the extent of compensation varied greatly. The Fund as a solution to civil law inadequacies should make use of the possibility of creating a uniform set of rules to end the current disparity.

An inspection of the damage at the instigation of the polluter should be the basis for the determining of the entitlement to claim and the extent of the compensation. The emphasis should not be placed on the wrong committed but rather on the social aspect of compensation for those who suffer to a greater degree than the general public as a result of technical and industrial progress and life in urban agglomerations.(1)

Entitlement to claim can be founded, in general, on proof of "environmental damage". Proving that the damage is related to the effects of pollution does give rise to numerous problems. Such proof cannot, however, be fully dispensed with, otherwise all connection with pollution as the cause of damage would be lost. The problem can be overcome in part by a generous appreciation of evidence.(2)   A further help is that the investigation of the case is not undertaken by the applicant himself, but is carried out by the Fund administration. To this extent, the evidential burden of the claimant is greatly reduced. It is the Fund that appoints experts and pays their fees.(3)  This is already a great improvement on the traditional procedure for the enforcement of claims.

1) Cf. Kötz, Sozialer Wandel im Unfallrecht (1976); Bullinger, VersR 1972, 599 (606); Langelaar, Milieu en Recht 1974, 75: "égalité devant les charges économiques".
2) As in the Dutch Air Pollution Fund;  cf. interview with the Fund administration on 6th October 1976.
3) As in the Dutch and Japanese systems.

Compensation should cover as fully as possible the damage suffered but claims for damage that is only trivial should not be allowed. The basis for this is the principle that slight environmental damage must be accepted as part of the general risk of life in a modern industrialised society. A resident in an urban concentration must accept certain noise, dust and fume levels. The fact that a car owner in an industrial area needs to repaint his car more often than an owner in a rural area must be regarded as part of that general risk of life. The same applies to less significant injury to personal well-being. Petty claims should not be included at all. In effect, in view of the current adjustment to and toleration of environmental deterioration, this type of damage would in any case be of no great importance, but to avoid the necessity of dealing with trivial claims, a lower limit for liability should be fixed, as in the Dutch Air Pollution Fund.(1)

Some funds, in particular those for the settlement of damage caused by oil pollution, go even further and are equally applicable to damage to the general public. The cost of pollution control and clean-up operations is reimbursed. The Maine Coastal Protection Fund, moreover, finances State research and development projects. The inclusion of costs to the general public is justified as these claims are plagued by similar enforcement problems as individual civil law claims in tort. Also, by this means, it is possible to extend the scope of the Fund to cover more of the actual social cost of pollution. The method of levying taxes does, to some extent, include already such expenses. The existing effluent taxes in France and Germany, for example, are used for water protection and thus for the purpose of preventing damage.(2) The complete answer would be a system that included both damage to the individual and to the general public. This would also have to encompass damage that will not become apparent for years to come. Only in this way could a comprehensive inclusion of the indirect social cost of pollution to society be embraced. Admittedly this cost cannot be calculated. Accordingly, a "field of risk" would have to be ascertained upon which an estimation of the cost could be based. The "field of risk" could be calculated with reference to statistic and economic computation models.(3)

---

1) Cf. the French Fund for hunting damage: there the minimum is F.100 (art. 14, para. 6, al.1. of the law of 27th September; Art. 15 of décret of 26th February 1974).
2) France: art. 14 of the law of 16th December 1964 (No. 64-1245); art. 17-21 of décrèt no. 66-700 of 14th September 1966 (I.O. of 24th September 1966); cf. also Despax. 53; Federal Republic of Germany: Abwasserabgabengesetz of 13th September 1976 (BGBl. I 2721); cf. also Der Rat von Sachverständigen für Umweltfragen Sondergutachten Abwasserabgabe (1974).
3) Cf. OECD, Problems of Environmental Economics (1972); OECD, Environmental Damage Costs (1974).

## II. Inter-relationship with civil law liability and other claims for damages

The question arises whether a compensation fund should intervene merely in a subsidiary capacity and only if individual actions fail (i.e. in cases of unidentified polluter, damage caused by multiple-source pollution, exclusion of liability, limited liability, inability to pay on the part of the polluter or if tracing the polluter would necessitate unreasonable effort or cost), or should it act in all instances of pollution? On balance, it would seem best that a claim be allowed against the Fund in all cases. This would mean the establishing of a clear rule making the enforcement of a claim conditional only on the declaration of damage on the part of the claimant. Funds that only play a subsidiary role and require that a claimant first seek redress from the particular polluter or that he first attempts to trace the polluter do not give the best results possible.

The Dutch Fund, for example, requires that the claimant first makes a reasonable attempt to elicit damages from the polluter himself.[1] This unspecific legal requirement has led to problems of interpretation: what are the requirements of reasonableness? Is refusal to pay on the part of the polluter sufficient? How much effort need the individual put into tracing the polluter? It is to be feared that an opening for restrictive application, or at least an element of legal uncertainty, has been built into the Fund, a fear that has not been allayed by practical experience.[2] If in every case proof is to be demanded that an individual claim for damage is not possible, then the claimant would be burdened with the risk of preliminary trial, which would frustrate the intention of relieving the claimant of the risk of litigation, the need to conduct proceedings and the burden of proving causality.[3]

It is not only in cases of unidentifiable or impeded identification of polluters that the interest of injured parties need protection. As stated, even in seemingly obvious cases of pollution damage by an identified polluter, enforcement can still be fraught with problems. The great inequality between the injured farmer and the apparently all-powerful industrial concern, the uncertainty as to the strength of the evidence of causality, the risk of litigation, the financial burden, the general reluctance to take a case to court at all (the problem of "access to justice"), all contribute to the situation that even in clear-cut cases judicial enforcement is frequently not pressed for, or is only possible in the face of great difficulties. It seems therefore worth considering whether perhaps a claim should be admissible, on principle, in all cases.

---

1) Cf. also the Canadian Maritime Pollution Fund.
2) Cf. above p. 17.
3) Cf. H. Westermann, 68.

In obviously clear-cut cases, the dispute could be left in the hands of the parties, as provided for in the Maine Coastal Protection Fund. Here, a claim can be raised against the Fund in all cases of oil pollution damage. If the polluter is identified, however, then negotiations are set in motion between the parties under the guidance of a "Board of Arbitration".

If the origin and extent of the pollution can be agreed, then it is the Fund and not the polluter that pays compensation. At the same time, recovery for this outlay is sought from the polluter. If agreement cannot be reached on the course of the pollution incident, or the extent of compensation, or if there are problems in identifying a polluter, then the Board of Arbitration decides the claim.

As well as the Maine Coastal Protection Fund, the Japanese Fund for the Compensation of Pollution-related Health Damage also admits claims irrespective of whether the polluter is known or not. Even if the polluter is obvious, the injured party is not obliged to first proceed against him.

The argument against the replacement of civil law liability by a compensation fund is that the individual responsibility of the polluter lapses and that there is no preventive effect. This objection is unfounded in view of the right of recovery or the consequent adjusting of the levy assessment (see below).(1)

III. Allocation of cost

All the Funds are financed by levies, by means of which the community of potential polluters bears the cost of the damage they cause. This method conforms with the "polluter pays principle", which exists as a prevailing feature in most countries' environmental policy and should be preserved.

The view that the State should make itself responsible for pollution and draw finance for this purpose from general taxation sources should not be heeded.

The idea underlying such views is usually that, from the point of view of public assistance considerations, pollution damage should

---

1) That the French Air Traffic Noise Fund has had wide effect is
   shown by the following statistics: By July 1976, eight of the
   nine schools near the airport Charles de Gaulle had already been
   equipped with soundproofing at a cost of F.3 million. Of the 72
   schools in the area surrounding Orly airport, 54 had already been
   provided with double-glazing costing more than F.36 million. A
   further F.2 million have been spent on soundproofing medical institutions. Compensation for private house-owners is being made
   gradually. Goussainville, an area near Roissy was the first area
   to be dealt with. Of 150 householders, 109 were interested in
   having their property bought and finally 101 decided to sell. All
   told, the Fund has paid out F.85 million.

be better compensated than has hitherto been the case.  For this reason, certain types of pollution damage should be drawn into a State compensation scheme.(1)  Such ideas have also been put forward in France.(2)  In American discussion on legal policy, this solution, which precludes the effective enforcement of the principle of internalisation of social costs, has been totally ignored.

The opinion that the compensation of damage to the individual in a highly industrialised society should be increasingly regarded as a social problem concerning the general public is to be endorsed.  The social role of the settlement of damages would be reasonably fulfilled by the fixing of compensation regulations.  In this sense, funds provide comprehensive compensation.  The existence of "social" compensation rules does not,however, necessarily entail that they be financed from public sources.  The socialisation of compensation does not automatically mean a socialisation of the risk.  The allocation of the costs of compensation should be determined according to the most effective apportionment of the marginal social costs possible or the greatest preventive effect possible.  State compensation payments financed from general taxation sources, on the principle of a common burden, provides no preventive effect, and can only be considered as second best when compared to solutions that attempt to enforce the "polluter pays principle".  Admittedly, this principle cannot always be applied.  If damage could not even remotely be attributed to a polluter, then to burden an individual or particular branch of industry would no longer be economically meaningful - it would be arbitrary.  However, here State contributions could supplement the "polluter pays principle" without turning it on its head.(3)

A further argument against State compensation is that for budgetary reasons there is always the tendency to keep compensation payments within strict limits and, for example, to take the cost rather than environmental-political objectives into consideration in the setting of conditions for the entitlement to claim (e.g. level of noise as a basis for a claim for compensation based on para. 42 BImSchG).  In funds, this tendency is not so prevalent.  In most cases, the Fund is so financed that no limitation on the claimant's right of recourse to the Fund need be set.

All in all, the financing of the fund by levies seems preferable.  As is the case in existing funds, large-scale polluters could be

1) Cf. Heussner, Verhandlungen des 49. Deutschen Juristen Tages, Vol. VI, 18; Wulfhorst DRiZ 1972, 267; cf. also Bullinger, VersR 1972, 599 (606).
2) Cf. Rodière, Rév. de Droit Comp. 1959, 10; Nonnenmacher, Vers.un Droit Atomique (1956), 44 for the law concerning atomic energy; Derrida, D. 1965, J. 222 (232); Kiss, A.F.D.I. 1970, 769 for air traffic noise (sonic boom); cf. also Girod, La Réparation du Dommage Ecologique, 124 and 259.
3) Cf. Bullinger VersR 1972, 599 (606); H. Westermann 71.

taxed according to the volume and noxiousness of the emission.(1)
Small-scale polluters such as motor-vehicles, domestic oil-fired heating, could be correspondingly taxed.  The Japanese system of appor-
tioning a percentage of the motor-vehicle tax to the compensation fund
seems to recommend itself.  This would, however, raise the question,
to what extent the rate of motor-vehicle taxation helps to achieve
environmental-political objectives.  Local authorities, too, would
have to be made responsible for their contribution to pollution (refuse disposal, sewage works).

Levies should be so assessed that they reflect the possible harm
of a product, material or an emission.  Assessment is not a simple
matter, but existing funds have demonstrated that this is not an in-
surmountable problem.

## IV.  Preservation of the preventive effect

Apart from guaranteeing reasonable compensation, pollution law
also has as its aim the prevention of damage.  In the context of a
compensation fund, this can be achieved in two ways:  through the
assessment of levies and by the provision for a right of recovery.

Levies placed on products, production processes and materials
can have a favourable effect on the environment inasmuch as products
damaging to the environment become so expensive that the consumer
will turn to cheaper, less damaging products.  The objective can, on
the one hand, be to force polluting materials and products from the
market (high sulphur content oil, non-returnable bottles), and on the
other hand, to motivate manufacturers to make a particular product
less pollutive (development of motor-vehicles with less pollutant
exhaust fumes) or to alter production methods to reduce emission
values (electric steel process instead of Bessemer process).  The
levies raised in existing funds achieve this object only to a limited
extent.  This is due to the method of levy assessment rather than the
underlying principle.  Levies can only maintain a deterrent function
if they differentiate between individual emissions both quantitatively
and qualitatively.  This differentiation is fully overlooked by, for
example, the French Air Traffic Noise Fund.  The levy is assessed
according to the number of passengers and destination (internal or
external flight) with the effect that environmentally preferable types
of aircraft (e.g. Airbus with 300 passengers) are often more heavily
taxed than environmentally undesirable aircraft (e.g. Concorde with
120 passengers).  The Japanese levy on motor-vehicles similarly fails
to link taxation to the extent and noxiousness of the exhaust of
individual motor types, but is dependent rather upon the weight of
the motor vehicle.  Only in the assessment of levies on industrial

1) Cf. Westermann 71;  Bullinger VersR 1972, 599, 606.

polluters does the Japanese compensation system make the necessary
differentiation in terms of extent and type of emission. Even there,
assessment is related to the expected needs of the Fund, and in most
instances the possibility of setting levies so high that pollution
control would be cheaper for the manufacturer than to pay the levy
has not yet been exploited.(1)

None of the existing systems has attempted to implement a
theoretical possibility that seems to suggest itself: to finance the
settlement of pollution damage from levies, but to separate the amount
of the levy from the purpose for which it is to be used. A change in
thought is here necessary: a preventive effect could be achieved by
linking taxation not to the needs for compensation, but rather to the
marginal costs of pollution, thus encouraging the polluter to undertake preventive measures. To this extent, the aims of a levy system
could be united with those of social insurance.(2)

Alongside levies, the inclusion of a right of redress offers the
possibility of preserving a deterrent effect for the Fund and at the
same time, quite rightly placing the burden of compensation on the
individual polluter. Of course, it would not always be possible to
claim redress in practice. If the majority of cases before the Fund
relate to multiple source pollution and cases in which causality is
difficult to prove, then redress would be correspondingly difficult
to obtain. All the same, a Fund with experts at its disposal, and
less inhibited psychologically (less intimidated by big companies,
less likely to be worried by the possible financial consequences of
a lawsuit) would have a better chance of enforcing claims than the
private individual.

The greater a compensation fund's field of intervention in cases
that could be fought by the individual, the more the right of redress
gains in significance. The form of the right of redress is dependent
on whether the Fund is regarded chiefly as a "help in need" making
payment in anticipation, but then itself enforcing the civil law
claim, or whether one considers the Fund as a form of "insurance",
which does away with liability in tort and which is financed by levies
calculated in advance to meet all expenses.

---

1) Only in one case, in that of the Chisso concern, the company responsible for the serious quicksilver pollution in the Minamata
   case, was the levy raised to such a level that its deterrent effect
   was felt. In this special case, however, the preventive effect
   came too late. It should have come much earlier, in the sixties,
   when new and better production methods for the production of
   acetaldehyde had been developed. The company should have adopted
   these methods as long ago as 1968. In this way, damages arising
   in the past are having to be settled now.
2) Cf. Gresser 127; OECD, Problems of Environmental Economics (1972);
   Franklin, 53 Va. L. Rev. (1967) 774; Calabresi/Melamed, 85 Harv.
   L. Rev. (1972) 1089.

Most funds take the former view.  The Dutch Air Pollution Fund,
for example, has full right of redress.(1)  The Japanese Fund has no
right of redress, but the levy for an identifiable large-scale polluter can be increased to such a level that this amounts to recovery.(2)
The Maine Coastal Protection Fund also reserves full right of redress.(3)

The alternative view is taken only by the Brussels Liability
Agreement supplementing the compensation fund for oil pollution damage,
which gives oil companies an insurance-like cover through the payment
of levies.(4)

On first sight it would seem more sensible to give the Fund the
right of redress the individual injured party would have had, in order
to preserve the preventive effect.  In all events, this effect would
scarcely ever be achieved, because the polluter could always pass the
expense of damages on to his insurance company.  Only if insurance
cover does not apply can a preventive effect be achieved.  It should
therefore seriously be considered whether the right of redress should
not be restricted to those instances in which there is normally no
insurance cover.  Such an arrangement would have certain advantages:
the cost of many expensive and otherwise unavoidable actions for recovery would be spared.  Bearing in mind experience with similar insurance-like solutions in other fields (motor-vehicle insurance, industrial insurance), in which civil liability has been abolished, a
substantial decrease in the cost of processing claims (especially in
administrative costs) could be expected.(5)  This experience should
not be ignored in the establishing of compensation funds.

The question then arises, in which instances does insurance cover
become inapplicable and redress can be had?  Although a single answer
is not possible, in view of the various regulations and developments
in individual fields and countries, it can be ascertained that insurance cover is invalid if the occurrence of damage was predictable
and cannot be regarded as sudden or chance.  This is the overriding
principle behind hazardous insurance, as it manifests itself in manufacturers' public liability, and constitutes the starting point for
non-liability for pollution damage.  Even if there is a discernable
tendency to extend insurance to cover constant and steady pollution,
the predictability of the occurrence of pollution damage remains a
determining factor with regard to the limits of cover.  In particular,

---

1) Art. 64, sect. 2 of the wet zake de luchtverontreiniging, cf.
   above, p.
2) Cf. Gresser, 116.
3) Cf. above, p.
4) 9 Int. Legal Materials Mod. 45 (1970), cf. above, p.
5) Cf. von Hippel, Schadensausgleich bei Verkehrsunfällen 99 ff;
   von Hippel, ZRP 1976, 252 f concerning the New Zealand general accident insurance:  the administrative costs are only 5.95 per cent
   of the total income.

that the technology used was up to standard and has been inspected in accordance with regulations are important conditions of cover.(1)

## V.  Simplification, acceleration and reducing the cost of the compensatory process

The enforcement of a claim against a compensation fund is significantly easier than proceeding against a particular polluter.  The problems of tracing the polluter, negotiating the extent of compensation, going to court, and enforcing the claim no longer arise. Only proof of pollution damage is required, and even here the burden of investigation is assumed by the Fund.(2)

Claims against compensation funds can generally be dealt with more rapidly than those against particular polluters, which can be drawn out affairs frequently taking several years to complete.(3)  It should, however, also be realised that in the past even compensation funds have faced certain teething troubles and claimants have had to suffer long delay if difficulties in proving causality arose.(4)

The question whether a compensation fund is able to resolve claims for damages more cheaply than the traditional system cannot be answered definitively in the absence of the relevant statistical data. Yet here are indications that this is the case.(5)  Expensive court proceedings, with lawyers', court and experts' fees can largely be dispensed with and need only arise in the context of exercising the right of redress.  As far as can be judged, the cost of administration would seem to be less than that of, for example, the enforcement of car accident damage claims.(6)  The cost of levying the motor-vehicle tax is slight, as all that is required is the transfer of a proportion of a tax, the collection system for which is already established.(7)

1) Cf. Bulletin du Comité Européen des Assurances, 2629; cf. also Grell, Versicherungsmässige Deckung bei Umweltschäden, Zeitschrift für die gesamte Versicherungswirtschaft 1976, 73 (80 ff.); Goujet, Versicherungspraxis 1976, 66; Huré, Pollution et Assurance, la Réassurance 1972, 269;  Environmental Pollution Management (1974), 138, Insurance policy covers industry against liability.
2) As in the Dutch Air Pollution Fund and the Japanese compensation system.
3) Cf. para. 1 of the Japanese Compensation Law:  "This law has as its aim ... the allocation of fast and just aid";  regarding the Maine Coastal Protection Fund, cf. Post 540.
4) The longest case lasted two years;  interview with the Fund administration, 6th October 1976.
5) Cf. experience with the system of general traffic accident insurance and general accident insurance:  see v. Hippel, 99ff or ZRP 1976, 252 (253).
6) According to Gresser amongst others, the administration costs for the compensation system for pollution-related health damage amounts to 30 per cent of the total income ($6 million in 1974), $16 million in 1976).  On the other hand, the administration costs for car accident damage (not regulated by a fund) amount to 40 per cent.
7) Gresser amongst others, p. 29.

The cost of the Dutch Fund can be considered as low inasmuch as the raising of a general air pollution levy shows a profit, an adequate part of which is used for compensation purposes. As the number of instances of damage has been small, only a small staff has been needed to run the Fund.(1)

VI. Effect on the economy and the consumer

The financial consequences of improved compensation for pollution damage can only be correctly understood on the basis of extensive investigation - research that has not yet been undertaken. Only in individual instances are definite indications to be discerned.(2) The Japanese system has shown that individual large concerns can be so burdened that prices and their competitiveness can be affected.(3) In general, however, the burden is not excessive.(4) In the final analysis, the net result is a reshuffle of prices. Price rises in consumer goods are balanced out by a reduction in expenditure on medical care, repairs, etc. The increase in the cost of environmentally harmful products is also balanced out by goods that become cheaper (e.g. drinking water). It should be pointed out that compensation funds scarcely extend the liability for pollution damage - they are chiefly intended to make the enforcement of claims easier. Put another way, this means that additional burdens are placed on individual fields of industry only where, in spite of all the principles of environmental policy, the passing on to the general public of the costs of pollution remains a part of legal reality.

E. CONCLUSION

Experience to date shows that compensation funds represent a valuable and practical means of overcoming the inadequacies of traditional individual liability in tort. Numerous arguments speak in favour of their application:

1. The filling of substantive law gaps in the protection of pollution victims (negligence as a prerequisite of liability, conformity to environmental standards as a defence, non-liability in the event of an Act of God, financial limits on the extent of liability, limitations on the awarding of nominal damages).

---

1) For the investigation of cases, the Fund can deploy factory inspectors. Similarly, the collecting of the levy rests in other hands.
2) Cf. the cost of noise standards near highways, in e.g. v. Heyl, annotation to BGH DöV, 1975, 601.
3) One of the leading steel manufacturers paid levies amounting to 2,000 million yen ($6 million). This represented 20 per cent of its annual turnover.
4) Gresser, 29.

2. Improved enforcement of claims ...
   a) in cases where the individual polluter cannot be
      identified;
   b) in cases of multiple-source pollution from small-scale
      emitters;
   c) in cases in which the polluter is identifiable, but a
      claim is in fact unenforceable (lack of insurance cover,
      or pollution stemming from abroad);
   d) in other cases in which enforcement of individual
      damages is impeded by difficulties (improved "access
      to justice" by guaranteeing a right to claim against the
      Fund).
3. Financing of self-help measures to prevent damage (double-
   glazing, removals costs) in particularly affected areas
   (airports, highways, industrial installations).
4. Economically sensible internalisation of social costs.
5. Simplification, acceleration and reduction in the cost of
   the compensatory process.

The objections brought to bear against the Fund (additional administration, additional financial burden on industry and consumer,
socialisation of the risk and the loss of individual responsibility)
are unconvincing in the face of the advantages.

As has been stated, the additional administration required is
matched by reductions in personnel and expense in terms of courts,
lawyers, insurance, experts, etc. By incorporating the Fund into
existing administrative organs, the cost of administration can be
kept within modest limits. Neither socialisation of the risk nor a
decrease in individual responsibility need be feared. Individual responsibility is kept alive by the right to redress and graduated levies.

Additional expense to industry and the consumer will only occur
where the cost of damage, in contradiction to the principles of liability in tort, is still passed on to the general public.

All in all, seen in the context of other comparable solutions,
the compensation fund seems the most competent to ensure effective
compensation for pollution damage. If the general development of
tort liability is examined, the general tendency towards collective
compensation systems is unmistakeable. There is much in favour of
regarding collective compensation legislation as the solution of the
future for environmental control, especially as in environmental
control because of the exceedingly volatile nature of the individual
relations between polluter and victim, the preconditions for such a
solution are extensively present.

COMPENSATION FOR DAMAGE DUE TO TRANSFRONTIER POLLUTION

by

P. Dupuy (1) and H. Smets (2)
Environment Directorate, OECD, Paris

1. Following the United Nations Conference on the Human Environment, held in Stockholm in 1972, it could be thought that public international law, and more particularly that concerning State liability for transfrontier pollution, would come to play a vital role in the matter of compensation for international environmental damage. In fact, included among a variety of provisions, of obvious political content, but of less clear legal implications, two affirmations stood out in the Declaration of Principles adopted at the end of the Conference:

Principle 21

"States have, in accordance with the Charter of the United Nations and the principles of international law, the sovereign right to exploit their own resources pursuant to their own environmental policies, and the responsibility to ensure that activities within their jurisdiction or control do not cause d damage to the environment of other States or of areas beyond the limits of national jurisdiction".

Principle 22

"States shall co-operate to develop further the international law regarding liability and compensation for the victims of pollution and other environmental damage caused by activities within the jurisdiction or control of such States to areas beyond their jurisdiction".

2. It can be seen that, strictly speaking, only the second of these two principles directly concerns the international liability of the State, and even then is somewhat potestative in intent, since it implicitly acknowledges the inadequacy of existing rules of international law regarding liability to compensate for environmental damage.

1) Professor of International Law, University of Paris, Val-de-Marne (Paris XII).
2) Lecturer, University of Liège.

It was, however, possible to consider that over and above a purely incentive legal value, Principle 22 expressed a firm political determination on the part of States present at Stockholm (1) to develop this branch of law into an instrument meeting the present requirements of pollution control.

3. Such a conclusion was supported by an analysis of Principle 21. This does not deal with the legal liability of the State itself, i.e. with the international obligation to compensate, but in asserting the international "responsibility" of all States to protect the environment beyond their frontiers, it formulated a primary obligation in law, the violation of which would amount to an unlawful act giving rise to liability on the part of the State. Principle 21 thus tells us both about the content of the obligation of prevention (although the term "responsibility", little used in continental law, leaves room for some uncertainty as to the nature of such an obligation)(2) and about the basis of the international liability of the State for environmental damage. From these two points of view, Principle 21 constitutes not so much an innovation as a confirmation.

(a) As for the content of the obligation, it in effect embodies, adapting it to the new environmental context, the principle today regarded as custom-based by virtually all legal writers, namely that of the harmless use of territory, a principle relied on by the United States Supreme Court in many federal cases as well as by the Court in the Trail Smelter Case and by the International Court of Justice itself in the Corfu Channel Case.(3)  This rule affirms "the obligation of every State not to allow its territory to be used for acts contrary to the rights of other States".

(b) As for the basis and nature of liability, Principle 21 reiterates the rule according to which non-observance of this "responsibility" for harmless use amounts to an unlawful act and, as such, makes the State to which the act can be imputed internationally liable. We thus remain within the framework of the ordinary law of international liability, now being codified through the work of the International Law Commission, and according to which any internationally unlawful act by a State makes it internationally liable (Article 1 of the proposal).(4)

4. Recent developments in State practice or the trend of on-going negotiations, particularly in the Third United Nations Conference on the Law of the Sea,(5) support this finding, although it is refuted by certain States, who do not always seem to use the same yardstick for problems of legal theory and technique as do legal writers, which partly accounts for the fact that opposite conclusions are reached.

5. Be that as it may, the finding that international damage to the environment is a matter for the traditional rules of international liability, except where there are special agreements between States,

is not absolutely conclusive from the standpoint of the present study, which is concerned not with the _basis_ of liability but its content, i.e. the obligation to provide_redress for the damage.

6. Under both the ordinary system of liability for unlawful acts or under a strict liability regime, the legal rules remain in principle the same. If the victim's access to compensation is facilitated in the second case, this is because he is spared the necessity of proving an unlawful act on the part of the State which he claims is responsible for his loss.

But in all cases, the victim still has to establish a causal link between the act complained of and the damage. It is precisely in this respect that the inadequacy of international law, even its most recent developments, is to be seen in the field of compensation for ecological damage, or more generally for any damage caused to the human environment. Contrary to what could reasonably be expected after the Stockholm Conference, efforts by States to develop environmental law have not been mainly concerned with improving arrangements for compensation at international level, but almost exclusively with cooperation to prevent damage. We thus have to fall back on the general rules of international law.

7. Here, however, an elementary perception of causality still prevails. Since the celebrated case of the "Alabama Arbitration" (1872), it is acknowledged that compensation will not be awarded for "indirect damage". This conclusion is correct, especially if this expression is taken to mean damage "on the rebound", i.e. damage sustained by individual B as a result of loss suffered, in the first place, by individual A. Such a situation is by no means rare in cases of pollution damage.

8. As regards what should perhaps be called "second-degree" damage, i.e. attributed to a single original occurrence but where the first damage causes subsequent damage and so on (and where the sequence of events is thus "transitive", unlike damage "on the rebound" mentioned above), such as "loss of earnings" (lucrum cessans), this is not generally compensated except when the chain of events linking the damage to the original occurrence is still very short.(6)

Furthermore, in cases involving complex causality, where several acts have contributed to the damage, serious difficulties have often been encountered in case law in regard to the sharing of liability, which Courts and arbitration tribunals prefer to avoid as far as possible.

Pollution damage, however, is very often (even in many cases of accidental pollution) cumulative, deferred or indirect, or all three at the same time.

9. This is why it has been thought necessary in the present study to examine existing or proposed ways of adapting compensation

to the specific nature of environmental damage, <u>without relying on the often arbitrary procedures relating to the international liability of the State</u> (especially those cases where diplomatic protection is first invoked)(7) and without finishing up with a situation where compensation for damage which is nevertheless very substantial is inadequate, if not, in many cases, non-existent.

10. Such arrangements for compensation may be found within some legal framework outside public international law (I).

But legal remedies remain of <u>limited</u> application (II) and must hence be backed up by mechanisms of an economic nature (III).


# I. LEGAL PROCEDURES

## A. <u>Equality of treatment</u>

11. The work undertaken by the OECD in 1975-78 concerning non-discrimination and equality of treatment (8) has shown that the development and wider application of equality of treatment between victims of domestic pollution and victims of transfrontier pollution may, in many cases, make it possible to settle compensation problems directly If each State had a <u>non-discriminatory environmental policy</u>, whereby every possible effort was made to reduce both transfrontier and domestic pollution, and if each State also ensured that victims of both domestic and transfrontier pollution were guaranteed equal access to their administrative or legal procedures, both to prevent pollution and remedy its effects, incidents of transfrontier damage would diminish and compensation could be awarded to victims of transfrontier pollution by the courts of the polluting State on the same basis as for a victim of domestic pollution. The causes of disputes as between States would then be largely eliminated.

12. Indeed, where a State practises equality of treatment, the victims of transfrontier pollution emanating from that State who bring cases before its courts would be assured of obtaining the same compensation as victims of domestic pollution. Thus, having obtained compensation through the domestic legal channels of the State where the pollution originated, victims of transfrontier pollution would have no need to ask their own State to exercise the right of diplomatic protection on their behalf. This solution would be all the more advantageous in view of the fact that, in any event, the State asked to afford such protection (the polluted State) is never bound by international law to grant it.

13. However, it is at once apparent that this is a satisfactory solution only on certain conditions:

(a) First, the damage to be compensated must be specific, i.e. it must be sufficiently limited to be the subject of compensation in an action brought by the victim, or a homogeneous group of victims, in accordance with the procedures of general law in the courts of the State in which the transfrontier pollution originated. On the other hand, if the damage assumes the dimensions of a catstrophe, it will be necessary to find other solutions that will require the intervention of the State of which the victims of the transfrontier pollution are nationals (claim for compensation lodged at diplomatic level).

(b) Secondly, the compensation obtained in the polluting State must be comparable in extent and amount to that which the victim sould have obtained in his own State, otherwise it will be to the victim's advantage to bring the action in his national courts. However, enforcement of the judgement may then perhaps (5) give rise to difficult problems.(9)

In practice, the principle of equality of treatment is of optimum value only when it applies as between States which have comparable environmental policies and a legal system based on similar substantive rules (particularly as regards the extent of damage which can be compensated). However, the principle of equality of treatment might, by means of treaty provisions, constitute a minimum that may be required of the polluting State and be incorporated in the duties to take curative action which are binding on such a State under international law.

## B. Concurrent application of two sets of laws(*)

14. In order to go beyond the principle of equality of treatment and its shortcomings, it is possible to imagine a system where both the law of the victim and the law of the polluter would be applied concurrently, by making a sort of "mixture" in the best interests of the victim so that he does not find himself in a more unfavourable situation as a victim of transfrontier pollution than he would as a victim of domestic pollution originating in the polluted State.

However, in order to achieve a fair balance between the interests of the victim and rights of the polluter, it would also be necessary to ensure that this mixed system did not result in the punishment of the polluter for the emission of a level of pollution that would be regarded as permissible under his own law.(**) The victim of transfrontier pollution might therefore be offered the following alternative on an optional basis:

---

*) The intrinsic difficulties and novelty of this approach should not be underestimated.
**) "Permissible pollution" is pollution which does not exceed the maximum threshold allowed by the regulations in force in the polluting State. However, the fact that this pollution is permissible does not mean that the victim will not be compensated. Thus, authorisation to set up a plant emitting pollution may be granted by French law under certain conditions but always without prejudice to the rights of third parties.

15. (a) <u>In cases where the damage is caused by pollution not exceeding the permissible limit in the polluting State</u>, the principle of equal treatment may be adopted purely and simply, i.e. the compensation will be determined in accordance with the law of the polluter.

(b) <u>Alternatively, in cases where the damage is caused by pollution that is unlawful (i.e. in excess of the limits allowed) in the polluting State</u>, the victim of transfrontier pollution might then have recourse to his own national law to <u>determine</u> the compensation for the injury sustained.

16. This system has the following advantages: <u>From the standpoint of the polluter</u>: he has the guarantee that damage caused to a victim of transfrontier pollution will not be more severely penalised than damage to a victim of domestic pollution, at any rate insofar as the pollution is kept within the limits allowed in his State. <u>From the standpoint of the victim of transfrontier pollution</u>: he has the guarantee that the compensation received for damage by transfrontier pollution will be the same as he would have obtained for equivalent damage caused by domestic pollution in his own State, at any rate insofar as the damage sustained by transfrontier pollution is caused by a level of pollution which is <u>unlawful</u> in the State of the polluter.

17. The penalty imposed on the polluter for exceeding the permissible level of pollution (10) will therefore be to compensate the victims of transfrontier pollution in accordance with the scale in force in the victim's State in cases where this scale is more severe. To the extent that this mixed system would be organised by means of international agreements between the States concerned – which would be unavoidable in practice – such States could decide which court would be competent to settle any disputes arising in cases going beyond the strict application of the principle of equality of treatment /see paragraph 20(b) above7. For simplicity's sake, it would seem advisable to choose the <u>court of the polluting State</u>, even in cases where the law of the victim is to be applied. It is, in face, quite common practice for national courts to apply the law of a foreign State in cases of private international law.

18. The same "mixed" system might also be <u>strengthened</u> if, under the conditions laid down previously, application of the law of the victim were to be extended not only to the determination of the amount of compensation but also to the <u>rules of evidence</u> or to the <u>definition of compensable damage</u> (indirect or deferred damage, loss of amenity, etc.), insofar as such a development would be to the victim's advantage.(*) Here, too, it must be noted that it would be necessary to institute such mixed systems of compensation by means of <u>very specific</u>

---

*) On the use of the more favourable law, see A. Rest: The More Favourable Law Principle in Transfrontier Environmental Law, E. Schmidt Verlag, Berlin, 1980.

agreements between the States concerned. A large number of varients can be found to the suggestions made here, since the aim is not so much to formulate an inflexible uniform system as to illustrate the possibilities offered by the combined application of the laws of polluter and victim.

19. Instances of international agreements providing for the combination of laws in this way are still rare,(11) but they are quite conceivable, especially in a bilateral context. An interesting example is the agreement concluded between Germany and Austria on 19th December 1967 for the compensation of individuals living in the vicinity of Salzburg airport, which is very near the German border. The solution adopted is similar to those described so far but differs in some respects.

20. First, the agreement is based on a legal fiction whereby, with respect to the protection of individuals living on the German side of the border in the vicinity of the airport, Germany will act as if the airport were located on German territory, i.e. by taking the measures required in conformity with its own legislation (particularly as regards the creation of safety zones). As regards compensation, if the company managing the airport is required to pay compensation under the German legislation on air traffic and safety or on aircraft noise abatement, the German Government will assume the company's liability for compensating the victims.

Any litigation resulting from the use of the airport in a way that is detrimental to persons, property or rights situated in Germany will come before the ordinary German courts, which will opt for the application of either German or Austrian law, whichever is more favourable to the victims. Once the German Government has paid the compensation in lieu of the company managing the airport, the Austrian Government will reimburse the German authorities for all relevant expenses and for the amount of compensation paid.(12)

21. A comparable system of substituting the national authorities of the victim for the liable foreign polluter, with the subsequent subrogation of these authorities as successors to the rights of the victim, is also practised under the law of some countiies, a specific case being the "Fisherman's Assistance and Polluters' Liability Act" in force in the Canadian Province of Manitoba.(13)

## C. Compensation for continuous pollution

22. Lastly, one other type of solution deserves consideration. It is based largely on socio-economic considerations, although it comes within the context of substitutes for traditional international liability insofar as it, also, takes as its starting point - like the previous solutions (paragraphs 16 to 26) - the principle that there is a sole and identified polluter. This solution might be said to

replace compensation for damage occurring in the past by "offsetting"
the damage perpetuated in the future.(*)

23. There are, indeed, cases where making good damage of technological and industrial origin gives rise to difficult problems, since
the only means of putting a complete stop to the damage would be to
terminate the polluting activity, a solution that is sometimes imprac-
ticable because it would entail unacceptable economic or social consequences for the community (unemployment, stoppage of essential economic production, etc.). Thus, the victim in the Trail Smelter case
were compensated on several occasions (1926, 1931 and 1937) because the
transfrontier pollution did not stop.

It must then be accepted that the cause of the damage is to be
allowed to subsist for a time, but an effort will be made to reduce
the injurious effects by providing the victims with some form of compensation or mitigation, without however giving them any guarantee
that such effects will cease once and for all.

24. "Offsetting" would be a form of making good in equivalent
value, as it were, corresponding to compensation for the exercise of
a public or private right or easement - something akin to the purchase
of a "right to pollute" - and seeking to strike a balance between
maintaining an activity in the public interest and safeguarding
private rights.(14) A very similar solution has already been adopted
in the national law of several countries (15) to attenuate the injurious effects suffered by people living near airports (payment for
the right to make noise, fitting of soundproofing material, anti-noise
screens, etc., without abating the nuisance at source).

25. At international level, the case of the lower Frickthal area
is a very clear-cut example of "offsetting" by a specific polluter in
favour of identified victims.

Smoke and fumes from an aluminium plant located in Germany pol-
lutes the air of two villages situated in the Canton of Aargau in
Switzerland. From 1954 onwards a joint commission tried to provide
various solutions and finally resolved the matter as follows: since
1965, the aluminium manufacturer has been paying a total of SF.100,000
to the victims each year, while at the same time trying to reduce the
disamenity, without entirely eliminating the polluting emissions.
It should be noted that the question of which law to apply is here
avoided, since the payment is determined by agreement between the
parties concerned. However, the system of "offsetting" can never be
more than a limited solutinn, warranted only in very special situations
which are doubtless of short duration.

---

*) The term "offsetting" is here used solely in cases where the dam-
   age is perpetuated; it may take the form of a compensatory payment
   or of mitigation of effects.

## D. Liability insurance to cover compensation for accidental damage

26. In cases where damage may accidentally assume such proportions that the economic survival of the polluting plant is at stake,(16) it is often found necessary to provide special machinery to ensure that the company's risk is covered and to guarantee full compensation for victims. Such machinery makes provision for payment of compensation in excess of the liable polluter's financial capacity and is sometimes combined with a system of liability derogating from the general law which, in effect, ensures compensation solely by virtue of the fact that damage has occurred.

Such machinery includes normal insurance systems (civil liability of the polluter), mutual schemes (liability for the damage caused by a polluter is shared by a group of polluters in the same sector of activity) or systems of compensation guaranteed by a State or States (cover of exceptional risks out of public funds).

### (a) Normal insurance

27. Normal insurance cover is common practice in cases of domestic pollution and is applicable in cases of transfrontier pollution. What it amounts to is that the possibility of having to pay compensation is replaced by the certain payment of insurance premiums of smaller amount before the occurrence of damage. In this connection, reference may be made to the OECD Convention on third-party liability in the field of nuclear energy (Paris, 1960) which fixes a minimum ceiling of liability of the nuclear operator at 5 million units of account and is the basis of a system of absolute liability for transfrontier radioactive pollution. When a transfrontier pollution incident of nuclear origin involves two contracting Parties, the insurance pools assume responsibility for paying compensation for the damage up to an amount that was considered high at the time ($5 to $15 million). Should the transfrontier pollution incident involve a contracting and non-contracting Party, difficulties may arise with respect to compensation since the victim will usually have to invoke the traditional rules of private or public international liability, which are considerably less favourable.(17)

28. (b) The essential feature of mutual schemes for compensation is that the payment of compensation for any damage caused by pollution is shared by the group of potential polluters, including the polluter whose activity caused injury to the third party. As a precaution, these potential polluters agree to set up a mutual guarantee fund which will pay the victim the amount due. The rates and ceilings of compensation and amounts of contributions will usually be determined by members of the scheme. Such systems already operate successfully

in an international context, either on the initiative of the polluters themselves, or under an international convention.

29. In the first category, for example, there are the agreements between oil companies for the compensation of damage caused by oil pollution of the seas, i.e. such agreements as Tovalop, Cristal and, more recently, Opol (18)(19) in cases of accidental pollution.

Under the terms of the Tovalop agreement, which at present covers 9/10ths of the world tanker fleet, the polluter party to the agreement accepts a regime of presumption of fault and is liable to pay compensation up to a given ceiling for pollution control measures. Moreover, the complementary Cristal agreement provides a fund contributed to by member oil companies to meet their liability in the event of damage caused by one of their ships.

It is a typical system of mutual insurance in which the imputation of individual liability is not eliminated, but the award of compensation is ensured by the common fund.

30. A very similar system has been introduced in the same field – although on government initiative in this case – by the establishment of an international fund for compensation for oil pollution damage (Brussels Convention of 18th December 1971). Its aim is to provide cover for pollution damage in addition to the cover already provided by the 1969 IMCO Convention of civil liability of oil tanker owners for oil pollution damage. The Fund pays compensation for certain types of damage not covered by the 1969 Convention and in excess of the shipowner's maximum insurance cover.(20)

It is still funded on a mutual basis, however, since the finance is essentially provided by oil importers in the Contracting States.

It should be noted that, while in practice "a Contracting State may, at the time it lodges its instrument of ratification ... state that it will itself assume the obligations" incumbent on any person required to contribute to the Fund, the system instituted remains private. In this connection, it would certainly appear to be a system which, in principle, makes it possible to avoid invoking the public international liability of the flag State with respect to such damage, although nothing in the texts prohibits such action.(21)

(c) Compensation guaranteed by the State

31. A solution somewhat similar to collective insurance which, though equally well known, differs from the former system in its method of financing, consists of the establishment of a compensation fund financed from the public purse. This system is practised by OECD Member countries which are signatories to the Supplementary Brussels Convention of 1973 on third-party liability in the field of nuclear energy, whereby compensation for damage in excess of a ceiling between 5 and 15 million units of account is no longer paid by the operator or

his insurer but by the State in which the installation is situated, and out of public funds.

Lastly, compensation between 70 and 12 million units of account is paid by the community of Contracting States in accordance with an allocation system laid down by the Convention.(22)  As regards these last two tranches, the initial liability of the operator is assumed first by the State (5-15 to 70 million units of account) and then by the international community (70 to 120 million units of account) in the event of damage of catastrophic dimensions.

32. Recourse to public funds has also been authorised by the law of certain countries (22) and could be the subject of studies with a particular view to examining the various possibilities for participation of the private and public sectors in jointly financing a fund for the compensation of large-scale damage by pollution.  Such a system would be a means of coping with damage on an exceptional scale (for example, the Seveso incident) and a new way of meeting the shortcomings of individualised legal liability.

## E. Particular problems relating to guaranteed compensation

33. The systems of insurance and guarantees may also be used for the purpose of compensating "victims of particular classes of pollution outside the scope of any liability within the customary meaning of the term.

### (a) Lack of insurance cover

34. If insurance of the pollution risk is compulsory but no insurance has been taken out, or if the insurance company of the person liable fails to meet its obligations with respect to victims (for example, bankruptcy) or even in cases where "liability" for the pollution lies with an insolvent third party, it may be agreed that responsibility for compensating the victim shall fall on the State, the pool to which the polluter belongs, or the pool of insurers.  Thus, under the Vienna Convention, the State of the operator causing the damage guarantees compensation for radioactive pollution.  Similarly, under the terms of the 1971 Convention establishing an international fund for compensation for oil pollution damage, the Fund pays the compensation in the event of the insolvency of the owner or insurer liable for payment under the 1969 Convention.

When the person liable for pollution not covered by a special system is insolvent or untraceable (pollution appearing after an enterprise has been wound up) the victims do not usually receive compensation.  In the case of transfrontier pollution, victims may both request assistance from their States (solidarity) or have the public international liability of the State of the person who caused the damage invoked.

(b) <u>Pollution originating in events entailing exoneration from liability</u> (for example, earthquakes or exceptional climatic conditions)

35. The likelihood of such problems arising is diminishing as a result of the adoption of systems of strict liability at international level and limitation of the grounds for exoneration from liability. The sharing of such risks among States or polluters (international fund for "catastrophies") would be an improvement on the present situation. It was accordingly decided that, in the event of oil pollution caused by a ship, the 1971 International Fund will intervene on a basis quite independent of the question of liability, provided the pollution does not result from an act of civil war or other hostilities nor involve a State-owned vessel. Generally speaking, however, victims of pollution on a catastrophic scale will merely receive aid from their own State, under the principle of national solidarity, while other States, or organisations devoted to humanitarian purposes, will intervene in only the most extreme cases.

(c) <u>Non-identification of the person causing the pollution</u>

36. In the case of pollution which does not reach exceptional proportions, it is often impossible - especially in industrialised regions - to identify the polluter who caused the damage, notwithstanding the fact that this polluter is clearly a member of a specific group (for example, a chemical industry - up-stream from the site of damage by water pollution).

Under private law, the aim will be to get one polluter to bear the cost of the damage on behalf of all polluters ("in solidum" liability), an economically hazardous solution which does not satisfy the requirements of equity, at any rate from the standpoint of the group of polluters. The other solution which entitles the victim to obtain compensation from the joint insurer of all potential polluters is practicable only in the rare cases where all the potential polluters have taken out civil liability insurance with the same company.

It has therefore been found advisable to organise compensation for pollution damage on the basis of special legal provisions. Thus, in Japan, all victims of certain types of damage in areas acknowledged to be polluted receive compensation from a fund financed mainly by the polluters. In other countries, the social security system, or the State, pays the medical expenses of victims or compensation for damage to persons.(26) Fishermen in Manitoba are compensated by the Provincial Government for any pollution damage sustained. In the Netherlands, victims of domestic or transfrontier air pollution may be compensated by the State if they are not entitled to compensation from other sources.(24) For this purpose, potential polluters in the

Netherlands pay a tax which varies according to the type of fuel and its sulphur content.  In the United States, a Bill on oil pollution has been introduced with a view to setting up a compensation fund of $200 million.(25)

These examples show how some States have managed to overcome the inability to establish individual liability while ensuring that victims are compensated.  In all these cases, however, it seems clear that national polluters causing transfrontier pollution do not contribute to the compensation of victims abroad (the provisions generally apply only to victims of domestic transfrontier pollution who are situated in the State which enacted them and not to victims abroad).

When such arrangements have been adopted by a large number of States in a given area (water or air), it will be possible to envisage their use at international level, notably on a reciprocal basis.

## II. THE LIABILITY TO COMPENSATE FOR POLLUTION AS AN INCENTIVE TO PROTECT THE ENVIRONMENT

37. The use of economic sanctions requiring a polluter to compensate victims of pollution can really help to protect the environment only if this instrument is genuinely brought into play and the financial burden borne by the polluter is proportionate to the damage caused by the pollution emitted.

Unfortunately, these conditions are not fulfilled in most cases of pollution, especially transfrontier pollution, owing to the fact that there are a large number of inadequately identified victims and their right to immunity from pollution is not always effectively protected.  These various difficulties are examined below.

A. The large number of victims who sustain slight injury

38. When pollution damage affects a large number of victims, most of them sustain relatively slight injury in relation to the costs involved in an action to have the polluter declared liable.  Many victims will not therefore seek compensation.  This situation will be improved if combined action by victims ("class actions" in the United States) is facilitated, or if private bodies assume responsibility for the defence of their interests.  For example, defence associations set up on an ad hoc basis, associations for the protection of natural resources, proceedings instituted by insurance companies on behalf of their clients (under the "legal proceedings" clause) or by public authorities.

39. Even greater difficulties arise in the case of transfrontier pollution owing to the higher costs of proceedings under international law and the limits imposed on action taken at international level by private associations or public authorities.  Some progress would be

made if States mutually recognised, on a treaty basis, one or more
official national agencies in each State as having the right to demand
and collect the total compensation for that State's residents who are
victims of pollution (aside from victims taking separate action) in
proceedings that such agencies would institute against the polluter
(or the polluting State).  These agencies would then compensate those
victims whose rights were protected under their domestic legal systems,
and any excess between the amount paid by the polluter and the compensation paid to victims would be allocated by these agencies to schemes
for improving the victim's environment (this situation may arise if
some victims do not demand compensation or if the law applicable in
the polluter's State is more favourable to victims than that applicable
in their own State).

Another solution more helpful to victims of transfrontier pollution is for the victims' State to compensate them and then exercise
the right of recourse against the polluter or the polluter's State
(cf. the Treaty between Austria and Germany relating to Salzburg Airport,(12) and compensation for damage caused by NATO aircraft).(27)

## B. Difficulty of identifying victims

40. Transfrontier pollution is not only a cause of direct and
personal damage, but it also affects amenities.  As the legal systems
of most States stand at present, it does not seem that the polluter
truly compensates all the damage to such amenities (destroyed wood-
lands, spoiled beauty spots, depletion of stock of fish in the seas,
etc.) because it is virtually impossible to identify all the persons
affected.  Failing such identification, the polluter might conceivably (28) be required to pay more than nominal compensation to
private associations or official bodies protecting such amenities, to
enable them to take steps to make good damage to the environment or
provide compensation in kind to the polluted State (the creation or
maintenance of natural parks, leisure areas, etc.), which would benefit both national and foreign tourists without any need for identification.

## C. Lack of legal protection for victims - Non-compensable damage

41. The above-mentioned loss of amenities and other forms of damage to the environment are not always actionable at law, even though
society recognises that these interests require protection.  This
shortcoming is being remedied by new laws to protect the environment
and the trend towards awarding higher compensation in the courts.
However, there are still many cases where the penalty imposed on the
polluter who infringes regulations (for example, the dispersal of
mercury in an international river or discharge of oil in the sea) is
limited to a relatively light fine.  If such fines were raised (or

even fixed by an international basin agency), it should be possible to offset the lack of compensation.

## D. Obstacles to full compensation

42. Owing to the fact that victims of pollution usually have to establish the origin of the damage, if not the fault of the polluter, polluters manage to pay lighter damages on average than they would have to pay in ideal situations of liability. The disadvantages suffered by the claimant in this legal situation is, in practice, compounded by the economic and financial inequality between polluter and victims and their unequal influence at policy-making and social levels. Although these legal or social aspects should not, in theory, carry any weight, they cannot be ignored by victims of pollution, especially transfrontier pollution, in view of the vicissitudes experienced by some cases brought in this field.

Moreover, the difficulties involved in estimating monetary damages for pollution often results in the award of a nominal sum, which clearly does not impose an economic sanction on the polluter nor represent an assessment of the real damage.

It is not therefore surprising that potential victims of future pollution usually prefer prevention of the pollution to "ex post" compensation for the damage, especially when such damage is irretrievable from the ecological standpoint. Conversely, polluters are hesitant about systems of prior compensatory action freely negotiated with victims (cf. the situation in Japan where organised fishermen have arranged with polluters to give up fishing rights in exchange for compensation).

## E. Deferred compensation

43. The time elapsing between the occurrence of the damage and payment of compensation (proceedings leading to final judgement and enforcement procedure) tends to reduce the dissuasive effect on the polluter inherent in the possibility of his liability being called into play. Such delays may be very lengthy in the case of transfrontier pollution, since the proceedings are long and delicate, or even hazardous. Thus, settlement of the Trail Smelter case took some ten years, while the plaintiffs in the Torrey Canyon case preferred an out-of-court settlement, although this was certainly less favourable financially. The effect of such delays is exacerbated by any depreciation in currency.

44. All the above observations suggest that, in the case of transfrontier pollution, the economic sanction for the polluter inherent in his liability for pollution is very often less effective in practice than the penalty for de facto pollution which opposes a single polluter and a single victim in the same ideal legal system.

This sanction has no real dissuasive power and is no incentive to the polluter to protect the environment when the probable amount involved is less than the cost of measures that he would have to take to control pollution.

With a view to remedying this situation, States have sometimes adjusted the system of liability, but they have mainly tightened up regulations (standards) and administrative procedures (permits) and increased penalties (fines).(29)  From the financial standpoint, States have realised that prevention of pollution is usually less costly to society than compensation for damage and have introduced "economic" machinery providing for more effective preventive action, to complement the machinery of liability.  These various schemes will be examined in the following section.


## III. ECONOMIC PROCEDURES COMPLEMENTARY TO LIABILITY

### A. Liability of the polluter and pollution charges

45. Traditionally, the machinery of liability was developed to regulate relations between individuals, in societies which largely ignored group relations and the protection of collective rights.  As environmental damage usually affects a large number of individuals and is often the result of the combined activities of several polluters, it has been necessary to seek mechanisms other than that of liability to resolve collective problems.

46. Such mechanisms, developed over the last twenty years, make a clear-cut distinction between the two functions:  "liability and economic sanction of polluters" and "making good damage and compensating victims", and they do not rely on causal relationship that is difficult if not impossible to establish.  Quite independent of any fault or individual liability, each polluter is required to pay an amount geared to the pollution emitted above a given level (sometimes zero).(30)  As a general rule, a legally constituted agency received this payment with a view to using the funds to carry out certain functions, such as financing supplementary measures to prevent pollution (aid for investment in communal or private sewage treatment plant, provision of equipment to control pollution in the event of accident), financing projects to improve the environment or make good damage, aid for research on pollution control techniques and, in some cases, even the payment of compensation to victims who have not received compensation from other sources /cf. the Netherlands air pollution Act (22) and the Maine and Florida legislation on oil spills and discharges7.(18)

In order to fulfil these tasks, charges (31) are levied on a pre-determined basis /a kind of insurance premium(*)7. Ideally, these charges are computed on the basis of the damage caused to society by the pollution emitted (31) but, in practice, a flat-rate estimate (33) of emissions is often used and may be multiplied by an equally fixed factor representing "gravity" of damage. In some cases, the charge bears little relationship to the damage (for example, the tax on air-craft noise which is paid for each passenger).

While it may be economically more efficient to gear the charge to the disamenity as an incentive to the polluter to protect the environment, it is sometimes advisable to establish the charge on such a basis that it does not modify the conditions of competition between polluters but still provides sufficient funds to fulfil the various tasks assigned to the agency collecting the charges. In such cases the charge will essentially serve to fund collective measures to protect the environment and make good environmental damage but will not be an incentive to the polluter to take special measures to control pollution.

47. Charge systems are part of global environmental protection policies which seek to ensure that specific quality levels are generally maintained. The payments by polluters provide the funds for carrying out this policy successfully in a coherent, continuous and effective way. On the other hand, liability is too often seen as a curative measure, operating case-by-case to penalise those polluters who allow themselves to be caught while letting the rest go scot-free.

Pollution charges are used on a national scale in many States,(34) especially in connection with water, primarily to finance supplementary pollution control measures. When the charge is paid without discrimination (35) by polluters causing transfrontier pollution and by polluters causing domestic pollution, the former try to control the pollution emitted in an attempt to reduce the charge and, accordingly, they reduce transfrontier pollution. Moreover, the agency collecting the charges (Basin Finance Agencies in France) initiate and partly finance activities which are also of benefit to international rivers flowing into other States. All the polluters in the upstream State on an international river therefore bear the pollution control cost both individually and collectively and, accordingly, reduce transfrontier pollution below the level that would have been achieved by invoking the civil liability of the polluters, or the public international liability of the State of such polluters (which is certainly not very effective and difficult to organise). The, the century-old

---

*) Charges are seen as the general use of premiums or taxes paid by polluters to finance a compensation fund which, in addition to providing the finance for compensation, has an important role to play in accident prevention.

pollution of the Espierre River is shortly to be eliminated as a result of the construction of the Grimonpont sewage plant in France,(36) a solution that had been sought for a very long time and was no doubt achieved by means of aid from the Basin Finance Agency, paid for out of charges on polluters.

Charges may also provide funds for equipment to control accidental pollution, such as oil slicks in inland waters, rivers and international lakes or in or near another country's coastal waters.(37) /cf. also the charges introduced by Canada (38) and Finland.(39)7

Lastly, charges may be used to finance research and development in the field of pollution control techniques and cover the operating costs of agencies monitoring pollution /cf. the Netherlands Air Pollution Act.(24)7 Such measures are also of secondary value so far as the victims of transfrontier pollution are concerned.

43. P llution charges have not yet been used on an international basis, although the Supplementary Brussels Convention, as regards radioactive pollution, and the Fund set up in 1971 for oil pollution illustrate that such a system is conceivable, at any rate for purposes of paying compensation for damage (charges based on the activities of polluters).

If pollution charges were levied internally on polluters situated in the different States in the same international basin,(40) pollution control measures could be taken jointly by the States or national basin agencies and financed by pooling part of the contributions paid by users of the basin with a view to ensuring more effective protection of the environment. Such a development will not be feasible, however, unless the principle of charging is adopted by the States of the basin and the amount does not vary appreciably from one State to another. In due course it would call for the establishment of some sort of international federation of national agencies serving the international basin.

B. Liability of the polluting State and government funding of pollution control

44. Just as the payment of charges by polluters enables them to prevent transfrontier pollution for which they might be held individually liable, so the financing of pollution control measures by a State enables it to prevent transfrontier pollution for which its public international liability might be brought into play.

Such measures have a more specifically "public" character when they are financed by government funds, i.e. by taxpayers. They come within the context of pollution prevention policies which States adopt on the basis of their domestic environmental policy, or on the basis of their "responsibility" to prevent transfrontier pollution, and lead to results deemed to be more satisfactory than the potential –

and considerably delayed - payment of compensation or other "offsetting action" in favour of foreign victims.

50. An approach of this kind was used in the case of pollution of the Rhine by salt (41) when France, Germany and Switzerland decided to provide up to 66 per cent of the finance required to bury 20 kg/second of salt in France.(*)  Similarly, the United States Government is financing a project to reduce the salt content of the Colorado River.(42)

51. The Norwegian Government offers another example (43) in providing aid to the Halden pulp and paper mill in the Iddefjord for the purpose of reducing transfrontier pollution flowing towards Sweden. It should be noted, however, that States implementing the "Polluter Pays Principle" adopted by the OECD (44) and other international bodies are subject to limitations on the measures taken to subsidise polluters.

## C. International solidarity and contributions by the polluted State to finance concerted action

52. The traditional definition of transfrontier pollution as the emission of pollution in the polluting State which causes damage within the State of the victims, should not obscure the fact that the dispersion of pollutants in the environment is one potential use of the environment which is incompatible with some other uses.  When the solution of a transfrontier pollution problem calls for a modification of the ways in which a river basin is used or requires concerted action, all the States of the basin may decide to share the costs involved.  In this case, the contribution of the downstream State, benefiting from concerted action to reduce transfrontier pollution, should not necessarily be regarded as an exception to a "principle of liability" of the polluting State for transfrontier pollution.  It would here be a subsidy borne by all taxpayers and/or users of the basin (including those of the downstream State) with a view to reorganising the uses of the international basin and putting right a de facto situation which is detrimental to the environment.

53. This financial solidarity, both upstream and downstream within an international basin, is the counterpart of national solidarity among all users within a national basin.  Thus in France, since issues relating to pollution (quality) and flow (quantity) are closely interrelated, the users (downstream farmers who irrigate their land) pay a charge for water drawn off (45) which, within the context of the Basin Finance Agency, can be used to finance pollution control projects

---

*) The remaining cost (34 per cent) is paid by the Netherlands on the grounds of international solidarity within the international basin (see paragraph 59).

further upstream with a view to improving water supplies. The same is true in the Netherlands. National solidarity can also take place through fiscal mechanisms when a State subsidises anti-pollution measures, a situation which arises to a limited extent in most OECD countries.

The involvement of all the basin's users in its management is conducive to the establishment of a proper balance between the rights and obligations of all users of the common resource. The funds collected from both polluters and beneficiaries of pollution control measures are used to improve the environment without the need being felt for a precise definition of the extent of the liability, rights or obligations of those concerned as regards pollution. It must be borne in mind, however, that the management of a basin with the collaboration of the different parties concerned – whose interests are sometimes conflicting – gives rise to certain problems.

54. On the international plane, there are very few cases in which a downstream State has contributed towards financing pollution control measures taken in upstream State. The Bonn Convention (41) constitutes a new departure in this respect since the Netherlands finances 34 per cent of the cost of burying in France the salt otherwise dumped in the Rhine, thus illustrating the fact that the notion of liability for transfrontier pollution may be combined, in some circumstances, with the very different notion of international solidarity in the context of an international basin. Such action should not be exercised to the extent of prejudicing the "polluter pays principle" (and exceptions) which is considered by some States to apply to transfrontier pollution.


IV. CONCLUSIONS


55. It is clear from the foregoing proposals that there are many ways of improving and supplementing the machinery of liability to ensure that it serves its preventive and curative purposes as fully as possible. These possibilities should offer the means of "circumventing" some of the problems raised by public international liability in matters of transfrontier pollution with respect to which certain States feel some hesitation, or even reticence. The main object would be to develop the insurance systems required to ensure payment of compensation to victims, and to establish charges outside the context of liability to provide the funds for more complete preventive measures. However, if such procedures are to take shape on an international plane, they must no doubt first be adopted more generally at national level.

56. _In the meantime_, it is noted that those States desirous of controlling transfrontier pollution are primarily trying to introduce international standards (46) and regulations, specifying the quantities of pollution which may be discharged, or prohibiting specific emissions or any increase in pollution (standstill). It is implicit in such agreements that the polluter (sometimes with State and in the form of subsidies) should bear the cost of pollution control (the Polluter Pays Principle),(44) and they do in effect replace the potential obligation to pay compensation by an obligation to prevent pollution.

The _liability_ of the polluting State for damage to the environment would be replaced by the establishment or strengthening of a "responsibiiity" whereby this State would be required to act in such a way as to prevent transfrontier pollution, combined with an obligation to cover the cost of the relevant measures. The liability of the polluting State still remains, however, and should be the last means of redress if all other methods are found to be inadequate for compensating victims of transfrontier pollution.

57. Many States have opted for the positive approach which consists primarily of developing mechanisms for _international co-operation_ whereby every possible effort is made to prevent damage by transfrontier pollution. These mechanisms call for the joint examination of the environmental impact of major projects likely to have effects beyond national boundaries, consultation between States and the setting-up of special pollution control agencies, such as international commissions. States should ensure that measures are taken to control pollution, showing no discrimination with respect to transfrontier pollution, and offer victims of transfrontier pollution real opportunities to defend their rights to a decent environment. If such measures are carried out in the spirit of the good neighbour principle, the difficult problems involved in invoking the international liability of States should not arise in practice.

58. However, there will still be cases of _accidental transfrontier pollution_ for which it would be advisable to establish a system of international liability making provision for rapid, effective and full compensation of victims of pollution (abnormal disamenity caused to neighbours) in all circumstances. The Conventions on liability for radioactive pollution or oil pollution of the seas could serve as the starting point for deliberations with a view to requiring polluters to bear the total cost of environmental damage accidentally caused by them and reducing, as far as possible, the cases in which it might be necessary to invoke the international liability of States. Such an approach would be especially needful in cases of pollution caused by _toxic chemical substances_ which may give rise to damage on a scale beyond the polluter's financial means, as evidenced by the Seveso incident, in particular.

1) Several States, including the Soviet Union, were not present at the Stockholm Conference. It will be noted that Principle 21 is not limited to transfrontier pollution, but also deals with the pollution of areas beyond the limits of national jurisdiction.

2) See "Observations on the Concept of the International Responsibility of States in Relation to the Protection of the Environment" in <u>Legal Aspects of Transfrontier Pollution</u>, OECD Paris, 1977, pp.380-408. See also the First Interim Report of the Environment Committee to the Council on the International Responsibility of States for Protecting the Environment Against Transfrontier Pollution and the Second Report of the Environment Committee on the same subject (restricted).

3) See P.M. Dupuy, "International Liability of States for Damage Caused by Transfrontier Pollution" in <u>Legal Aspects of Transfrontier Pollution</u>, OECD, Paris, 1977, pp. 345-368.

4) See International Law Commission Yearbook, 1977, p. 10.

5) See for example E. Langavant, Droit de la Mer I, Ed. Cujas, Paris 1980.

6) See B. Bollecker Stern, "Le préjudice dans la théorie de la responsabilité internationale", Paris, Pedone, 1973.

7) Which the State can refuse to grant at its entire discretion, as the International Court of Justice has had occasion to re-affirm in the Barcelona Traction Case (1970).

8) See Legal Aspects of Transfrontier Pollution, OECD, 1977 and Non-Discrimination in matters of Transfrontier Pollution, OECD, 1978, in which the texts of OECD Recommendations on transfrontier pollution are reproduced. See also commentaries by

- I. Seidl Hohenveldern: "Transfrontier Pollution and Recommendation C(74)224 of the Council of the OECD", A contribution to "Mélanges in memoriam Garcia-Arias", Revista Temis, Saragossa, 1973-74 (pp. 273-85).

- S.C. McCaffrey: "The OECD Principles Concerning Transfrontier Pollution: A commentary", Environmental Policy and Law, 1, 2-7 (1975).

- R.E. Stein: "The OECD Guiding Principles on Transfrontier Pollution", Georgia Journal of International and Comparative Law, 6, 245-58 (1976).

- I. Seidl Hohenveldern: "Alternative approaches to transfrontier environmental injuries", Environmental Policy and Law, 2, 6-9 (1976).

- P. Dupuy: "The OECD Recommendation C(74)224 on Principles concerning Transfrontier Pollution", Revue Juridique de l'Environnement", No. 1, pp. 25-30 (1977).

- S. Van Hoogstraten, P. Dupuy and H. Smets: "Equal Right of Access: Transfrontier Pollution", Environmental Policy and Law, 2, 77 (1976).

9) When victims of transfrontier pollution may be heard by the courts of their own State and these courts apply the national law in cases of transfrontier pollution, problems will undoubtedly arise in connection with enforcement of the judgement if the victims receive more favourable treatment under this law than they would under the law of the State of the polluter. What view is to be taken of the situation in which victims of the State of the polluter would not receive compensation, whereas the victims in the polluted State would receive compensation owing to more favourable rules of evidence or liability? Would it not be contrary to public policy for a foreign court to require the polluter to take costly pollution control measures, while the corresponding national court dealing with the same action brought by national victims could not take such a decision (Duty to act, or to abstain from acting, in international law)?

10) Where no permissible level of pollution has been specified, this approach could be extended to cases where pollution is an offence under the national law. If the polluter is punished by a fine, the foreign "civil claimant" could then demand application of the law of the polluted State to compensate for the foreign damage. In cases where an offence is established and a conviction ensues, the 1954 London Convention makes provision for the criminal court of the State in which damage occurs to award damages for oil pollution of the seas.

11) Pursuant to Article IX of the IMCO Brussels Convention (1969), the courts of the State in which damage occurs are exclusively competent, whereas Article 14 of the OECD Paris Convention (1960) confers exclusive jurisdiction on the State in which the polluting installation is situated and lays down the principle of non-discrimination in matters of compensation.
According to a recent interpretation placed in connection with transfrontier pollution on the Convention on Jurisdiction and the Enforcement of Judgements in Civil and Commercial Matters (1968), the victim may bring an action in the courts of the polluter or in his own courts. If the law applicable is the national law of the court, or the most favourable law, the victim may benefit from the most favourable law. The enforcement of judgements within the Community should not give rise to any difficulty. The Hague Convention on the law applicable with respect to product liability (Article 6) states that the law to be applied is that of the State of the person liable, unless the victim bases his case on his national law. Article 10 of the Convention on Civil Liability for Oil Pollution Damage resulting from Exploitation for and Exploitation of Seabed Mineral Resources (London, 1976) provides for a choice by the victim between the court of the State in which the damage occurs and the court of the controlling State. One of the proponents of recourse to the law most favourable to the victim of transfrontier pollution is A. Rest, in "Convention on compensation for transfrontier damage to the environment", E. Schmidt Verlag, A 53, Berlin 1976. It should be noted that the " most favourable law" criterion ensures equal compensation for transfrontier pollution in identical and symmetrical cases of transfrontier pollution between two States. This balance of rights and obligations cannot be achieved by the system of equality of treatment, since this system does not ensure equal treatment of victims of transfrontier pollution, but equal treatment of both national and foreign victims of the same pollution. As regards recourse to the law most favourable from the standpoint of protection of the environment, refer to the usual practice of the CERN (F. Schmid and J.M. Dufoux, "Le CERN, exemple de coopération scientifique européenne", J.D.I., February/March 1976, p.100).

12) A full analysis of this Agreement is provided by Ignaz Seidl-Hohenveldern in "A propos des Nuisances dues aux aéroports limitrophes. Le cas de Salzbourg et le traité austro-allemand du 19 décembre 1967", Annuaire français du droit international, 1973, pp. 890-894.

13) 17th June 1970.

14) P.M. Dupuy: "La responsabilité internationale des Etats pour les dommages d'origine technologique et industrielle". Paris, Pedone. 1977 (p. 278).

15) P. Girod: "La réparation du dommage écologique", Paris, LGDJ 1974, p. 266. French legislation (Decree No. 73-193 - J.O. 27th February 1973); German legislation: Federal Law of 30th March 1977, B.G.BL., I. p. 282, and Federal Law of 15th March 1975, B.G.BL., I, 721, 1193; Swiss legislation: Cantonal Law on Zurich airport, 27th September 1970.

16) The Seveso incident (Italy) is a case where the operator may be incapable of meeting its financial liability for pollution. Only the non-compulsory intervention of parent companies offers any likelihood of the victims (individuals and the State) receiving compensation for damages (probably in excess of French F.100 million). A parent company has already paid French F.12 million (2 billion lire), but there is talk of limiting these payments to Swiss F.8 million. In France, an industrial polluter (electro-plating and treatment of metals) was recently ordered to pay F.803,090 in damages to the Prefects of two Départements and 15 fishing associations for pollution of the Sandrine, a tributory of the Garonne.

17) Issues concerning third-party liability in the field of nuclear energy have been dealt with in a number of reports by the OECD Nuclear Energy Agency, especially in the "Nuclear Law Bulletin" published periodically by the OECD. Also see "Nuclear Legis-lation" Nuclear Third Party Liability", Vol. 1 (1967), OECD, which is currently being revised.

18) M. Rémond: "Compensation for marine pollution": this book, pp. 56 et seq. For a critical study of international Conventions and other provisions applicable in cases of oil pollution of the waters of the United States and Canada, see J.L. Pedrick: "Liability, compensation and prevention of oil spills, a North American Pers-pective", Earth Law Journal, 1, 301 (1975). The inadequacy of international Conventions on oil pollution is clearly demon-strated in the case of the Boehlen, a 10,000 ton tanker which foundered off the Ile de Sein in 1976. The limit of liability if F.6 million. F.30 million have already been spent and it is expected that a further F.50 million will be required to recover 9,000 tonnes of oil, at a depth of 100 metres, with a view to protecting the Brittany coast. Another example is provided by the case of a Yugoslav vessel, carrying 250 tonnes of tetraethyl lead, which foundered off the Italian coast. The Italian Govern-ment has made available 10 billion lire (F.57 million) for the recovery of the toxic drums (R.G.D.I.P. 81, p. 868, 1977)

19) In December 1976, a new Convention on Civil Liability for Oil Pollution Damage from Offshore Operations was opened for sig-nature. It provides for a system of absolute liability of the operator with a ceiling of 30 million SDRs (40 million after 1983), and a requirement that the operator should have and main-tain insurance of at least 22 million SDRs (35 million after 1983). However, nothing prevents a State from imposing higher ceilings of liability on operators in the zone in which it exercises sovereign rights over the natural resources.

20) J. Ballenegger: "La pollution en droit international", Lausanne, 1975, pp. 115-131.

21) P.M. Dupuy, op.cit., pp. 140-156.

22) P.M. Dupuy, op.cit., pp. 122-128. The IMCO Convention of 1969 has been in force since 6th May 1975 (32 ratifications), but the 1971

204

Convention (ratified by 11 States: Algeria, Bahamas, Denmark,
Germany, Japan, Liberia, Norway, Sweden, Syria, Tunisia and
the United Kingdom) has not yet entered into force as the prerequisite tonnage has not been attained (MEPC VII/2, 19th April
1977).

23) For example, "The Act to amend Section 28 of the Mineral Leasing
Act of 1920 to authorise a trans-Alaska oil pipeline and for
other purposes", 16th November 1973, P.L.93.159. The Belgian Act
on toxic wastes, 22nd July 1974: "Le Moniteur belge", 1st March
1975, p. 2365 et_seq. The United States Price Anderson Act on
nuclear damage /The Government guarantee of $120 to $560 million
is to be gradually replaced_by operators' financial security of
$5 million per installation/.

24) Air Pollution Act (WLV) /adopted in 1970 (Staatsblad 580) and entered into force in 1972/ - Section 64. An air pollution fund
has been set up to compensate persons who suffer damage as a result of pollution of the air over the Netherlands in cases where
such persons cannot obtain compensation elsewhere. From 18th
September 1972 to 31st December 1973, 103 claims were submitted
and decisions were taken in 25 cases (22 claims were rejected and
three compensatory payments of Fl.250, Fl.7,446 and Fl.2,455 were
granted). In particular, the Fund paid compensation of Fl.7,446
to a Dutch market gardener whose glasshouses were covered with
cement dust which was apparently blown over from Belgium. The
Fund is trying to obtain reimbursement of this amount. The
charges levied on fuels (KB 23rd June 1972; Staatsblad 307) are
used primarily for the management of air pollution control and
financing preventive measures.

25) See the Bill on "Comprehensive Oil Pollution Liability and Compensation" submitted to Congress by the President of the United
States on 9th July 1975. It is proposed to set up a fund of
$200 million, financed by a charge on oil, which would make it
possible to pay compensation for damage caused by oil pollution
of waters, even if the source of pollution is not identified (one-
third of pollution cases in 1973, amounting to 100,000 tonnes, in
the United States). Provision is made for the Attorney-General
to act on behalf of all the victims with respect to the Fund and
for public authorities to obtain compensation for damage to
natural resources within their jurisdiction.

26) In the case of accidents caused by motor vehicles, several
countries (including France) have set up a "guarantee fund",
financed by contributions from insured motorists, which guarantees payment of compensation to victims of accidents caused by
unidentified or insolvent motorists. Similarly, several countries
have established systems whereby damages are paid to victims of
criminal acts /Council of Europe, DPC/CEPCXXIV(76)10/. Thus, in
France, victims of offences committed by insolvent or unidentified
persons may claim damages from the State up to a ceiling of
F.150,000 (J.O. 413177), if such persons suffer serious physical
injury, cannot obtain compensation by other means and, accordingly,
find themselves in a grave situation in material terms. It should
be possible to compensate victims of some types of chemical pollution under such arrangements.

27) Agreement between the Parties to the North Atlantic Treaty regarding the States of their Forces (London, 19th June 1951).
Article 8.5 stipulates that claims for compensation for damage
shall be settled in accordance with the national law of the State
in which the damage occurs and paid by that State, and that the
State of origin (e.g. the State in which a milliary aircraft
causing sonic boom is based), shall reimburse the injured State
for 75 per cent of the amount of compensation that it has paid
to victims.

28) Such an approach is not as audacious as it may appear. Thus the President of the French Republic said in a speech at Vannes on 8th February 1977 that when nuclear power stations are set up near the sea, thus utilising existing open spaces, it would be reasonable to provide at the same time, other open spaces for the public, and that the body responsible for these power stations might contribute to the financing of programmes to protect the most sensitive or renowned beauty spots in the region concerned. The French Government has been asked to study proposals for implementing this principle which, in addition to paying compensation to the landowner, seeks to "compensate" the nation for the loss of "natural capital". By agreement (July 1977) between the commissioning firms and the Ministère de l'Equipement, it was decided that the utility should earmark part of the cost of constructing coastal power stations for the purpose of enabling to coastal conservation authority or local authorities to acquire land that would be left in its natural state and kept open to the public. In France, there is already a "green space" tax payable by developers in coastal Départements, and permission to clear land of trees may be subject to a requirement of reafforestation over an equivalent area.

29) Fines are often ineffective because they are fixed at a low level. In the United States, however, a Federal Court fined Allied Chemical Corporation a sum of $13.2 million (R. Train, CDSM, 1st October, doc. AC/274-R120).

30) Pollution charges might be levied only when a specific level of pollution is exceeded. To avoid establishing these thresholds (a right to pollute, as it were), charges are often calculated on the basis of the total quantity of pollution emitted, in which case the charge corresponds to a kind of collective liability and is not a payment in settlement of "liability" for pollution considered excessive beyond a specific level. The pollution charge is a means of implementing the "polluter pays principle", which is not based on the concept of liability but on the principle of cost-sharing.

31) The pollution charge is not the only mechanism that may be envisaged. Other systems depend on the purchase and sale of pollution "certificates" or "permits" on a market which involves both polluters and the agencies responsible for protecting the environment. A review of the possible economic systems can be found in "Economics of Transfrontier Pollution", OECD, 1976, and, more particularly, in the reports by the OECD Secretariat: "Problems in Transfrontier Pollution", OECD, 1974 and "The Polluter Pays Principle", OECD, 1975.

32) The "ideal" charge is such that the polluter bears the exact cost of the damage that he inflicts on society, but it is very hard to calculate since it is extremely difficult to put a price on such damage. In practice, charges are lower than the "ideal" charge and the polluter is at the same time subject to a regulatory system (norms not to be exceeded), a pricing system (charges) and a system of civil liability and penalties. In the case of transfrontier pollution, the liability of the polluting State might be brought into play, but there are only a few cases in which the State of the polluter has paid compensation for transfrontier pollution (excluding pollution relating to military activities and other activities of a specifically governmental nature). The Trail Smelter case is the exception to the rule.

33) The charge is computed by multiplying a base depending on the pollution by a rate depending on the effect of the pollution on the environment. The base is a flat-rate estimate when it is fixed "ex ante" according to the probable polluting characteristics of a plant, and is specific when it is obtained by measuring effective emissions of pollution. The rate of the charge is often fixed

on the basis of the tasks assigned to the collecting agency rather than on the basis of the damage. If the polluter can vary the amount of the charge by taking certain pollution control measures, he will be induced to take such measures insofar as they cost less than the amount by which the charge is reduced.

34) A review of the use of pollution charges is given in: "Pollution Charges: An Assessment", OECD, 1976. Also see "Water Management Policies and Instruments", OECD, 1977 and "Principles and Methods for the Provision of Economic Incentives in Water Supply and Waste Water Disposal Systems", ECE/WATER/16 (1976).

35) However, it should be noted in this connection that basin charges were not introduced to solve international problems; and the tightening up of emission standards in basins can also have international effects when these standards are adopted on a non-discriminatory basis. National policies serve to prevent transfrontier pollution when the principle of non-discrimination is applied (see also Section A.1 and the OECD Recommendations on non-discrimination: notes 1, 3 and 4 above). When a State levies charges on its polluters for the purpose of compensating its pollution victims, the victims of transfrontier pollution in a neighbouring State do not usually benefit from this system, as the compensation fund is restricted to national territory. On the other hand, when pollution charges are used to prevent pollution, victims of transfrontier pollution benefit from the reduction of such pollution.

36) "The Espierre Problem: A Case of Transfrontier Pollution" by J. Delos and F. Lentacker, published in Environmental Protection in Frontier Regions, OECD, 1979. N.B. The State provides a subsidy of 50 per cent, while the Agency and the regional or local authorities respectively pay 25 per cent.

37) Oil importer could be required to pay a charge per tonne of oil imported with a view to financing land-based pollution control facilities (cf. the Maine and Florida Acts) and such charges could even be adjusted according to the characteristics of the tankers from the standpoint of pollution of the seas and coastal waters. The initial adoption of such an approach at national level could be developed to provide an effective means of action at international level. The French charge on aircraft noise at Paris-Roissy Airport would have a considerable incentive effect if other airports were to adopt the same instrument (see "Charging for Noise", OECD, 1976).

38) The Canada Shipping Act of 1970 (Part XX – Pollution, Sections 748-750) makes provision for a tax of 17 cents per ton on oil imported by, or loaded on, tankers. The Fund intervenes only as the "guarantor of last resort" in matters of compensation. The tax was suspended owing to the large amounts collected as compared with the claims lodged with the Fund, which were rare and for small amounts up to 1976. In South Africa, a Fund for the Prevention of Oil Pollution was set up in 1971 and is financed by the State (grants, fines) and owners of ships causing pollution.

39) Finland's Act No. 668 on the financing of oil pollution control measures (22nd September 1972) provides for the establishment of a national fund of F.Mk.10 million financed by a charge of F.Mk.150 per thousand tonnes of oil imported. The fund is used to cover compensation for damage, the cost of measures to prevent damage and the purchase and maintenance of preventive equipment. It may also serve to finance the cost of making good damage to the environment. The Fund is managed by the State but is independent of the general budget. The Fund acquires by subrogation the rights of victims to whom it has paid compensation. In France, a contingency fund has been set up for emergencies (Mr. Giscard d'Estaing's speech in Vannes, 8th February 1977 and the Decision

of the Council of Ministers of 25th May 1977, earmarking F.10 million for this fund in 1977).

40) As regards the Rhine Basin, charges are already levied in France and the Netherlands and are to be levied in Germany in 1981. At the Interparliamentary Conference on Pollution of the Rhine (The Hague, February 1977), it was recommended that the efforts to establish a European system of charges on waste water discharges should be pursued energetically. The French Delegation has proposed that an International Basin Agency should be set up, primarily to provide funds for pollution control measures on an international basis.

41) Convention on the protection of the Rhine against pollution by chlorides (Bonn, 3rd December 1976). Env. Pol. Law 2, pp. 182-4 (1976). Ratification of this Convention by France caused difficulties. Other solutions are now investigated.

42) H. Brownell and S.D. Eaton: "The Colorado River Salinity Problem with Mexico", A.J.I.L., 69, p. 255 (1975).

43) Transfrontier pollution of the Iddefjord (Report by the OECD Secretariat based on proposal St. Prp. 130 submitted to the Norwegian Parliament by the Minister for the Environment on 11th April 1975): published in Environment Protection in Frontier Regions, OECD, 1979.

44) "The Polluter Pays Principle": Definition, Analysis, Implementation, OECD, 1975.

45) Article 18 of Decree 66-700, amended by Decree 75-998 of 28th October 1975 (Official Journal, 30th October 1975, France):

"I – Charges may be levied on public or private bodies which render action by the Agency either necessary or desirable by:
- contributing to the deterioration of water quality;
- drawing off quantities from water resources;
Charges may also be levied on public or private bodies which benefit from projects or construction work carried out with the assistance of the Agency.

II – Premiums may be paid to those responsible for commissioning public or private works when they incorporate arrangements for preventing deterioration of water quality."

46) One serious difficulty arising in connection with the establishment of international quality standards is that such standards might be tantamount to giving the polluting State a kind of standing right to pollute. Such an approach is sometimes deemed undesirable since it is only right and proper that the pollution emitted by a State should be related to need and to use of appropriate pollution control techniques. The closure of some polluting plants in the polluting State should not result in an increase in pollution "permits" for other plants. One solution is to establish emission standards, undertake concerted action (construction of certain types of waste treatment plant) or finance projects of common interest (e.g. underground disposal of salt from the Rhine).

# OECD SALES AGENTS
# DÉPOSITAIRES DES PUBLICATIONS DE L'OCDE

**ARGENTINA – ARGENTINE**
Carlos Hirsch S.R.L., Florida 165, 4° Piso (Galería Guemes)
1333 BUENOS AIRES, Tel. 33.1787.2391 y 30.7122

**AUSTRALIA – AUSTRALIE**
Australia and New Zealand Book Company Pty, Ltd.,
10 Aquatic Drive, Frenchs Forest, N.S.W. 2086
P.O. Box 459, BROOKVALE, N.S.W. 2100

**AUSTRIA – AUTRICHE**
OECD Publications and Information Center
4 Simrockstrasse 5300 BONN. Tel. (0228) 21.60.45
Local Agent/Agent local :
Gerold and Co., Graben 31, WIEN 1. Tel. 52.22.35

**BELGIUM – BELGIQUE**
LCLS
35, avenue de Stalingrad, 1000 BRUXELLES. Tel. 02.512.89.74

**BRAZIL – BRÉSIL**
Mestre Jou S.A., Rua Guaipa 518,
Caixa Postal 24090, 05089 SAO PAULO 10. Tel. 261.1920
Rua Senador Dantas 19 s/205-6, RIO DE JANEIRO GB.
Tel. 232.07.32

**CANADA**
Renouf Publishing Company Limited,
2182 St. Catherine Street West,
MONTRÉAL, Quebec H3H 1M7. Tel. (514)937.3519
522 West Hasting,
VANCOUVER, B.C. V6B 1L6. Tel. (604) 687.3320

**DENMARK – DANEMARK**
Munksgaard Export and Subscription Service
35, Nørre Søgade
DK 1370 KØBENHAVN K. Tel. +45.1.12.85.70

**FINLAND – FINLANDE**
Akateeminen Kirjakauppa
Keskuskatu 1, 00100 HELSINKI 10. Tel. 65.11.22

**FRANCE**
Bureau des Publications de l'OCDE,
2 rue André-Pascal, 75775 PARIS CEDEX 16. Tel. (1) 524.81.67
Principal correspondant :
13602 AIX-EN-PROVENCE : Librairie de l'Université.
Tel. 26.18.08

**GERMANY – ALLEMAGNE**
OECD Publications and Information Center
4 Simrockstrasse 5300 BONN Tel. (0228) 21.60.45

**GREECE – GRÈCE**
Librairie Kauffmann, 28 rue du Stade,
ATHÈNES 132. Tel. 322.21.60

**HONG-KONG**
Government Information Services,
Sales and Publications Office, Baskerville House, 2nd floor,
13 Duddell Street, Central. Tel. 5.214375

**ICELAND – ISLANDE**
Snaebjörn Jönsson and Co., h.f.,
Hafnarstraeti 4 and 9, P.O.B. 1131, REYKJAVIK.
Tel. 13133/14281/11936

**INDIA – INDE**
Oxford Book and Stationery Co. :
NEW DELHI, Scindia House. Tel. 45896
CALCUTTA, 17 Park Street. Tel. 240832

**INDONESIA – INDONÉSIE**
PDIN-LIPI, P.O. Box 3065/JKT., JAKARTA, Tel. 583467

**IRELAND – IRLANDE**
TDC Publishers – Library Suppliers
12 North Frederick Street, DUBLIN 1 Tel. 744835-749677

**ITALY – ITALIE**
Libreria Commissionaria Sansoni :
Via Lamarmora 45, 50121 FIRENZE. Tel. 579751
Via Bartolini 29, 20155 MILANO. Tel. 365083
Sub-depositari :
Editrice e Libreria Herder,
Piazza Montecitorio 120, 00 186 ROMA. Tel. 6794628
Libreria Hoepli, Via Hoepli 5, 20121 MILANO. Tel. 865446
Libreria Lattes, Via Garibaldi 3, 10122 TORINO. Tel. 519274
La diffusione delle edizioni OCSE è inoltre assicurata dalle migliori
librerie nelle città più importanti.

**JAPAN – JAPON**
OECD Publications and Information Center,
Landic Akasaka Bldg., 2-3-4 Akasaka,
Minato-ku, TOKYO 107 Tel. 586.2016

**KOREA – CORÉE**
Pan Korea Book Corporation,
P.O. Box n° 101 Kwangwhamun, SÉOUL. Tel. 72.7369

**LEBANON – LIBAN**
Documenta Scientifica/Redico,
Edison Building, Bliss Street, P.O. Box 5641, BEIRUT.
Tel. 354429 – 344425

**MALAYSIA – MALAISIE**
and/et SINGAPORE - SINGAPOUR
University of Malaysia Co-operative Bookshop Ltd.
P.O. Box 1127, Jalan Pantai Baru
KUALA LUMPUR. Tel. 51425, 54058, 54361

**THE NETHERLANDS – PAYS-BAS**
Staatsuitgeverij
Verzendboekhandel Chr. Plantijnnstraat
S-GRAVENAGE. Tel. nr. 070.789911
Voor bestellingen: Tel. 070.789208

**NEW ZEALAND – NOUVELLE-ZÉLANDE**
Publications Section,
Government Printing Office,
WELLINGTON: Walter Street. Tel. 847.679
Mulgrave Street, Private Bag. Tel. 737.320
World Trade Building, Cubacade, Cuba Street. Tel. 849.572
AUCKLAND: Hannaford Burton Building,
Rutland Street, Private Bag. Tel. 32.919
CHRISTCHURCH: 159 Hereford Street, Private Bag. Tel. 797.142
HAMILTON: Alexandra Street, P.O. Box 857. Tel. 80.103
DUNEDIN: T & G Building, Princes Street, P.O. Box 1104.
Tel. 778.294

**NORWAY – NORVÈGE**
J.G. TANUM A/S Karl Johansgate 43
P.O. Box 1177 Sentrum OSLO 1. Tel. (02) 80.12.60

**PAKISTAN**
Mirza Book Agency, 65 Shahrah Quaid-E-Azam, LAHORE 3.
Tel. 66839

**PHILIPPINES**
National Book Store, Inc.
Library Services Division, P.O. Box 1934, MANILA.
Tel. Nos. 49.43.06 to 09, 40.53.45, 49.45.12

**PORTUGAL**
Livraria Portugal, Rua do Carmo 70-74,
1117 LISBOA CODEX. Tel. 360582/3

**SPAIN – ESPAGNE**
Mundi-Prensa Libros, S.A.
Castello 37, Apartado 1223, MADRID-1. Tel. 275.46.55
Libreria Bastinos, Pelayo 52, BARCELONA 1. Tel. 222.06.00

**SWEDEN – SUÈDE**
AB CE Fritzes Kungl Hovbokhandel,
Box 16 356, S 103 27 STH, Regeringsgatan 12,
DS STOCKHOLM. Tel. 08/23.89.00

**SWITZERLAND – SUISSE**
OECD Publications and Information Center
4 Simrockstrasse 5300 BONN. Tel. (0228) 21.60.45
Local Agents/Agents locaux
Librairie Payot, 6 rue Grenus, 1211 GENÈVE 11. Tel. 022.31.89.50
Freihofer A.G., Weinbergstr. 109, CH-8006 ZÜRICH.
Tel. 01.3634282

**TAIWAN – FORMOSE**
National Book Company,
84-5 Sing Sung South Rd, Sec. 3, TAIPEI 107. Tel. 321.0698

**THAILAND – THAILANDE**
Suksit Siam Co., Ltd., 1715 Rama IV Rd,
Samyan, BANGKOK 5. Tel. 2511630

**UNITED KINGDOM – ROYAUME-UNI**
H.M. Stationery Office, P.O.B. 569,
LONDON SE1    9NH. Tel. 01.928.6977, Ext. 410 or
49 High Holborn, LONDON WC1V 6 HB (personal callers)
Branches at: EDINBURGH, BIRMINGHAM, BRISTOL,
MANCHESTER, CARDIFF, BELFAST.

**UNITED STATES OF AMERICA – ÉTATS-UNIS**
OECD Publications and Information Center, Suite 1207,
1750 Pennsylvania Ave., N.W. WASHINGTON D.C.20006.
Tel. (202) 724.1857

**VENEZUELA**
Libreria del Este, Avda. F. Miranda 52, Edificio Galipan,
CARACAS 106. Tel. 32.23.01/33.26.04/33.24.73

**YUGOSLAVIA – YOUGOSLAVIE**
Jugoslovenska Knjiga, Terazije 27, P.O.B. 36, BEOGRAD.
Tel. 621.992

---

Les commandes provenant de pays où l'OCDE n'a pas encore désigné de dépositaire peuvent être adressées à :
OCDE, Bureau des Publications, 2, rue André-Pascal, 75775 PARIS CEDEX 16.

Orders and inquiries from countries where sales agents have not yet been appointed may be sent to:
OECD, Publications Office, 2 rue André-Pascal, 75775 PARIS CEDEX 16.

OECD PUBLICATIONS, 2, rue André-Pascal, 75775 PARIS CEDEX 16 - No. 41797 1981
PRINTED IN FRANCE
(1350 CQ 97 81 04 1) ISBN 92-64-12214-1